FIRST STEPS IN
CHRISTIAN RELIGIOUS RENEWAL

RUDOLF STEINER (1923)

FIRST STEPS IN
CHRISTIAN RELIGIOUS RENEWAL

Preparing the Ground for The Christian Community

Six Lectures and Two Discussions Held in Stuttgart
June 12–16, 1921

TRANSLATED BY MARSHA POST
INTRODUCTION BY CHRISTOPHER BAMFORD

RUDOLF STEINER

SteinerBooks

CW 342

SteinerBooks
Anthroposophic Press
610 Main Street
Great Barrington, Massachusetts 01230
www.steinerbooks.org

This book comprises volume 342 in the Collected Works (CW) of Rudolf Steiner, published by SteinerBooks, 2010. This is a translation of shorthand reports unrevised by the lecturer from the German *Vorträge und Kurse über christlich-religiöses Wirken I. Anthroposophische Grundlagen für ein erneueretes christlich-religiöses Wirken*, published by Rudolf Steiner Verlag, Dornach, Switzerland, 1993.

Library of Congress Cataloging-in-Publication Data

Steiner, Rudolf, 1861-1925.
 [Anthroposophische. Grundlagen für ein erneueretes christlich-religivses Wirken. English]
 First steps in Christian religious renewal : preparing the ground for the Christian community, 1 : six lectures and two discussions held in Stuttgart June 12-16, 1921 / translated by Marsha Post ; introduction by Christopher Bamford.
   p. cm. – (The collected works of Rudolf Steiner ; 342)
 Includes bibliographical references and index.
 ISBN 978-0-88010-622-1
 1. Anthroposophy–Relations–Christianity 2. Christianity and other religions–Anthroposophy. I. Title.
 BP595.S894A59513 2010
                        299'.935—dc22
                                      2010022453

Printed in the United States

CONTENTS

Mysteries: Gospel reading, offering, transubstantiation, communion. Working through the picture or image: pictorial speaking, symbol. On the translation by Rudolf Steiner of the Catholic Mass. Boundaries of natural scientific ideas in the example of the human being becoming physical (cell of the egg). Why renewal of religion through Anthroposophy? Discussion of practical aspects: Financing (*Der Kommende Tag*, Hermann Heisler). Preparation for pictorial speaking. Fourteen-day course possible. Legends.

4.

STUTTGART, JUNE 14, 1921 (EVENING)

Questions and answers. Form of the ritual. Ritual acts of Freemasonry. How do symbols arise, and how is symbolism possible today? Living into the genius of language and speech; pictorial soul life. A modern ritual must be simple and be the expression for the inner transformation of the human being. Forming a mantra. Music in the ritual. Rituals given by Rudolf Steiner. Concerning the baptism ritual. Seven sacraments: for every evolution-form of the human being there is also an involution-form. Laying on of hands. Priest vestment.

5.

STUTTGART, JUNE 15, 1921

The sermon. The picture element must pass over into the feeling and into the will impulses. The significance of rhythmical repetitions. About John 1:3: the eternal and the temporal; existence and subsistence. Meditation as preparation for the sermon. Cardinal Newman's wrestling for Christian truths. Anthroposophy as bearing the element of religious life. An example of pictorial speaking. Overcoming imaginations bound to space; the innocence of nature and the becoming guilty of the human being. Immortality and pre-existence. The *Gloria*. Christ brings about balance between Lucifer and Ahriman.

Discussion

Preparation of a further course: place, financing, participants, promotional means, Central Office, required education. Discussion about Anthroposophy and religion.

6.

STUTTGART, JUNE 16, 1921

About the nature of human memory. The astral body as reader of the esoteric script. The sacred art of writing in ancient times. The origin of the art of printing books. Goethe's relation to color. The significance of judgments out of the folk nature, of sympathy and antipathy for a particular folk soul.

APPENDIX

SPIRITUAL WORLD

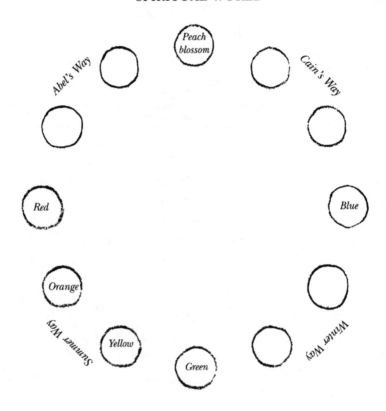

EARTHLY WORLD

Beneath this sketch drawn for Professor Hans Wohbold in Munich (undated, ca. 1923), Rudolf Steiner wrote: The summer way is the way of The Christian Community in memory of a community (pre-natal) in the spiritual world (Abel's way). The winter way is the way of Anthroposophists through cold solitude to knowledge (Cain's way).

INTRODUCTION

CHRISTOPHER BAMFORD

Held in June 1921, the present lectures and discussions, the first of the five "Priest Courses," record the first steps of the remarkable journey taken by a small group of dedicated souls, who, out of their own impulse, guided and advised by Rudolf Steiner, sought a path to Christian religious renewal. Only a year later, in September 1922, this same small group, joined by others of like heart and mind, would become the founding members of the Movement for Religious Renewal. To this movement, Rudolf Steiner, acting as "the mediating agent" and drawing as an individual on the spiritual world, gave new sacraments, including a new Communion Service ("The Act of Consecration of Man [Humanity]"), and the name: "The Christian Community."

The deed was a unique gesture for Rudolf Steiner, who, for pragmatic as well as principled reasons, while he placed the Christ Being and the Mystery of Golgotha at the heart of Anthroposophy, always clearly distinguished the initiation stream of spiritual science from institutional Christianity—or "religion"—and was extraordinarily careful in his own work as a spiritual teacher not to infringe upon the territory of the Church. Thus, for example, though he would give funeral eulogies, he would not conduct funeral services, but always ensure that a priest officiated. We might also note that, prior to this moment of destiny, Rudolf Steiner rarely spoke theologically or of theology, for the most part carefully restricting his teaching to cosmological questions.

Mindful of this, in the present case, as he put it in his own words: "I gave what I was in a position to give with respect to what future theology needs; and I also gave the contents of the ceremonial and ritual required for building a new community of this kind." He did so, he explained, "as a human being to other human beings," a private individual. What he gave to those founding The Christian

Community, therefore, from this point of view, had "nothing to do with the Anthroposophical Movement," or Anthroposophy, which therefore should not be looked upon as its "founder." Nevertheless, as he also emphasized: "this has nothing to do with the fact that the advice that makes this religious movement into a real spiritual community in a form suited to the present stage of human evolution was given in all love and also in all devotion to the spiritual powers who are able to place such a movement in the world today." Clearly, subtle issues are involved here.

From Steiner's perspective, then, Anthroposophy or spiritual science did not need a religious renewal, "but religious renewal [was] needed in the world." In this sense, Rudolf Steiner did not in any way "found" a church or a denomination. He guided and helped others to create a wholly independent Christian religious movement—not out of Anthroposophy, but out of Christianity itself and the spiritual world—and did so only in response to their request. Rudolf Steiner did not himself ordain the priests, saying he would not and could not do that. Thus the process of ordination was unusual. Acting as the mediator, Rudolf Steiner "mediated" Friedrich Rittelmeyer's ordination from the spiritual world and then, Rittelmeyer, an ordained Lutheran priest and the dean of Evangelical theologians in Germany at that time, ordained the first group of priests, who, in turn, then ordained the rest. Obviously, many difficult and perhaps unanswerable questions—for example, the future of religion as such—arise here.

None of these considerations, however, affected the reality that, two and a half years after the initial approach to Rudolf Steiner, the first celebration of the Act of Consecration was a momentous and historic experience for all those involved. And yet to those participating it also seemed entirely natural: "For those who remembered what some churches teach about the so-called apostolic succession, the event was astounding, but the reality was as plain as sunrise. You do not dispute the Sun. You bow to its rays..." (Alfred Heidenreich) Rudolf Steiner, too, was moved:

At the end of September and the beginning of October (1921), a number of German theological students, who bore in their hearts the impulse for a religious renewal in the Christian sense, assembled at the Goetheanum. The work begun then found its fulfillment in September 1922. The hours spent in September 1922 with these students in the small hall of the south wing— the very spot where later the fire was first discovered—were for me an experience I cannot but reckon as one of the solemn festivals of my life. There, together with a group of men and women who were fired with a noble enthusiasm, it was possible to enter on the path that carries the knowledge of the Spirit into religious experience. (*Goetheanum II*, cited Heidenreich).

As unique and epochal (in its way) as it was, however, the founding of The Christian Community was by no means the only significant initiative guided or undertaken by Steiner during this time. This is not to lessen it. On the contrary, in the end perhaps what makes it most remarkable is that, in the context of simultaneously pursuing an enormous number of other tasks, Rudolf Steiner, with the aid of the spiritual world—and, it must be said, that of the group of souls with whom he was working—could so consummately and swiftly help to bring to its conclusion such a remarkable achievement.

That Steiner could do so is partly due to the fact that, though he was working on many fronts simultaneously, as in some ways he had always done, all these were now interrelated and interconnected in a new way by the historical conditions ushered in by the end of the First World War (and the treaty of Versailles). A rupture in Western civilization—and perhaps even human civilization—had occurred. Anthroposophy was not exempt from these conditions: it, too, had to respond to the rupture. Something had ended. The historical moment called for a new beginning. For perhaps a few moments or years, the opportunity "to make it new" would be present. As Steiner also recognized, the spiritual world likewise hoped and called for such change. So long as the opportunity—the *kairos* or opportune moment—lasted, it would support such ventures in any way it could. Therefore, recognizing the moment—the need on Earth and the support in Heaven (which, as he understood, was no guarantee of success)—Steiner immediately set to work. By any account, the scope of what he achieved in the seven years (1918-1925) remaining to him after the end of hostilities is overwhelming.

The First World War had ended on November 11, 1918. Eighteen months before, in response to a request from a German diplomat in Berlin, Otto von Lerchenfeld, to prepare something on what should be done when the war ended, Rudolf Steiner had prepared two Memoranda that called for a radical rethinking of social life on the basis of which a true and lasting peace might be built. In these Memoranda, Steiner outlined what would become known as "The Threefold Social Order."

Officially, the Memoranda came to nothing, and so, when the war ended, Steiner took his message directly to the people. On March 5, 1919, his "Appeal to the German People and Culture" appeared in newspapers all over Germany and was widely distributed. People were listening: his book *Towards Social Renewal*, published shortly after the "Appeal," sold eight thousand copies in its first year. In these works, Steiner gave voice to what many others felt: to rebuild society would take a completely new kind of social thinking. In the place of the centralized, monolithic state, he called for a "threefold-ing" of society and proposed the separation, on the basis of their own natures, of the three spheres of a healthy social life—the economic, the judicial-political, and the spiritual-cultural—in which each was independent, with the result that they could then interact, individually and interdependently, each performing its own particular function, as do the organs in our own bodies. Over the next three years, Rudolf Steiner would work tirelessly for the practical embodiment of this idea.

Virtually simultaneously, within days of the war's ending, as the German Revolution (that led to the Weimar Republic) was taking place, Emil Molt, a Stuttgart social reformer and industrialist—he was the owner of the Waldorf Astoria Cigarette Company—was in Dornach, where he heard Steiner lecture on Marxism and Threefolding as polar alternatives for the future. A week later, talking to someone about the problem of educating his workers' children, Molt had the idea of founding a school for his factory workers' children. He spoke to Rudolf Steiner about it, and asked him to be the adviser. Steiner agreed. Nine months later, in September 1919, the first Waldorf school opened its doors. That, too, took enormous time, and energy.

As important a deed as educating children for the future was, it was still only a beginning. Higher education—by means of which scientific, epistemological, and cultural paradigms were established—was equally important. Not surprisingly, then, in 1920, Steiner turned toward the universities—university students—and the professions. That year the first Medical Course was held for doctors and Steiner gave important lecture courses on the "Boundaries of Natural Science" and "Anthroposophy and the Different Branches of Learning." A "Union for Anthroposophical College Work" was founded. And, finally, in the autumn, the first anthroposophical "College Course" was held.

These new activities began to draw a new, different group of people: bright, idealistic, educated students. In the universities and colleges in Germany, Switzerland, and Austria, anthroposophical student groups began to form, and aspiring philosophers, doctors, scientists, and theologians began to appear at Steiner's lectures and at the Goetheanum. In a word: the Youth Movement began. This, too, in itself and in its consequences also took enormous energy, for it almost split the Anthroposophical Society, which was being forced to change to meet the changing times in ways foreign to the older members.

In other words, during this whole period, as the ongoing background and context to all that was going on, a profound metamorphosis in the life of Anthroposophy and the Anthroposophical Society was in process. For the first time Anthroposophy was being called upon to truly open its doors to the world. It was being called not only to go out into the world, but to meet the world at home in the form of the new, younger seekers, who were coming toward it in increasing numbers. Steiner recognized that this new situation meant Anthroposophy would have to be reframed. It would need to be communicated in more or less ordinary language—the language of experience. It would have to move from what had become its cozy, privileged domain into the domain of more public discourse.

Thus, almost without warning, what had been more or less an "esoteric school" with its roots in nineteenth-century occultism and Theosophy was transformed into a still esoteric but now broader movement for spiritual, social, and cultural change. Older members found themselves being asked to change. Not only was this difficult in itself, it was psychologically difficult—and often impossible—for them. Thus, from the beginning, a tension arose between the old and the new, which came above all in the form of a new generation.

Born around the turn of the century, these young people came of age as the war ended. They were both the first post-Kali Yuga (post 1900) generation and true "Michaelites"—for the Michael Age had begun in 1879. And they brought something new. They came to Anthroposophy innocently, out of their hearts' needs, without any connection to traditional esotericism. They did not think of themselves as "occultists," but rather as spiritual *activists*, practical philosophers, scientists, and theologians. They wanted to be *pioneers* in their fields. They wanted to change the world as well as change themselves.

Steiner welcomed them. He had been waiting for this moment, for these young people, all his life. Here were educated, seeking, young people who agreed with him, and who wished to make a difference with their lives. They wanted to develop spiritually *and* intellectually. They yearned to overcome the separation between everyday life and the disciplines of science, art, history, psychology, theology, religion, and so on. They wanted learning to be *real*. They wanted spiritual, professional, and personal life to be a one, a continuum, lived from the same source. Above all, they wanted life to be *whole* and saw Anthroposophy as just that: as a *holistic* way of life—self- and world-transformation in one.

The founding of The Christian Community belongs to this "youth" impulse and also to the reality of social "threefolding," which, in the cultural sphere, as Steiner always stressed, depends upon the coming together again as in the ancient Mysteries of the threefold unity of science, religion, and art.

✳

As with the other cultural and spiritual initiatives that Rudolf Steiner helped bring into the world—whether eurythmy, threefolding, Waldorf education, anthroposophical medicine, or bio-dynamic agriculture—the initiating impulse for the founding of The Christian Community came not from Steiner himself but from a person, and later, a group of people, who felt a need or had an idea that the times seemed to call for, and who asked for Steiner's aid and counsel in realizing it.

In other words, the process that leads to a new creation begins with a question. Steiner's role was always—initially, at least—to respond with his whole being out of the spiritual world in as helpful and responsible a manner as possible. Once an initiative, set in motion by a question, reached a kind of sustainable momentum, Steiner would give himself completely to the opportunity offered him by the spiritual world through the person or people asking the question—an opportunity that, in nearly all cases, at least in retrospect, it seems he had been waiting for.

In the present instance—which makes an interesting, and in some ways exemplary story—the first, and in that sense seminal, person was a philosophy student, Johannes Werner Klein. Klein, as it later turned out, was not perhaps the emissary Steiner would have chosen in an ideal world. His biography shows him to have been somewhat unstable and inwardly and deeply conflicted: he would later leave both The Christian Community and the Anthroposophical Society (and the First Class) to join the National Socialist Party.

The son of a Dusseldorf lawyer and a pastor's daughter, Werner Klein, in 1915, at the tender age of 17, full of enthusiasm and patriotic idealism, volunteered for the army, fighting bravely in Russia and France. He became an officer. Then, in 1918, in a military hospital in the Ardennes, he experienced the shattering of his ideals. He realized Germany had lost the war. He was plunged into despair. Compounding his life crisis, when the war finally ended, the woman he loved—whom he had met on leave, and whom he had never spoken to but only written to—decided to marry someone else. Klein considered suicide, but, standing before a mirror, pistol in hand, his own image terrified him, and he put the pistol down. Life, as it does, went on. At College, studying law, he oscillated between being swept along by student life and falling into deep depressions, which he endured by taking long, solitary walks. After one of these, perhaps, he decided to change direction. He decided to study evangelical theology in Marburg, following a conversation with Friedrich Rittelmeyer— his first "anthroposophical" connection, though he probably knew nothing of it, for he consulted him only as one of the most renowned people in the field. But soon he left Marburg for Munich. Leaving Munich again shortly after arriving, he returned thence to Marburg, where he turned from theology to philosophy and, through a professor there, met the Anthroposophist Martin Borchart. Finally, then, with Borchart—and his wife, Elisabeth—Klein began to study Anthroposophy. In this way Werner Klein was led inexorably toward Rudolf Steiner and in February 1920, together with his new friends, traveled to Dornach to hear Steiner lecture.

Evidently, one does not choose one's emissaries. They have their destinies. Even if Rudolf Steiner had been able to see what lay in store for this young man, which may well have been at that time still an open question, he was bound as an initiate to disregard what he knew: to honor the freedom of others and not interfere with another person's destiny out of his own knowledge of what lay in the future. In that sense, given the question, which was a profound and good one, it was his task only to respond to it authentically and in the moment. On another level, it seems clear, too, that human ventures, even spiritual ones, are inevitably messy affairs, as human beings themselves are, and that to believe that they can be otherwise is unrealistic.

Certainly, Rudolf Steiner had nothing to do with choosing this particular emissary. In fact, the present instance shows that it is the timeliness of the question that is important in such cases, not its bearer or the quality of his soul life or the nature of his destiny. Citing, almost certainly to Steiner's approval, the philosopher Schelling's division of Christianity into three periods (the Petrine, the Pauline and the Johannine) in which Rudolf Steiner would have heard the echoes of Joachim of Fiore's similar schema of the progressive unfolding of Christianity through Ages of the Father, the Son, and the Holy

Spirit, Klein asked: "Has the time come to prepare the way for a third Christianity, Johannine Christianity?" To which Rudolf Steiner replied with great seriousness, for the question was surely a good one: "If you want to do this and find the necessary forms for it…. It would have great significance for humanity." But, he added: "My task is a different one. I must bring spiritual science and speak out of it. I must stay with that task. What you see is great and necessary, but you must do it." With this, Klein felt himself affirmed. At the same time, in retrospect, he mentions that there may have been a "misunderstanding," that his understanding of "Johannine" Christianity—this "third stage of Christianity"—may not have been Rudolf Steiner's. But the process had begun: the question had been stated.

Meanwhile, in Zürich, Gertrud Spörri was studying theology. The daughter of the owner of a small weaving mill, she had left school early to help her father. During the war, working as a social worker, she had become engaged to the son of a factory owner. The engagement did not last. Her fiancé's father insisted they break off the engagement. By then, however, his sister had introduced her to Anthroposophy. After reading *How to Know Higher Worlds*, she began to travel to Dornach on weekends, where she enjoyed several conversations with Rudolf Steiner. They became close. Then, while attending a church service on Reformation Day 1916, she heard a sermon on the topic, "We need a new Reformation!" Is that all? She thought. A year later, during another sermon she saw—inwardly in vision—someone at the altar and a pulpit or lectern for making prophecies. To her horror, she realized it was herself she was seeing. This image stayed with her. Gradually it ripened into the decision to study theology. She returned to school, graduated and, by 1920, Gertrud Spörri was the only woman among fifty other students studying theology in Basel. Each weekend found her in Dornach, wrestling with such questions as: Who is God, what is God, where is God? Is there a spiritual foundation for baptism, for the eucharist?

In May 1920, then, two months after Werner Klein had posed his question, Gertrud Spörri, studying theology in order to serve Anthroposophy, posed her question to Rudolf Steiner. She asked him whether he thought there was any possibility of Anthroposophy working within the church. Could one become an anthroposophical minister? He responded that something might indeed be achieved within the church if a sufficient number of anthroposophical theologians were to become ministers and take up the pulpit. Later, during the first lecture course for architects, he mentioned to her in a private conversation that, if he were to do a similar course on theology it might be possible to "speak with young people in a much more intimate manner than is possible yet with doctors."

At this time Werner Klein and Gertrud Spörri did not yet know each other, and neither had spoken to others of their conversation with Rudolf Steiner. Although they had been present together at a lecture in February 1920, they had not spoken to one another. However, in autumn of that year (1920), at the opening of the first Goetheanum, during the first College Course (CW 322), Gertrud Spörri did meet Martin and Elizabeth Borchart, as well as Gottfried Hüsemann and Rudolf Meyer, who would also be part of the founding group (although Meyer would not be ordained until later). But she did not meet Werner Klein.

Finally, in April of the following year (1921), during a College Course in Dornach, they met, and, since Gertrud Spörri was a theology student, Werner Klein felt impelled to tell her of the idea— ideal—that had been consuming him. Sitting in a café, according to Heidenreich, Klein poured his heart out. He questioned the validity of theology as it was studied. At one point, to emphasize the importance of religion in relation to Anthroposophy, Klein suddenly produced a mimeographed copy of *Cosmic and Human Metamorphoses* and read out the following passage:

> In the highest sense, spiritual science, particularly as regards the Mystery of Christ, may be taken as a support or foundation for the life and exercise of religion, but it should not be made into a religion. For we must be clear that religion in its living form and living practice is what enkindles the spiritual consciousness of the human community. If this spiritual consciousness of community is to become a living thing in us, we cannot possibly stop at merely abstract ideas of God or Christ, but must be

renewed amidst the religious practices and activities (which, in different people, may take various forms) as something that provides us with a religious center and appeals to us as such. If this religious sentiment is only deep enough, and finds means of stimulating the soul, it will soon feel a longing—a real longing—for the very ideas that can be developed in spiritual science. If spiritual science may be said to be a support for a religious life, as, objectively speaking, it certainly is—subjectively the time has come today when we may say that a person with true religious feelings is driven by these feelings to seek knowledge. For spiritual consciousness is acquired through religious feeling and spiritual knowledge through spiritual science, just as knowledge of nature is acquired by natural science. Spiritual consciousness leads to the impulse to acquire spiritual knowledge. It may be said that an inner religious life may today subjectively drive a person to spiritual science.

In this context, Gertrud Spörri at last felt able to confide what Rudolf Steiner had said to her privately regarding a possible course for young theologians. Together, they realized two things would be needed for this to happen: first, a real question or request to Rudolf Steiner would need to be formulated; second, more people would need to be found. He would undertake the former, she the latter. Thus, she went first to Berlin, where she hoped to study. There she met Emil Bock, who took the new idea to his circle of friends. From Berlin, she went to Stuttgart, where, with Werner Klein, she met with Ludwig Köhler and Gottfried Hüsemann. Then in May, at Whitsun, all those interested gathered in Stuttgart and an official letter was drafted. Finally, on May 24, Rudolf Steiner, in conversation with the bearers of the question—Werner Klein and Gertrud Spörri—agreed to hold the course in the middle of June. He told them that free communities must be founded, a ritual established, and women must hold an equal place with men. He added that, in preparation for the meeting in June, all those interested should gather in Stuttgart to hold preliminary conversations on these issues in preparation for the course.

(Gertrud Spörri went on to play an important role in the subsequent courses. She organized the first two (and the last) meetings, arranging lodging and meals, doing all the correspondence, taking care of the finances, and organizing the travel plans. After a hiatus, during which she nursed her dying father, she returned to the work and was among the forty-five persons prepared by Rudolf Steiner for the priesthood. She became the first titular "Oberlenker" ("bishop" or "coordinator"), warranting this honor, according to Rudolf Gädeke, by the inner certainty and strength she had gained through nursing her father and intensely studying Rudolf Steiner's *Truth and Science* (CW 3).

Together with Friedrich Rittelmeyer and Emil Bock, she founded The Christian Community in Stuttgart and was an active participant in the burgeoning movement. She was especially active in the development of rituals and through her ongoing relationship with Rudolf Steiner, which, for instance, made it possible for her later to initiate the important course in Pastoral Medicine. Rudolf Steiner helped her, as the first female priest, in many ways and through many conversations. At his suggestion, she focused in her sermons and lectures, particularly on gender issues, and later wrote books on *The Woman in the Priesthood* (1929) and *The Woman at the Altar* (1931). Being the first female priest among so many men was not easy! Clearly, she was a strong woman and this strength finally got her into trouble when she broke her solemn vow not to change the ritual. As a result, Friedrich Rittelmeyer had to suspend her and release her from her priestly duties and she left The Christian Community on March 6, 1933. Thereafter, she was socially active in various ways, ending her days working for the Red Cross in Switzerland and in a tuberculosis clinic. Gertrud Spörri died of a heart attack after a hip operation in 1968.)

*

So much for the context, the brief recounting of which thus far has omitted any consideration of a question that may perhaps already have loomed large in some readers' minds.

Clearly, The Christian Community is different in kind from the other initiatives Steiner midwifed. Though "spiritual" activities in the form that Steiner renewed them, today such fields as education, agriculture, medicine, art, and social theory are worldly or "secular," not religious, as they were in ancient times. Likewise spiritual science, like natural science, as a path or method is "secular"—even though spiritual and initiatory—which is precisely why Steiner calls it "science." The Christian Community, on the other hand, whatever these two words mean today, is self-evidently both "Christian" and "religious."

As Steiner emphasized, Anthroposophy or spiritual science (like Theosophy) is not a religion. And yet he often added that, if one has a religion, the study and practice of Anthroposophy will only deepen it. In some sense, then, Steiner believed that religion and spiritual science were neither competitors nor mutually exclusive. Pursuing different paths toward the spirit, they were in some sense related. Certainly, the religious "mood" of reverence and devotion was a key element in the meditative path as Steiner taught it; and also, the Lord's Prayer, which he prayed daily; and also, for those ready for it, the love of Christ. He also spoke frequently of what we might think of as religious virtues such as grace, trust, gratitude, and love. But all these were to be practiced within the "secular," but initiatory, setting of Anthroposophy. Consequently, he was surprised and disappointed when, after the founding of The Christian Community—which he had imagined as working in the religious sphere in the larger world— it became evident that its membership would be drawn primarily not from the outer world, but from among Anthroposophists, who thereby indicated that spiritual science was failing to satisfy all their spiritual longings.

Here we enter a realm of paradox, ambiguity, and mystery.

Steiner himself often referred to the relationship between spiritual science and religion in terms of the biblical figures of Cain and Abel. He spoke of the "mystery," known to the Rosicrucians and lying at the basis of Masonic lore and ritual, according to which Abel was born of Adam and Eve; but Cain was born of Eve by one of the Elohim or Gods. Cain, then, according to this legend, is divine-human, while Abel is purely human. In other words, we are presented with two "streams" of humanity or two types or orders of human service. One recognizes that human beings contain divinity, the uncreated spark of God—that they are "little gods." The other believes that they "receive" divinity from above. In this view, "Abel" represents the priestly, receptive, mystic, feminine function of those who receive everything from the divine; while "Cain" represents those who create everything out of themselves, the artists and scientists: the creators. As Steiner explains in his lectures on Freemasonry, *The Temple Legend*:

> Among the descendents of Cain are all those who have been creators of art and science, as, for instance, Methuselah, the inventor of the Tau script, and Tubal-Cain, who taught the use and working of metal ores and iron. All those who trained themselves in the arts and sciences were in this line. Hiram [the architect of Solomon's Temple] also descended from the race of Cain, and he was the inheritor of all that had been learned by the others of his line in technology and art.

Solomon himself, of course, was of the Abel or priestly stream. This is to say that, in the persons of Solomon and Hiram, the founding myth of Freemasonry (known also to the Rosicrucians)—that of the building of Solomon's Temple—tells of the story of the collaboration of these two streams. That is, the two can and do work together.

However that may be, for Rudolf Steiner, then, we may say, at least metaphorically, that there are two basic human approaches to the spirit—one scientific-artistic-creative (Cain) and the other religious (Abel). I say "metaphorically" because, from one point of view, these are essentially two different traditions or ways of approaching the spiritual world—we may call them, borrowing a Buddhist expression, "own power" and "other power"—the one striving upward from within, the other receiving from above. After all, there are not two kinds of human being. There is only one kind of human being: made in the image and likeness of God and constituting the tenth hierarchy. Within this humanity, the Abel tradition or approach stresses the transcendence of divinity, available by grace to human beings who prepare their souls to receive its gifts. We may call this path "religion," though religion is obviously more than this single definition. The Cain tradition, for its part, stresses initiation, the awakening to the immanence of the divinity in the human heart that makes the human being a "second" God or creator on Earth.

From another perspective, the distinction Rudolf Steiner makes between the Abel and Cain paths is similar to the ancient Indian distinction between the Brahmans or priests and the Kshatriya or warriors. In the "Golden Age," it is said, there were no distinctions: every one had a direct connection to the divine. Then, in the "Silver Age," the system of the four castes—priests, warriors, merchants, and craftspeople—came into being. It worked well, and people lived together in harmony, constituting as it were an earthly reflection of the Heavenly Human. But in the "Bronze Age," strife arose between the castes. The warriors began to compete for primacy with the priests, a tension that has continued, more or less, into our own time, the "Iron Age."

Historically, in the West, what in the East is called the Kshatriya or warrior path goes under the sign of Hermes and is called Hermeticism or the "Royal Art." This tradition has to do with knowledge and initiation that is not metaphysical or theological—that is, priestly—but cosmological in both "macrocosmic" and "microcosmic" senses. Hermeticism, according to this definition, has to do with the science of the subtle states mediating between the divine and the earthly realms, and eschews any theological or "first" principles, which are the province of theology as such.

The designation "Hermetic" here of course derives from the Greek God Hermes, the messenger and interpreter of the Gods, who links Heaven and Earth and whose primary symbol is the Caduceus. Hermes in this sense is a universal symbol, the same (more or less) as the Egyptian Thoth, the Roman Mercury, the Hindu Budha, the Northern Odin or Wotan, and the Mayan Quetzalcoatl. This tradition, emanating from the ancient Mysteries, enters the West under the sign of *Hermes Trismegistus*, the legendary first teacher of Hermetism, called Thrice Great because he is master of the three realms—the earthly, the sublunary, and the celestial, at least to the sphere of the fixed stars.

Now, the aim of these Lesser ("hermetic") Mysteries—so-called because they are cosmological, and hence derivative, in contrast to the principal Greater (or "theological") Mysteries—is nothing other than the realization of the primordial human state—that of the *Anthropos* or the Archetypal Cosmic-Divine Human. In other words, Rudolf Steiner, using different language, implicitly—and esoterically— placed Anthroposophy under the sign of Hermes and the Royal Art, that is, the Cain stream.

One may note, however, that the distinction between Cain and Abel seems to reflect the mystery of nature and grace, which, as the wisest philosophers have always concluded, are but two aspects of the same reality—grace descending as far as nature ascends. Despite this, "priests" and "warriors"—"organized religion" and alchemical, Hermetic, Rosicrucian and Masonic initiates—have frequently been in conflict, both sides in the long run contributing equal venom and provocation. Here again, however, as with nature and grace, a little reflection will show that they are two sides of a single coin. Even where "own" power is emphasized, nothing happens without grace, as Steiner himself repeatedly affirms.

Nevertheless, Rudolf Steiner himself clearly felt—or at least affirmed—that there was a fundamental difference between the Abel and Cain streams, that is, between "religion" and "spiritual science" and that this distinction should be maintained. That is, he held to the distinction between the Lesser and the Greater Mysteries. He never spoke about theology: all his lectures and writings are essentially cosmological. The two realms and paths were for him as distinct as "summer" and "winter"; and yet, paradoxically again, as related and united as these are by being part of the year.

Rudolf Steiner indicated as much when, around 1923, he made a sketch (see the image at the beginning of this introduction) for Professor Hans Wohlbold, a science teacher and student of his since 1904, and beneath it he wrote:

The summer way is the way of The Christian Community in memory of a community (pre-natal) in the spiritual world (Abel's way).
The winter way is the way of Anthroposophists through cold solitude to knowledge (Cain's way).

From his earliest lectures through the *Calendar of the Soul* to *The Cycle of the Year as Breathing Process of the Earth* (1923, around the time of this sketch), a golden thread weaving through Steiner's teaching connects the profound meaning of the experience of the year to cosmic, earthly, and human soul life and shows how the soul, like the Earth, expands receptively into the cosmos during hot summer months and then draws into itself in the cold winter months, having, like the Earth, in-breathed the forces of the cosmos. The Summer Mysteries are filled with communal poetry, dance, and ritual. In the Winter Mysteries, individual contemplation and inwardness prevail. But heat and cold have other meanings, too. Steiner suggests one such meaning, when he connects "cold solitude" to "knowledge" and warm summer to prenatal, spiritual, and earthly "community"— for community depends upon the polar counterpart of knowledge, namely, love. Perhaps if the winter path is the path of knowledge, the summer path is the path of love. Yet, is true knowledge possible without love? Or love without knowledge? And is not the Rosicrucian goal to unite love and knowledge, the cross and the roses? Love, of course, we may connect with "soul" or "feeling," often symbolized by water; knowledge we may connect with "spirit," often symbolized by "fire." Thus, in the two paths of The Christian Community and Anthroposophy, we also have an echo of the difference described by the ancient alchemists as the wet way and the dry way—the first slower, but perhaps more sure, the second faster, briefer, but more dangerous.

Still another interpretation is suggested by a comment made by Rudolf Steiner in a discussion during the Agriculture Course. Asked, "What is the best time to sow seeds for bread-making?" he replied: "Planting dates are extremely important, of course, and it makes a great difference whether you sow close to the winter months or further away from them. If you sow close to winter, you induce strong reproductive capacity; if you sow further away from winter, you induce a strong nutritive force in your grains." He goes on to speak of the difference one experiences when meditating in winter or summer: reproductive—that is, creative—capacity in winter, nutritive—that is nourishing, healing—power in summer.

But perhaps, after all, things are simpler than this. In a note to the sketch in *Freemasonry and Ritual Work* (CW 265), Hella Wiesberger cites a work by Jan K. Lagutt, "The Foundation Stone of Freemasonry":

> Priesthood in all religions [Abel's way] rests on consecration, by means of which higher, impersonal powers, which can be regarded as the out-flowing of divine grace, are bestowed upon the bearer. Consecration brings it about that divine effects of grace can be carried into the physical world through the priest. Clearly stated: the consecrated priest becomes a channel through which divine effects can flow into the earthly world....
>
> The stream to which, among other movements, Freemasonry belongs, leads in a different direction [Cain's way]. Here no ordination occurs in the sense of the conferring higher powers, but an initiation or awakening, the nature of which is marked by an activation of powers already inherent in the human being. The symbolic ritual actions usually associated with initiation have the sole intention of awakening latent powers and bringing them into activity.

Lagutt then goes on to speak of the relationship between—and even ultimately the union of—these two paths. If priesthood starts with grace, initiation should end in grace. If impersonal powers are given to a priest on ordination, he or she must become worthy to awaken, to achieve initiation, through them. Initiation, for its part, when it is not empty ceremony, calls on one's deepest individual powers, but through these one should become ripe to enter those spheres where divine grace resides. Priests may thus become initiates and initiates in turn may gain priestly dignity, if they allow their deepest human qualities, the divine within them, to unfold. Thus the opposites can come together. The one does not exclude the other. Both are paths to true being—which is divine.

And yet: Steiner held firmly to their difference and their independence from each other. And yet...

✳

Undoubtedly, the relationship of Anthroposophy to The Christian Community—of spiritual science to Religion—raises many questions. Underlying and perhaps illuminating these is the question of Rudolf Steiner's own relationship to Christ and the Mystery of Golgotha and to Christianity, both as a religion and as "what is greater than a religion." For some readers and students of his work, Christ is seen as secondary to the primacy of the "method" or inner path of spiritual science, which is, as it were "neutral" with regard to religion. For others, that same path, which Steiner himself took and taught, cannot be separated from the Christ impulse, whose fruit it is. From this latter perspective, Christ and Christianity are central to and in fact are the very heart of Anthroposophy.

But this still leaves open the question of what part Christianity as a religion—in a sense, religion itself—plays in Rudolf Steiner's thinking.

It is often disputed, for instance, that religion played any part at all in Steiner's formation. And yet it is clear that, in addition to his better-known clairvoyant gifts—his consciousness of the suprasensory world—and his determination to forge a scientific, cognitive-thinking, and, we might add, artistic approach to the spiritual nature of reality, Rudolf Steiner was also from the beginning, even if inchoately, always "Christian" and possessed what we might call a "religious" sensitivity, one which understood the spiritual importance of religion. As he himself tells us in these lectures, religion, science, and art—still separate today, but ever striving to recreate the unity they enjoyed in ancient times—make up the cultural sphere of the threefold social order. These three, which were one in the ancient Mystery cultures, were in a sense also one in Rudolf Steiner: a single seed which he sought all his life to develop into a fully formed whole.

In this regard, we can learn a great deal of the consistency of the beginning of his trajectory from his *Autobiography*.

The Steiner family was Catholic by culture and origin. Thus the infant Rudolf was baptized in the parish church of St. Michael in Drascovec. By then, however, his father, who had "spent his childhood and youth in close contact with the Premonstratensian Monastery in Geras…[and] always recalled this period of his life with great pleasure…[and] liked to tell how he served in the monastery and was taught by the monks," had become a freethinker, who would have nothing to do with the Church (though later he would return to it).

Religion therefore played no active role in Rudolf Steiner's home life. It was not much talked about, except when it was disparaged. Nevertheless, because it was everywhere, traces of religious activity made their impression on the boy. He fondly remembers the liberal, tolerant, jovial priest, who used to visit his parents and who taught them how to bake acacia blossoms. He remarks how he loved to walk alone up one of the local mountains to Saint Rosalie's Chapel and how, on another walk, passing by the monastery of the Order of the Most Holy Redeemer, he would meet the monks and wished they had spoken to him—a feeling that germinated within him until, in his ninth year, he "became convinced that there were very important matters connected with the tasks of these monks and that [he] had to learn what they were."

Recalling his tenth year, Steiner wrote:

The proximity of the church and surrounding cemetery was profoundly significant for my life as a boy. Everything that happened in the village school was connected to the church… As schoolboys we acted as servers and choir members at Mass, memorial services for the dead, and funerals. My youthful soul gladly lived in the ceremonious nature of the Latin language and the cult. Until my tenth year I participated intensively in serving in the church, and this often enabled me to be in the company of the priest, whom I revered so deeply…

My most vivid memory of childhood…is of the cult and the solemn liturgical music and how it caused the questions of existence to arise with moving power before my spirit. The priest's Bible instruction and the catechism had much less effect on my inner life than did his actions as celebrant of the ritual in mediating between the sensory and suprasensory worlds. From the beginning, this was never a mere form to me, but was a profound inner experience. And this was even more so since it made me a stranger in my own home. Nevertheless, my home environment did not diminish the spiritual richness I received though the ritual....

Serving at Mass, of course, meant participating through image, symbol, and gesture in the Mystery of Golgotha enacted through the stages of the proclamation, sacrifice, transubstantiation, and communion. Thus, in freedom, unconditioned by family or preconception, Rudolf Steiner was able to absorb the ritual memorial of the "turning point of time" and its human-earthly-cosmic consequences. Funerals and memorial masses for the dead will have given him some added sense, in addition to his own experience, of the "communion of saints" and of the reality of humanity on both sides of the threshold as a single community. And, above all, as he writes, the whole ritual confirmed and conveyed the possibility of mediating between sensory and suprasensory worlds.

At the same time, however, to place this in context, it is important to recall an astonishing fact that Rudolf Steiner told Friedrich Rittelmeyer, namely, that it was not until much later that he, Steiner, actually read the Gospel accounts. He knew nothing of the Bible in his childhood. For instance, he says that, until led to them by his own investigations, he knew nothing of the Gospel descriptions of the events connected with the Resurrection, which he then found agreed in every detail with what had been revealed to him. In other words, the early intimations described in the Autobiography are just that: the preparation of the vessel, the planting of seeds.

A few years later, at fourteen, when his philosophical-scientific path of thinking was already well established—and arithmetic, geometry, physics were his delight and sustenance—he tells how he discovered and began an intensive study of Kant's *Critique of Pure Reason*. Though difficult for him to understand, the book posed what was already for him the overriding problem: namely, as he puts it, "to what degree human reason is capable of understanding the nature of things." Over the summer holidays, therefore, he set himself the task

of developing "a judgment on the relationship between human thinking and the creation of natural phenomena." Two things, he wrote,
influenced his feelings toward these efforts in thinking:

> First, I wanted to develop my own thinking so that each thought
> would be completely clear and surveyable, unbiased by any arbi-
> trary feeling. Second, I wanted to establish a harmony within
> myself between such thinking and religious instruction. This
> was also vitally important me at the time. We had excellent
> textbooks in this particular field. With tremendous devotion, I
> absorbed from them dogma and symbolism, the description of
> ritual and church history. I lived in these teachings with great
> intensity...

For the moment at least, this surprising anecdote is the last extended
and explicit reference in the *Autobiography* to matters of religion or
Christianity. Steiner's attention and energy are turned to questions of
epistemology, freedom, science, Goethe, and a philosophical, cogni-
tive-intuitive approach to the spirit. This was his great task: opening
science and thinking to the suprasensory through the transformation
of consciousness. Faced with this, one might be tempted to think that
Steiner changed radically, that Christ and Christianity are no longer
important to him—that they are no longer in his mind or heart at all.
Yet he gives us clues that this is not the case.

First, there is his initiatory friendship with Felix Kogutski (1833-
1909), the herb-gatherer, naturopath, and mystic—"a simple man of
the people"—whom he met on the train to Vienna. Steiner was going
to school; Kogutski was traveling to the city to sell his medicinal
herbs to pharmacies. "From our first meeting I had a deep affinity
with him," Steiner writes. Meeting Kogutski, a living Rosicrucian,
who could apprehend clairvoyantly the inner worlds of nature
("contact with the spirits of nature was something self-evident to
him") was a turning point in Steiner's life, for it was Kogutski who,
acting as the "agent," would lead Rudolf Steiner to his meeting with
the M[aster], most likely Christian Rosenkreutz. But Kogutski also
provided another service: he was the first person with whom Steiner

could share his suprasensory experiences. Nor was that all: Kogutski was also a deeply grounded "esoteric" Christian of great personal piety and it is not hard to imagine that spiritual and theological questions relating to Christianity also figured in their conversations.

At the same time, his vocation was taking him ever more deeply into both the philosophy of the German idealists Fichte, Hegel, and Schelling, all of whom were recreating what we might call Christian mystical-gnostic philosophy in a rationalized form, and the worldview of Johann Wolfgang von Goethe, the origins of whose thinking and method lay in the same Rosicrucian and alchemical philosophers—above all Paracelsus, Boehme, and Basil Valentine—who not only underlay the intuitive world of Felix Kogutski, but also introduced him to what we might call the world of esoteric Christianity. When he began to read people like Meister Eckhart, Nicolas of Cusa, and the other medieval "mystics" is unknown, but certainly he was well versed in them by the time he came to give his first "theosophical" lectures in 1900.

Steiner's continuing interest in religious-theological questions during this period is confirmed anecdotally by three conversations that Rudolf Steiner—now established in the inner work of his philosophical and Goethean studies, and moving easily between groups of freethinkers, esotericists, and progressive theologians—reports having had with Wilhelm Neumann, a Cistercian priest of "encompassing scholarship." Steiner recounts that, among the many stimulating talks he had with this "ideal learned person, who was also a true son of the Church," two were specially significant to him":

One concerned the being of Christ. I expressed my view that Jesus of Nazareth, through an extra-earthly influence received the Christ into himself, and that Christ as a spiritual being, lives with human evolution since the Mystery of Golgotha. This conversation remains deeply engraved in my soul: it was deeply significant to me and has often surfaced in my memory. The conversation really took place between three individuals—Professor Neumann, me, and an invisible third, who was the personification of Catholic Dogma and appeared to the

spiritual eye behind Neumann, accompanying him and reprov-
ingly tapping his shoulder whenever the scholar's subtle logic
led him to agree with me too much. [Here] I was face to face
with Catholicism as expressed in one of its finest representatives;
through him I learned to respect it, but also to thoroughly recognize it for what it is.

The second concerned reincarnation:

On another occasion we talked about repeated earthly lives. The
professor listened and spoke of all kinds of literature that discuss
this subject. He shook his head several times, but seemed to have
no intention of going into the details of what to him seemed
a strange topic. Nevertheless, this conversation also became
important to me. Neumann's discomfort at not expressing his
opinions about my statements has remained deeply inscribed in
my memory.

And the third concerned the "Angelic Doctor," the great scholastic
philosopher and theologian Thomas Aquinas, whom Pope Leo XIII
had enjoined all Catholic students to study in his encyclical, issued in
August 1879, *Aeterni Patris*. No wonder, then, that, at the opening of
the Michael Age, the spirit of Aquinas hovered over the salon hosted
by Marie delle Grazie where Steiner made friends with priests such
as Laurenz Müllner and Wilhelm Neumann and where Karl Werner,
the great biographer of Aquinas, presided over all like an invisible
presence. Rudolf Steiner's interest in and study of Aquinas must date
from around this time. In this context, he recounts the following in
The Redemption of Thinking, his 1920 lectures on Aquinas, about
how, in 1888, he gave a lecture on "Goethe as the Father of a New
Aesthetics," and Father Neumann was in the audience:

I had explained how we must regard Goethe's presentation of
art, and after my lecture... Father Wilhelm Neumann...made
this curious remark, "The germ of this address, which you have
given us today, is to be found in Thomas Aquinas." It was an

extraordinarily interesting experience for me to hear from Father Wilhelm Neumann that he had found in Thomism something like a germ of what I had said to be the consequence of Goethe's world-outlook in relation to Aesthetics. For Father Neumann was himself highly trained in Thomism...

These questions then—the meaning of the Mystery of Golgotha, the reality of reincarnation, and the relation of Steiner's own unfolding path of thinking to that of the Christian tradition—were still or already present as questions to Rudolf Steiner during the period when his principle focus was on developing a path of spiritual epistemology, growing out of and extending Goethe's worldview—a path by which he could unite human thinking and consciousness with the consciousness of the suprasensory world in and through his own experience.

But perhaps not too much should be made of these anecdotes. They should be taken for what they are: indications or traces of a continuing concern, but not central at the time; even perhaps peripheral: there as something he could and would return to. In this sense, we might say that they ran parallel to his growing awareness of the esoteric traditions—alchemical, Hermetic, Theosophical, occult, mystical, and spiritualist—to which his time in Vienna also introduced him. Later, when the time was right, he would bring these two concerns together. For the moment, however, his priority was the transformation—the initiation—of his own consciousness. And yet, paradoxically, it must be said that this path of initiation, after all, was finally "Christic," which is why he would speak of *The Philosophy of Freedom* as a "Pauline"—"not I, but the Christ in me"—path of knowing. From this point of view, then, Christ and Christianity were never peripheral.

Toward the end of the century, Steiner began to experience these paradoxes tightening. As he describes it, he had to find his own path, through his own experience. To remain true to himself, he felt compelled to reject Christianity and Christ as the churches and theologies of the time presented them: namely, as something otherworldly or outside or beyond what thinking or consciousness could approach and appropriate. Thus, during this period, as he admits, some of what he wrote began to sound positively anti-Christian. In a sense, this was his last initiatory trial. Inwardly, as he says, he was struggling with "ahrimanic" demons, who sought to entangle him in abstraction, and he had to forge a path through them to his own understanding:

> At that time I had to rescue my spiritual worldview through inner storms that took place behind the scenes of my everyday experience. I was able to make progress during that period of testing only by contemplating, through spiritual perception, the evolution of Christianity. The insight I gained is described in *Christianity as Mystical Fact*...
>
> The Christianity that I had to find was not in any of the existing confessions. After the severe, inner struggles of that time of testing I found it necessary to immerse myself in Christianity and, indeed, in the world where spirit itself speaks of it.
>
> My relationship to Christianity should make it clear that my spiritual science cannot be attained through the kind of research ascribed to me by many people. They suggest that I have assembled a theory of spirit based on ancient teachings. They suppose I have elaborated Gnosticism and other such teachings. The spiritual insight gained in *Christianity as Mystical Fact* is brought directly from the world of spirit itself...I took nothing from historical documents for the book's contents unless I had first experienced it in spirit.
>
> During the period when my statements about Christianity seemed to contradict my later comments, a conscious knowledge of real Christianity began to dawn within me. Around the turn of the century this seed of knowledge continued to develop. The soul test described here occurred shortly before the beginning of the twentieth century. *It was decisive for my soul's development that I stood spiritually before the Mystery of Golgotha in a deep and solemn celebration of knowledge.*

✳

With the turn of the century, later described by Steiner as the end of the Kali Yuga, the Age of Darkness, everything changed, both for humanity and for Steiner himself: "A climax had been reached in excluding spirit from human thought and activity. A complete change in human evolution seemed an absolute necessity."

Steiner by then was active in the literary and cultural life of Berlin. He was teaching in the Worker's College, editing the *Review of Literature*, and contributing articles to various periodicals. At the same time, he was active in progressive and anarchist circles, and becoming known as a lecturer and a radically independent thinker. For instance, relevant to our theme—and suggesting he had followed up on Father Neumann's suggestion regarding Aquinas—in a lecture to the fiercely secular Giordano Bruno Union, Steiner dared to compare modern, post-Kantian dualism unfavorably to what he called the "monism" of medieval Scholasticism. Uproar ensued. What was Steiner's intention with this "unrecognizable" Scholasticism? Did this "materialist" want to revive Scholasticism? Even worse: "People thought I was paving the way for Catholicism to enter the union." Some supported him; some attacked him; but everyone recognized his probity and knew such controversy was good for the Union and so Rudolf Steiner continued to participate in it, even giving his "foundational anthroposophical lecture" there.

By this time, it was becoming increasingly clear to Rudolf Steiner that he had an obligation to speak publicly about spiritual knowledge. His knowledge of spiritual realities, after all, was entirely the result of his own research, his own experience. He was beholden to no one, only the spiritual world, which responded immediately and affirmatively in the form of an invitation to lecture from Count and Countess Brockdorff, the leaders of a branch of the Theosophical Society. He spoke first on Nietzsche. Invited back, he spoke on Goethe's "Fairy Tale of the Green Snake and the Beautiful Lily" from an esoteric perspective. This, in turn, led to an invitation to lecture to members of the Theosophical Society, which Steiner accepted, with the proviso again that he would speak only from his own experience. He began with lectures on Christian mysticism at the dawn of the modern age, namely, medieval and renaissance mystics from Meister

Eckhart to Jakob Böhme (published as *Mystics after Modernism*). This was followed by the lectures that became *Christianity as Mystical Fact*.

The rest, in a sense is history or, at least, better known. The initiate stepped forth into the light of the world. Becoming General Secretary of the German Section of the Theosophical Society, Steiner did so on his own terms, out of his own mission: he would speak and teach Theosophy only out of what he had experienced—what he knew—and would do so from where he stood, as a central European, a bearer of the Western esoteric lineage. Thus, while assiduously, meditatively, and dedicatedly working through Theosophy and fully committed to its noble ideals—such as the "Brotherhood of Humanity," "No Religion Higher than the Truth," the "investigation of the unexplained laws of Nature and the powers latent in human beings"—Steiner, teaching "Anthroposophy" from the beginning, began to transform what he received in the light both of the Mystery of Golgotha and the evolution of consciousness as he experienced it. In other words, as was generally recognized at the time, Steiner entered the world of Theosophy as a "Christian mystic." More than that, right from the start, leading Western-oriented Theosophists like Bertram Keightly and G.R.S. Mead saw in the just published *Mystics after Modernism* "the whole of Theosophy"—that is, that the Western tradition possessed all that Theosophy strove for, but from a Western, Christian perspective. But that was only the beginning.

Consider, for instance, the following and astonishing very early statement, given in a "private" esoteric lesson and recorded in note form by Marie Steiner in 1903 or 1904:

There is a beautiful statement by Hegel: the deepest thought is concerned with the figure of Christ, the historical and the external. And the greatness of the Christian religion is to be seen in the fact that it exists for every level of education. The most naïve mind can take hold of it and at the same time it is a challenge for the deepest wisdom.

The history of the development of Christianity already teaches us that the Christian religion is understandable for every stage of consciousness. It is the task of the theosophical spiritual stream, or spiritual science altogether, if it understands its task, to show that Christianity calls us to penetrate the deepest wisdom teachings of humanity. Theosophy itself is not a religion, but rather a tool for understanding religions...

Steiner goes on to speak to the need to develop "spiritual organs" in order to understand spiritual realities. He describes how our human evolution has both made this task difficult and at the same time continuously provided teachers, leaders, guides and initiates to help us. Thus, initiation arose:

There was an initiation in wisdom, in the feeling life, and in the will. Christianity is the combination of all these stages of initiation. In ancient times, initiation was a prophetic proclamation, a preparation. Slowly and gradually, the human being was emancipated from his or her guru or initiate. Initiation first took place in full trance consciousness...in complete secrecy, in total seclusion...

Then initiation stepped forward out of the darkness.... in a great powerful personality, the bearer of the highest unifying principle, of the Word that expresses the hidden Father, that is, his manifestation, which by taking human form could therefore become the Son of Man and the representative for all humankind. It did so in the unifying bond of all the "I's": in Christ, in the life-spirit, in the eternally uniting, occurred historically—and at the same time symbolically—the initiation of all humanity at the soul level, at the feeling level. This event was of such might and power that it could continue working in every individual who followed him, into the physical body, even unto an appearance of the marks of the wounds, even unto the most penetrating pain. The profoundest depths of feeling were stirred. An intensity of feeling arose, such as had never before flooded the world with mighty waves. In the initiation of the cross, divine love brought about the sacrifice of the "I" for all human beings. The physical expression of the "I," blood, flowed in love for humankind. It has never been emphasized enough how much blood flowed in this way; people are no longer even aware of it, not even in theosophical circles. Nevertheless, the waves of enthusiasm that streamed out in this flowing blood have accomplished their task. They have become powerful impulse bearers. They have made people ripe for the initiation of the will. This is the legacy of Christ.

Around the same time (1904), Steiner also gave a public lecture—one of his lectures introducing Theosophy—entitled "Theosophy as the Servant of Christianity." Christ and Christianity were thus clearly at the heart of his mission from the beginning.

Naturally, however, Steiner could not do everything at once. The ground had to be prepared; obligations met. Theosophy had to be taught and refined and transformed from experience. The significance of Christ and the Mystery of Golgotha had to be introduced gradually. Preconceptions and antipathies regarding Christianity had to be slowly overcome. Nevertheless, the central significance of the being and deed of Christ began to permeate—now explicitly, now implicitly—everything that Rudolf Steiner taught. By 1907, with his series of lectures on the Lord's Prayer and the "Christian Mystery"—the Mystery of Golgotha and, through it, the purification of the blood from the passion of egotism—and the Whitsun Conference at which he placed the German Section squarely in the stream of Rosicrucianism—at the heart of which lay the mantra "Ex Deo Nascimur, In Christo Morimur, Per Spiritum Sanctum Reviviscimus"—the ground was prepared. At the same time, in addition to the more scientific-cognitive Rosicrucian path, Steiner laid down (and practiced) what he called the "Christian-gnostic path," centered more on feeling and sensations. This path, whose teacher was Jesus Christ himself, centered on meditating the Gospels (particularly in the form of the stations of the cross) and, one imagines, praying the Lord's Prayer, as Steiner himself did daily. The great Gospel courses followed. The return of Christ in the etheric was announced. The Fifth Gospel lay on the horizon. And, with the break from the Theosophical Society in 1912/13 over the "Krishnamurti Affair" (which showed the relative orthodoxy of Steiner's Christology), and the creation of the independent Anthroposophical Society, Christ and non-religious, spiritual Christianity could finally show itself at the heart of Anthroposophy or spiritual science. All this is traceable— from the beginning to the end—and is essentially self-evident.

The question of Christianity and, or as, religion, however, is more complex. Certainly, religion as such had no place in either Theosophy or Anthroposophy. It was a different stream—parallel perhaps, but different. And yet equally clearly for Rudolf Steiner personally at least the situation was more complex. Religion was not his task. As he said to Rittelmeyer, (echoing his words to Werner Klein, when the suggestion of religious renewal first arose): "In my life mission I must confine myself to the 'occult'—otherwise I shall not succeed. Your task is religion." Yet his unconditional love of Christ is evident everywhere; and not only the love of Christ, but also a deep love and appreciation of Christianity, despite the errors, materialism, and sheer egotism of the churches. We see this, for instance, when he speaks in *The Fifth Gospel* of the great fervor, intensity, enthusiasm, and warmth of heart feeling carried by the ordinary folk of Christendom through the centuries before our own. In other words, he understood the cosmic-earthly evolutionary function of religion, especially as creating "a community of the heart" and as transmitting images and symbols to human feeling that were transformative and cognitive in a different way from the more conceptual path of Anthroposophy. At the same time, his conscious sense of spiritual science or Anthroposophy as the "servant" of religion—which is the meaning of the oft-repeated statement that, if you have a religion, spiritual science will only deepen your understanding and practice of it—is constant. That is, he saw the two streams as working separately but together toward the same goal.

As to religion itself—or rather, what Steiner calls in these lectures "the religious"—while there is some ambiguity about its future in any form that would still be recognizable to us today, it is also clear that, as humanity (and the cosmos) evolved, religion, or what is religious in us, like all other manifestations of consciousness, would also continue to evolve—ultimately to the point where "science, art, and religion" were one again. It was as a contribution to such an evolution that

Rudolf Steiner, as an individual, counseled and helped the impulse that would become The Christian Community to come into being.

✳

In the end, after all it is the actual text before us, which readers can and should meditate and reflect on for themselves, that contains the answers to any questions it might raise. And surely, too, though some background knowledge—and knowledge of Rudolf Steiner and Anthroposophy—is useful, in the final analysis we must let all that go and simply listen to (or read) what is said without preconception and preformed judgment.

The lectures and discussions presented here in fact demand very careful reading. From one perspective, certainly, they are preparatory. Here a beginning is made, and participants get to know both each other and the vastness of the project that they are embarking on. Deeper issues of theology and ritual will be the focus of later volumes. The tone is introductory, intimate, improvisatory, and, above all, practical: we witness Rudolf Steiner as very much a person of action—the "practical, organizational initiate"—who knows from experience the real world tasks and obstacles that the young idealists before him will face in order to achieve their goals. But this is only a first reading. For in the interstices of what unfolds as an opening conversation, fundamental guiding principles are voiced and deep questions and issues of real, consequential substance are raised, from which we can all learn a great deal.

Steiner begins by framing the group's task not in theological terms—as a question of dogma or theology—but as the renewal of "the *religious*," that is, as he puts it, "the working of the religious element as such." For this, he says, the sermon—or language—is central, or at least a useful starting point. It must be used differently. The task of re-opening the spiritual worlds to human beings cannot be done starting from "old conditions." On the one hand, traditional religious life is too corrupted; on the other hand, modern culture has changed too much. While in the nineteenth century some people could still understand concepts such as "Christ," "grace," and "salvation," with the twentieth century everything changed. The new materialistic culture—based on science—was already pervasive and would increase among all sectors of the population, penetrating even the subconscious and causing "an inner resistance to grow against actual religious life." A new starting-point, therefore, was needed.

As always, Steiner is a realist. Christianity cannot be renewed within the dominant mechanistic-materialist cosmology proposed by science. People might think that the two worldviews—mechanical-physical and Christian-spiritual—can co-exist, as it were paralleling each other, but that is not the case. Human beings cannot live a split soul life, which separates faith and science. Consequently, as Steiner puts it, because human souls know better, gradually they will come to reject the possibility of mediation, of being split, and, with it, reject Christianity itself—especially so, if, on the basis of a split between faith and science, a split soul, one tries to develop a religious life.

To exemplify this, Steiner turns to the dominant school of Protestant thought emanating from Albrecht Ritschl, who radically excluded science from religion and allowed no scientific ideas to enter the sphere of faith. Religion, from this point of view, is solely experience that flows from faith. At this point, Ritschl encounters the problem of authority for, as a Protestant, for him there can be no outer authority. Christ is the only authority for the individual soul. But where is one to find him? Here immediately problems arise. Turning to the New Testament, one immediately finds one cannot take Paul's experiences, which are subjective, as a guide, for that would be to take Paul as an outer authority. As for the Christ of the Gospels, that too provides problems, for again there is little "general experience" there. The result is that in the end what remains for faith is only a kind of "general, nebulous God-experience."

Having excluded science and reduced faith in this way, Protestantism—Steiner is here addressing Protestants—finds itself in a very weakened position, especially in relation to Catholicism, which, at that time at least, minimized the Gospels, and worked more and more effectively through employing symbolism at every level. In other words, the group of young theologians faces two problems: how is religious renewal to relate to science (as we know it)—for instance, how can it develop a true ethics in a mechanical, cause-and-effect world—and how is it to understand the function of symbols and images in religious work?

Spiritual science shows a way out of these dilemmas, but it cannot be applied directly. Its sphere is different and its claim to validity is based on other grounds. Nor does it need anything from those who wish to regenerate religion. On the other hand, it can be helpful, especially with regard to certain fundamental principles, some of which were now manifesting in the recently established Waldorf School, which, like the religious renewal seeking to come into existence here, is not "anthroposophical" in the sense that it teaches Anthroposophy, but only in the sense that it depends on universal human experience, which is also the foundation of Anthroposophy. One of these principles embodied in Waldorf pedagogy, for instance, is that you cannot teach anything you do not believe yourself. For instance, you may wish to teach children about the immortality of the soul using the example of the butterfly emerging from the chrysalis, but if you are not convinced of its truth, you will never convince the children. In other words, teachers must learn to experience the image or symbol of the butterfly as reality: that it "corresponds in every detail and every word to reality," because, "for spiritual science, it is actually true that the same thing that appears as butterfly on a lower stage manifests at a higher stage as immortality." Image and symbol must be experienced as reality. This means that it is impossible to hold a split view that accepts modern science as it is and spirituality as it is. And the same holds for the sermon or religious instruction.

Following this somewhat startling opening, Steiner asked participants what concerns or questions they had. These turned on three areas—ritual; the sermon; and community building or the congregation—and the relationship between these. Additionally, there was the question of the extent to which everything should made conscious, as well as the relationship between the need for community and the striving to enliven the "I" or individuality. Then there was the practical question of how to create "the field of work," as well as secondary questions such as what sort of theological background should be required of future priests and also the important one of the kind of qualities required for the priesthood, that is, how people should be selected—even though, finally, the initial group at least would be self-selected.

Rudolf Steiner's response is interesting and, again, practical, if orthogonal. He will answer—or give his opinion—on every question, but his emphasis as always is surprising. He begins by pointing out that today one must take into account the reality that an increasing number of people feel the need to be much more conscious—for example, to "understand" the content of the ritual—while others feel no such need. Then he shifts to another, more primary question, which will become one of his concerns through the meeting: how to avoid conscious religious content from becoming abstract or intellectual and cut off from feeling. Too often, we confuse intellect with consciousness. Goethe, on the other hand, who was extremely conscious, could live in images without falling into intellectuality. He could think pictorially. Catholicism knows this and therefore works through symbolism, while Protestantism, for its part, has tended to become doctrinal, hence intellectualized and overly individualized, fragmented. One of the tasks is therefore to learn to work more with and through images. Ideas must be expressed in pictures. Anthroposophy tries to do this, and a similar, but different path must be found for religion. Humanity has the deepest need for images and it is tragic that humanity has come to deny the cognitive function of images, as it has denied the cognitive capacity of feeling.

The question of overcoming intellectuality—that is, the dominance of doctrinal content over a feeling cognition of spiritual reality—is primary in another way, for intellectuality individualizes in an egotistic way: it fragments—"subjectifies"—so that individuals believe that they can build their own church within themselves and the sense of true community is lost, whereas in fact community is the place where the religious must work. Certainly individual conviction is necessary, but it is not sufficient. For this reason, as Steiner says:

> We must raise the issue that, on the one hand, the "I" is there
> as the culmination of individual life and, on the other, Christ is
> the power and the being who unites himself with the innermost

being not just of Christians: Christ, as power and being, must be expected to unite with all human beings. We must attain the possibility of a bridge between the totally individual "I," which wants to believe what it can, and community with Christ.

Community building is therefore key. Mostly we try to do this through teaching, but teaching actually tends to fragment. Building community requires finding "what lives and weaves between human beings." For this, the group will have to abandon teaching or seeking to exercise power through words and concepts, and, instead of focusing on "knowledge of God" find a means to a "life in God"—that is, the experience of the divine in the soul—which means learning to live in a content that is more than and beyond what we speak.

Steiner's second lecture turns more explicitly to the "real groundwork," building community. He begins with the example of the Youth Movement. Young people, who had come together out of a yearning for association and community, have ended up as psychological hermits. Why? Because a distinctly religious impulse lay deep within them and was not met. The result was that instead of community, they formed cliques and "cliques dissolve; they are not lasting communities." Communities require a firm, shared belief in community life: that is, an inward bond arising from "a certain kind of brotherliness and sisterliness." Priests must be leaders, but their leadership must flow from their human personality, acting out of a consciousness of God, of divine service, and in a relation of loving unity with those whom they serve.

Here Steiner emphasizes the threefold nature of the priest's task: spiritual-cultural certainly, but also economic, and engaged in the rights sphere. "In economic matters, the decision rests with the priest." Therefore, "priests must live in heartfelt connection with the whole charitable, service-oriented life of their community." At the same time, they must know how to reconcile social differences: they must become counselors, free and independent, in all areas of life. Unfolding ideas such as these, Rudolf Steiner himself, practicing what he is speaking about, acts as a wise and friendly counselor, ranging over a wide sweep of topics—for instance, marriage—and constantly reverting to his own experience with Anthroposophy and the Anthroposophical Society. Speaking frankly, as it were, unguardedly, he seems the very epitome of practical wisdom and advice. Very different from his more structured presentations, here we gain a very real sense of Steiner, not now so much the initiate as the heart-centered servant of humanity and the spiritual world.

New, practical questions continually arise—for example, would it be possible work out of the existing church? Steiner's best answer is: perhaps, but not likely; after all, it is important that the new religious community be free. Besides, there would inevitably be opposition to anything connected to Anthroposophy. Not that the new community should arise out of Anthroposophy:

> We do not live as yet in social conditions that would allow the building of religious communities out of Anthroposophy itself. The building of religious communities must be taken up independently, and then the association with the Anthroposophical Movement be sought. I can say positively that the Movement will not fail to support this association. However, it would not be beneficial, so to speak, to build church communities out of Anthroposophical "communities."

In this regard, Steiner cites the example of the Waldorf School, where the task of religious instruction is delegated to the different denominations. Here, as always, the task is to discover what it is to be a free human being today. This means, for the group, gathering as many people as they can in freedom to create independent communities. Courage will be necessary for this—and fundraising, to which considerable time is devoted in the course of these discussions; also the question of whether those working to form such communities should take on jobs to support themselves or try to do so within the community-building process itself. From questions such as these, and the discussions arising from them, anyone working in the cultural-spiritual sphere today will learn much that is still useful today!

The third session, an extended discussion on these and other points, only amplifies the "contemporaneity" and continued relevance of what was happening in Dornach in 1921. Practical issues dominate—after all, without addressing them, nothing can happen—but interspersed, almost as offhand remarks, Rudolf Steiner offers some remarkable comments. For instance, regarding the relation of Anthroposophy to the incipient movement, Steiner emphasizes that it should be kept in the background:

> We should not imagine that, with a short lecture, we can quickly bring to Anthroposophy those people who seek to find their way to a religious worldview in the modern sense. Many will resist it. Above all, it will not be easy to get beyond their belief that certain results of anthroposophical research are out of the question because of their own dogma. Many will still believe that reincarnation is irreligious and not Christian. And yet, it is not to be wished that everyone who cannot yet accept this should be shut out, but the actual religious relationship should be held onto. Just as, at the time of the founding of Christianity, one could be a good Christian without knowing that the Earth is round or that America exists; and just as Christianity was not shattered with the discovery of America, so, too, can someone be a good Christian without having access to the truth of reincarnation. For basically, the essential thing with a Christian—I still want to speak about this tomorrow—is his or her relationship to Christ Jesus himself, to this totally objective being. That is the essential thing. A personal relationship to Christ Jesus is the essential aspect of Christianity. Any teaching or doctrine as such, which as a teaching is of course assured to be true but is simply a cosmological doctrine, cannot be the characteristic sign that a person is Christian. People are Christian through their own personal relationship to Christ, just as Buddhists are Buddhist through their relationship to Buddha. It is not through any teaching or doctrine. You need the content of a doctrine—as we will see—in the sermon, but you are not actually a Christian because of a doctrine. No one can be a Christian today, in the sense that we must understand it, who does not have a positive relationship to the suprasensible Christ-Being.

After this remarkable statement and much practical discussion, the following session shows Steiner amplifying much that has gone before. His focus—what draws what he has to say together—is the task of overcoming intellectualism, the prime task of our age, which is as present in ordinary theology and religious life as it is in all other areas of modern life. To do so, however, we must learn and use another form of knowing and experiencing the world—reality—than the intellectual one, for one cannot intellectually overcome intellectualism. This other form of knowing, as Steiner has mentioned before, involves communicating and acting through what is of a pictorial, symbolic, or image-nature, and therefore can naturally pass over and between the sermon and the ritual—with enormous consequence. For, as Steiner points out, all that we know intellectually—all that enters the soul through the intellect—dies when we die. It is subject to death, just as our bodies are. But what we have experienced in a living, participatory, feeling way passes into the afterlife with us. This, of course, is why an intellectual approach to education is not taken in the Waldorf school, where abstraction is eschewed and a concrete, pictorial approach to subjects is practiced. The same must occur in the new Christian community and therefore Steiner offers a first description from within and from an anthroposophical perspective of the symbolism of the central Christian ritual: the Mass. This is critical:

> In your practical work as priests, Anthroposophy should inspire you, so that you first enter into working with the symbolic, the ritual, and what belongs to the ritual, and through this gain the possibility of community building. Otherwise, it will only be possible for you to speak to individual people. Building community can never be achieved in abstraction from life.

Further discussions follow, touching on a wide variety of topics, but always framed by the organizational and spiritual tasks at hand. Above all, Steiner seems to be concerned with two things: that the group has its feet firmly on ground and that they grasp the need, in order to build community, of a different way of thinking, speaking, and acting: namely through image and symbol. Both these require simplicity and directness. For instance:

> When you approach a congregation or community with the ritual, you must make the ritual extremely simple. A complicated ritual would not satisfy people today. Thus, you must form it so that is extraordinarily simple. Above all, throughout the ritual, there must be an expression of the inner transformation of the human being. We could call this inner transformation of the human being the en-Christing of the human being, or the imbuing of the human being with Christ. Human beings are not born imbued with Christ beforehand by way of inheritance; they must find the Christ in themselves. This transformation, this "en-Christing" of the human being, can be expressed symbolically in a multitude of ways through simple, but effective, ritual acts.

As an example of a simple, direct way of communicating spiritual realities imagistically, Steiner then gave the following verse used in the Waldorf School to express the reality of the threefold human being:

May Light—your thinking—shine through you
May Life—your feeling—penetrate you
May Fire—your will—strengthen you through and through

Thus, as the lectures and discussions unfold and participants begin to know each other, many themes are touched on, now briefly, now more elaborated. All circle around the great theme: how to renew Christian religious practice—not out of, not even drawing directly from, but somehow in parallel with Anthroposophy, in the spirit of Anthroposophy, and learning from its experience. One topic leads to another: for instance, the need to overcome intellectualism through the development of a pictorial, imagistic, symbolic mode of thought, speech, and action leads to a profound consideration of imagination, which in turn leads to the need to place human beings in a cosmic context: cosmic citizens, not cosmic hermits. Other topics, such as music and the sacraments, as well as a little theology, seem just to slip in, but again, in a profound manner. The whole tapestry—including the extended discussions of practical issues such as fundraising, outreach, and so on—is extraordinarily rich and demands slow, considered reading.

Readers therefore should not be misled by the low key, almost casual tone. Meeting for the first time with this group, it is truly amazing how Rudolf Steiner, with the gentlest of guidance and without the exercise of power, accomplishes the remarkable task of preparing at once a vessel and a ground for a Christian religious renewal that is at once deeply spiritual and founded in spiritual realities and fully incarnated in the present, in the world.

Reading this document, those drawn to Christianity, Anthroposophy, or Rudolf Steiner himself, as an initiate and teacher, will learn a great deal, find themselves thinking in unaccustomed ways, and, I dare venture, find themselves transformed.

*

As for the thorny questions mentioned earlier, they remain, as they must, paradoxical and resoluble only by one's own experience. In a certain sense, it might be said that Anthroposophy stands under or begins with the old Theosophical principle, "No religion higher than the Truth," and in that sense is "scientific," while the incipient Christian Community bases itself on "love of Christ Jesus," his being, deed, and presence. Whether these are one or two is a question that can be answered only in one's own life and how one lives it. From another point of view, it might be said that Anthroposophy represents "esoteric" Christianity, while The Christian Community, in some sense at least, represents "exoteric" Christianity. But so-called esoteric and exoteric spiritual paths have always stood in an ambiguous and painful relation. And here again, finally, the answer can only be found in one's own life and how one lives it. So the questions, as they must, remain open.

Further Reading

RUDOLF STEINER:

"Anthroposophy and Christianity," lecture of July 13, 1914, in
    Christ and the Human Soul, Anthroposophic Press, 1985
Autobiography, SteinerBooks, 2006
Awakening to Community, Anthroposophic Press, 1974
Boundaries of Natural Science, Anthroposophic Press 1983
The Christian Mystery, Anthroposophic Press, 1998
Christianity as Mystical Fact, SteinerBooks, 2006
"Christianity in Human Evolution," lecture of February 15, 1909,
    in *The Principle of Spiritual Economy*, Anthroposophic Press, 1986
"Freemasonry" and Ritual Work, SteinerBooks, 2007
Mystery of the Trinity and the Mystery of the Spirit, Anthroposophic
    Press, 1991
Mystics after Modernism, Anthroposophic Press, 2000
Reverse Ritual, Anthroposophic Press, 2001
The Temple Legend, Rudolf Steiner Press, 1985
Towards Social Renewal, Rudolf Steiner Press, 1992

OTHER AUTHORS:

Heidenreich, Alfred, *Growing Point: The Story of the Founding of the
    Christian Community*, Floris Books, 1979
Hindes, James H., *Renewing Christianity: Rudolf Steiner's Ideas in
    Practice*, Anthroposophic Press, 1995
Madsen, Louise, *The Christian Community: an Introduction*, Floris
    Books, 1995
Ravetz, Tom, *Free from Dogma: Theological Reflections in the Christian
    Community*, Floris Books, 2009
Rittelmeyer, Friedrich, *Rudolf Steiner Enters My Life*, The Christian
    Press, 1963
Welburn, Andrew, *The Beginnings of Christianity*, Floris Books, 1991

FIRST STEPS IN
CHRISTIAN RELIGIOUS RENEWAL

Rudolf Steiner

Lecture 1

My dear friends! You wished to gather here to discuss things inwardly connected with your vocations. I assume that your wish proceeded from the recognition of the seriousness of the situation of our time—a seriousness that manifests above all when one seeks to work in contemporary cultural life from a religious viewpoint. And I assume further that this is not for you primarily a question of theology, but a question of religion. The true burning question of our time is undoubtedly not just theological. You might even think that, with a little goodwill, some people could clearly grasp the theological question in a relatively short time. What everyone who looks at our time in an unbiased manner must understand, however, is not a question of dogma or theology. It is the question of the sermon and all that is connected to it. It is the question of the *religious*, that is, of the working of the religious element as such. And with the question of religion we asking a much broader, more comprehensive question than any theological question could ever be.

If we begin from the outset from a religious perspective, the task is one of regaining the possibility of making the spiritual worlds, with all their manifold effective forces, available once more to human beings—available initially at least, if we restrict ourselves to the religious, through the word. In this context we must already be conscious of the fact that a quite new evolutionary development here poses a very serious question. Anyone who believes that starting where older people among us still stand will have any other consequence in modern civilization than the actual and complete corruption of religious life does not see or fully grasp the question. Whoever believes he or she is able to rescue religious life by starting from the old conditions assumes an impossible position. I am not saying this as an introduction because I want to start from some spiritual scientific dogma; I shall certainly not do that. What I am saying is simply what reveals itself to unbiased observation of life today. We must be aware of this when we speak of what must be spoken of in real, true Christianity, irrespective of whether our sermons resonate today in the hearts of our contemporaries.

As for our days here, I expect they will be spent in question-and-answer and in discussing what lies in your hearts: the things that are actually important to you. Today, however, as an introduction, I wish to outline some of what we have to consider.

We must be clear that what has emerged in humanity during the last three or four centuries as scientific education has already created a wide circle of influence around it. Those who are older can still notice the difference between what existed in the 1870s or 1880s and what surrounds us today. In the 1870s and 1880s one could still speak to a larger number of people about questions of spiritual life as these arose out of the traditions of the various confessions or denominations, as well as out of the different sects. One could still find hearts and souls in which such [traditional] talk found resonance. Basically, today we face a different time. Certainly there are still many people who have not absorbed much of what culture and education have recently brought into our civilization. One can still speak to them about such concepts as Christ, the effect of grace, salvation, and so on, without an immediate resistance asserting itself in their hearts. But this will not last much longer. A new kind of popular culture is spreading at breakneck speed through broad masses of the population by means of newspapers and popular magazines, and above all—when all is said and done—through the education in our schools. Even if ideas specifically antithetical to religion are not expressed in this current educational situation, feelings flourish there that rebel against such concepts as Christ, salvation, grace, and so on. So we should not forget that the ideas that are taken up in contemporary education are being poured into forms which, in the widest circles, cause an inner resistance to grow against actual religious life. Therefore we must seek a new starting point. We must not allow ourselves any illusions about this.

You see, when people seriously take up the now widespread "scientific" view that describes the universe as having a mechanical origin, and that organic life developed out of some mechanical mass and that the outer human physical body evolved out of some similarly mechanical agglomeration—and when the facts leading to such hypotheses are followed so that one constructs an imagination of the end of the world that corresponds to them—under such conditions, you see, Christianity cannot possibly thrive. That this is not generally noticed today indicates a lack of inner honesty in human beings. They simply allow the mechanical-physical natural order and Christianity to exist beside one another, one on one side, the other on the other. Then they attempt to prove theoretically that these two things can coexist. The only problem is that in this process what asserts itself in every unbiased soul as a feeling is covered up. And even if the intellect tries to find all the possible harmonies between Christianity and modern science, ordinary human hearts and minds (*Gemüt*) will reject all these attempts at mediation. The result can only be that the hearts and minds of our fellow human beings have less and less of a place for religion.

If we do not consider the religious question from this deeper point of view, we do not truly appreciate the seriousness of the situation in which we are today. We do not encounter the difficulties I have just mentioned only in theology. We encounter them mostly where they do not express themselves clearly—in the subconscious of our fellow human beings. We encounter them precisely when we wish to cultivate religion—not theology. This is what is important and must, above all, be understood.

In this area it is the Ritschl school of thought[†] with all its fringe theories that is especially characteristic of what has happened recently. The Ritschl school—as you most likely know—is held to be extraordinarily great by many of those who work in the field of religion.

Yet what is the Ritschl school actually? It is the school of thought that takes the view that the last centuries—especially the nineteenth century—have yielded a great sum of scientific knowledge, and that this scientific knowledge is dangerous for religious life. It is clear to the Ritschl school that if we let scientific knowledge, whether as criticism or for the development of dogma, into religious life, scientific knowledge will corrupt religious life. Therefore, they say, we must seek a different basis for religious life: we must start with faith.

Yes, well, but with that the soul is split into two, as it were. On the one side, we have the theoretical cognitive forces of the soul that deal with science; and, on the other, we establish a part of the soul that develops out of itself capacities that are totally different from those of cognition. That is the sphere of faith. And now a battle is fought, not to build harmony between science and religion, but to exclude science from religion. The battle is for a sphere in which the soul can move without admitting scientific thinking at all. The ideal of those who belong to the Ritschl school is to allow as few scientific ideas as possible—if possible, absolutely none—to play into religious life.

Now, irrespective of whether you can ascertain such a view theoretically or convince yourself that such a division of the soul into two could exist, it is nevertheless true that for the actual life of the soul many forces rebel against this two-part soul out of the subconscious and that precisely because of that, religious life is undermined. But we can ignore all that. We need only to look at what is positive in the Ritschl theory in order to see how in the end, as far as religious feeling is concerned, it loses all content.

Consider the most important forces that play a role in religious life. First, there is the sphere of faith—whether it leads to knowledge or not we will discuss later. Second, there is the sphere of actual religious experience—this also we will want to consider in greater detail later. Third, there is the sphere of religious authority. Since Luther, Protestant life has done extraordinarily much to correct and to explain the concept of authority. In its struggle against the Catholic Church, Protestant life aroused, one could say, a clean feeling with regard to the concept of authority. Within Protestantism, it is clear that one should not speak of an outer authority; only Christ Jesus can be the authority for the individual soul. And yet at the very moment when, according to the viewpoint of the Ritchl school, one comes to the content of religious life—that is, to the second point, actual religious experience—one immediately encounters an immense difficulty, one that, as you know, confronts all the more recent followers of Ritschl in a profoundly meaningful way. Ritschl himself does not want a nebulous, dark, mystical experience of faith; he wants to make the Gospels the soul content of religious life. A religious person should be able to experience the content of the Gospels. That is, in other words, one should also be able to use the content of the Gospels for one's sermons.

Right away, however, Ritschl's newer followers find themselves in a difficult situation. Take, for instance, the Letters of Paul. In the Letters of Paul there is, naturally, quite a lot of Paul's own religious experience, which, from a certain point of view, is quite subjective; it is not simply religious experience for all people generally. One can only relate to it by saying, Paul had this experience and put it into his Letters. And I can only have a connection to it when I tell myself, I look to Paul; I attempt to find my way into his religious experience and attain a relationship to it. But this is precisely what the newer Ritschlians want to exclude. They say that this kind of subjective religious experience cannot be the actual content of general Protestant belief, because it leads to simply acknowledging an outer authority, even if it is a historical authority. According to them, one should appeal only to what can be experienced in every individual human soul. From this point of view, Paul's Letters would have to be omitted from the Gospels.† Therefore, as far as contents for sermons are concerned, the Letters of Paul would have to be left out. One would simply not be able to include the Letters of Paul in the content of the general sermon.

Now, if you consider the matter impartially, you will hardly doubt that what the Ritschl school today counts as objective experiences can also count, to unbiased examination, only as a subjective experience. For example, the presentation of the life of Christ Jesus, as it is told in the Gospels, can be relived by everyone, but not, for instance, the teaching of his taking on—on behalf of humanity—the sins of the world and attaining their remission. You would have to accept for the general sermon what refers to the experiences of Christ Jesus, but not, however, what has to do with the taking on, and the attaining of forgiveness of sins on our behalf, or anything connected with that. In fact, considering the matter impartially, you will find that you can hardly say that there is, with regard to Christ Jesus, any such a kernel of general experience on which you can call for the general sermon. If they were only impartial and open enough, in the end the Ritschlians would find it necessary to let piece after piece fall away, until finally there was basically very little left of the content of the Gospels.

However, if the content of the Gospels is left out completely as content for the sermon, even for religious instruction, then no concrete content remains that can be shaped. The only thing that remains is what would be designated as a general, nebulous, mystical God-experience. We meet this more and more among individuals today who believe that they can nevertheless be good Christians. We encounter the fact more and more that every content that can be shaped—and even when it comes from the depths of the human being, a content must lead to a certain formulation—that every such content is rejected, and actually only a particular direction of feeling toward a universal divine element is looked to. Indeed, in many cases honest religious Christian striving today is in many ways already on the way toward becoming such a blurred feeling-content.

Here especially Protestantism has reached an extremely significant turning point, one indeed where there is the greatest danger that it could get into an extraordinarily bad position in relation to Catholic teaching. You see, Catholic teaching never set much store in the content of the Gospels. Catholic teaching has always worked— including in the sermon—with symbolism. You will notice even today how strongly symbolism comes to life again among Catholic priests who are equal to their task as preachers—even more so where Catholicism strives for regeneration. You will notice how dogmatic content, certain contents about facts and beings of the suprasensible life, are clothed in symbols, as it were. There is full consciousness even among the relatively lower clerics that symbols live extraordinarily deeply into the soul, much more deeply than dogmatic or doctrinal content. They are aware that they can contribute to the spreading of religious life much more when truths of salvation are expressed in symbolic form—when these truths are given a completely pictorial nature—and no actual doctrinal content is let in. You know, too, that in the Catholic Mass, the Gospel is only read; the sermon in the Catholic Church avoids introducing the contents of the Gospels as an object of teaching for its believers.

Whoever can assess what power lies in a new development of the symbolic content of the sermon will already understand that today in fact we are at an important turning point where the main results of Protestant life during the last centuries could face an intense quandary, an extraordinarily difficult situation, in relation to the expanding powers of Catholicism.

When you see, besides this, how, on the one hand, Protestant life itself is losing its connection with the content of the Gospels, and how, on the other hand, a kind of nebulous mysticism is all that remains as its content, then you can also say that the power of faith itself stands on very shaky ground. One must be clear about this: the power of faith today stands on very shaky ground. In addition, you cannot avoid having to say: No matter how great the barriers you erect to keep scientific ideas from penetrating into religious life, scientific ideas—which produce only irreligious life, not religious life—will, in the end, still tear down those barriers. All that the modern way of scientific thinking as it is officially practiced today can accomplish— you might not accept it at first, but after studying the matter historically, you will have to acknowledge it—is that, in the end, there will be books like David Friedrich Strauß' *Alter und neuer Glaube* [Old and new belief].[†] Of course, the book is trite and superficial; but such triteness and superficiality is the necessary consequence if one really takes seriously the scientific ideas that are considered valid today and wants to form any kind of religious or faith content.

Now, as I have already suggested, what we need in the religious sphere are such concepts as Christ, grace, salvation, and so on. Yet how can the unique effect of the Mystery of Golgotha be possible in a world that has evolved in the way natural science views it? How can you place a unique Christ in such a world?

You can present an exceptional human being, but you will see when you try to describe this person's life that you cannot remain honest without facing the question: how does the life of this most excellent person differ from that of a Plato, a Socrates, or any other excellent human being? You will not be able to come to terms with this question. If you are unable to see any other processes in earthly human evolution than those that science, when it is honest, can accept today, then you will also be unable to place the Mystery of Golgotha somehow into history. We have all experienced the significance of *"Ignorabimus"* ("we will not know") Ranke in relation to the question of Christ.[†] It seems to me that the *"Ignorabimus"* Ranke should play a more important role for us than all the attempts by Ritschl's followers or others to capture a special sphere for the religious life where Christ can be valid and effective, because one sets up barriers against scientific life.

You see, in these introductory words, I want to address our central question directly. I want you to contemplate the question: How can we speak in a world, which runs according to the laws that science must accept today, in such a way that somehow ethical impulses can be realized? Where should ethical impulses take hold when we have a universal causality in nature? At most, we can assume that, in the beginning, an ethical element did once intervene in the causal world of mechanical nature and gave rise, to a certain extent, to the general mechanical tendency that now continues automatically. But if we are honest, we must admit that we cannot imagine a mechanical nature of this kind as permeated by any ethical impulses.

We also cannot imagine, if we accept universal mechanicity and the universal mechanical causality of nature, that our own ethical impulses can affect anything in the world of natural causality.[†] People today are just not honest enough. If they were, they would say to themselves, if we accept the universality of natural causality, then our ethical impulses are certainly beautiful human impulses, but such beautiful human impulses remain nevertheless just illusions. We can say that we have ethical ideals living within us. We can even say that the radiance of a divinity, whom we revere and adore, shines upon these ethical ideas; but to ascribe a definite reality to this divinity, and even to ascribe any connection between our prayer and the divinity and its will, remains an illusion.

Certainly one must acknowledge the industriousness and goodwill that has been brought to bear from the most varied sides, in order, on the one hand, to be able to stand on the side of natural causality and, on the other hand, to reserve a special sphere for religious life. We must recognize this. But there is nevertheless a kind of inner dishonesty in doing so: if we are to be inwardly honest, we cannot allow this split to exist.

Now, most probably, as our deliberations continue here, we will not need to occupy ourselves too much with the results of spiritual scientific investigations. We will receive the content for our religious questions, as it were, out of the purely human element. Yet, to draw your attention to the central point, I want to make you conscious of the fact that spiritual science, with its absolutely real results that are just as valid as the results of natural science, cannot base itself on universal natural causality. Let us understand one another correctly precisely on this point, my dear friends.

You see, the latest thing the study of nature has brought is the law of the conservation of matter and energy. You know that this law of the conservation of energy has intervened in a devastating way in psychology. We cannot come to terms with soul life and its freedom, if we take this law of conservation of matter and energy seriously. And the foundations that science today gives us for the understanding of the human being are such that we can have no option but to think that this law apparently also applies to the whole human being.

You know that spiritual science—not as a preconceived dogma, but as the result of spiritual research—has insight into repeated earth lives.[†] In the light of such insight, between birth and death we live, on the one hand, with impulses deriving from heredity—we will come back to this—and, on the other, with impulses belonging to earlier lives and to life between death and rebirth.[†] Now, the world we live in between death and a new birth encompasses facts that are not subject to the law of conservation of matter and energy. When we seek, as it were, the spiritual connection between our present life and our next one and, going beyond that, to lives that do not occur in a physical body but take place spiritually after the end of the Earth's existence, then we encounter cosmic contents that are not subject to our laws of nature and, consequently, also not subject to the law of conservation of matter and energy. What is the connection between what plays into a later life from out of an earlier one and what a person then does in his or her deeds under the influence of earlier earthly lives? This connection cannot be grasped by natural laws, even if they extend right into the most inward structure of the human being.

Every predisposition that works into this life from previous ones is such that its lawfulness has nothing to do with universal natural laws. This means, if we have moral impulses in this life, we can say: In the end, these ethical impulses cannot complete themselves in the physical world. They can, however, live over from the present life into the next, because in between we pass through a sphere exempt from natural lawfulness.

By thinking in this way, we reach an admittedly transformed, but nevertheless thoroughly graspable, cognitive concept of wonder. Then the concept of wonder takes on meaning again. Wonder can only mean that not just natural laws have consequences, but that ethical impulses also have their consequences. True, if we are totally absorbed in natural causality, our ethical impulses do not flow into the natural order. However, if we are lifted out of natural causality, if we put time, so to speak, between cause and effect, the concept of wonder receives a completely cognitive content again; indeed in a still deeper sense, it then receives content.

If from the spiritual scientific standpoint, we look, for example, at the origin of the Earth, we do not see the forces that work today in universal nature at work in the origins of the Earth. What we see is that the laws of nature are excluded from the metamorphosis of the preceding Earth condition into the present Earth condition. And when we reach the end of the Earth's existence—when, as it were, the Clausius formula† is fulfilled and entropy has intensified to its maximum and the heat-death of the Earth has begun—then the same thing enters in again: that is, we see, both at the beginning and at the end of the Earth, natural causality excluded and another form of activity at work. It is precisely at such times when natural lawfulness is excluded—such as lie for us between death and a new birth and which lies for the Earth itself before and after its present stage of metamorphosis—that the possibility of intervention by ethical impulses exists.

Humanity has already, one might say, taken the first of two necessary steps. The first step is that all rational people—and also all religious people—have given up the old superstitious idea of magic that presupposes that we can intervene in the effects of nature through this or that machination. Today, instead of the magical view, we have the view that we must simply let nature run its course, that we cannot master natural causality by means of spiritual forces. We say that natural causality must run its course and we have no influence on it. For this reason, magic, in the old superstitious sense, is excluded from our spheres of knowledge.

However, as correct as this is for certain periods of time, it is just as incorrect when we consider greater periods of time. For example, from the point of view of spiritual scientific cognition, if we look at the time period that lies for us between death and a new birth, then we see that we pass through a region that appears somewhat as follows: Imagine for a moment that when we die at the end of our present life, we first leave the world in which we perceived universal natural causality with our senses and intellect. This universal natural causality continues to reign on the Earth that we have now abandoned through death. And, at first, following death, when we look from the other side to life on this side, we cannot say anything other than that effects grow out of the causes that were active during our life. Out of these effects then further causes arise, and out of these causes again new effects arise. Thus, after death, we see natural causality continue, persist.

If we have led a fairly normal soul life, life continues after death until all impulses active during earthly life have reached their conclusion in the working sphere of Earth itself, and a new spiritual impetus enters in—that is, until the last causalities cease and a new element is present. Only when the spirit provides a new impetus, so that the previous stream of causality ceases, do we reincarnate. We descend to a new life, not because we rediscover the effects of causes from our previous life. We do not find them, but we find a new rhythmic phase, a new rhythm, a new element or impulse. We have, as it were, spiritually crossed over a nodal point of rhythmic development. We cannot say in one life that causes that were present in a previous life are working themselves out. Rather, for our human life, they have all reached a nodal point where they have exhausted themselves. This does not of course as yet include the effects of the animal, plant, and mineral kingdoms, which will be exhausted only at the end of the period of the Earth stage of metamorphosis. But everything of an ethical nature that has to do with us human beings has entered a zero point, and a new beginning is needed. We take the impulses for this new beginning with us out of the spiritual life we pass through between death and a new birth, and we do so in order thereby to be able to connect ourselves with the impulses that form the Earth out of the ethical-divine. We can connect with them when we ourselves are in that world out of which the new impulses flow. So, we must say, if we look at our life between birth and death, certainly no superstitious magic is present, but the connection with the next life nevertheless comes about in such a way that we can actually speak of magic. However, it is impossible to speak of a direct influence of the spiritual into the physical. The important thing is that we learn through spiritual science that there is not simply a connected, constant stream of causality from beginning to end. There are causality-rhythms that pass through certain time periods that are not so terribly long in comparison with the whole development of the Earth. These causality-rhythms come to a null-point, a zero-point; then a new causality-rhythm enters in. When we enter into a new causality-rhythm, we do not find the effects of the previous causality-rhythm. On the contrary, we must bring them over into our soul through those after-effects that we must carry over into our present earthly lives because of karma.

With this, I wanted only to indicate that in reality spiritual science has no need to accept anything from those who want to regenerate religion today. To do so would mean for many accepting a new dogmatism. I only wanted to point out that, without harming the apparently necessary validity of the laws of nature, spiritual science can give the science of the outer world a form or paradigm that human beings can fit into again so that they can again really call their ethical impulses world impulses and will not be forced back into mere, powerless beliefs. You must at least take this into your consciousness as a possibility. Without this possibility in your own consciousness, you will not be understood by those to whom you must deliver a sermon.

I would also like to present something to you that I have often used for the teachers in the Waldorf school. It forms an important pedagogical principle. You see, if we want to teach children that something is valid, we should not expect that children will understand this validity if we do not believe it ourselves, that is, if we ourselves are not convinced of it. I usually give as an example the fact that it is good to use a symbol to teach children about the immortality of the soul. We tell the children about the butterfly that crawls out of the chrysalis and make the comparison that, just as the butterfly lives in the chrysalis, so also our soul lives in us: it is just that we cannot see it. This soul then flies away when death comes. Two things can happen when we do this. For one thing, we can fancy ourselves to be very clever and can think that, though this symbol says nothing about immortality, "I will use it for the children anyway, because they are ignorant of the facts, and in this way I can make them understand it." If we are objective enough, however, we will soon recognize that our feeling of superiority over the childish view cannot lead to fruitful instruction. What we are not convinced of ourselves will not convince the children. This is how imponderables work. My instruction bears fruit for the children only when I can believe that my symbol corresponds in every detail and every word to reality. Spiritual science, of course, provides reasons for this, because for spiritual science the butterfly that crawls out of the chrysalis is not a made-up, imaginary symbol. For spiritual science, it is actually true that the same thing that appears as a butterfly on a lower stage manifests on a higher stage as immortality. The cosmic powers themselves have ordained that the transition of the soul into immortality should manifest in the image of the butterfly crawling out of the chrysalis.

Thus, if we look upon the image as a reality, our instruction will bear fruit. It will not, however, bear fruit if we think ourselves to be a clever person who fashioned this image himself or herself. It will be successful when we know that the cosmos itself gives us this image. This is how imponderable forces work between the soul of the teacher and the souls of the children. And the same is true in religious instruction, in the sermon. We must carry in our own souls the foundations—all the fundamentals—of whatever it is we want our listeners to understand. And we must never have any concepts in our minds that contradict the matter at hand. Let me put it this way: Assume that you are like the modern followers of Ritschl or others who are complete believers in the immortality of the soul, in the existence of God, and so on, but at the same time are weak enough to accept the Kant-Laplace theory,[†] and indeed do so in the way that modern science teaches it. The fact that the Kant-Laplace theory sits in your mind and soul and objectively contradicts the content of your Christian creed or the belief that you have to represent immediately adversely affects the power of conviction that you must have in order to give an effective sermon. Even when you do not know that a contradiction is there, the contradiction works and has an effect. This means that those who want to preach a sermon must bear within themselves all the elements that make their worldview consistent, that is, without contradiction. Certainly theology will not help much with the sermon, yet we must have it within us as something noncontradictable and not as something that exists merely *beside* the science of the outer world. Theology must be able to encompass science; that is, it must be able to conduct itself in relation to it with complete understanding.

We can also look at the matter from another side. You see, philosophy and science speak today of the most varied relationships of human beings to the world around them. However, you hardly ever find what philosophy and science speak of among ordinary and uncultivated people, even urban people, who listen to our talks and sermons today. Take, for example, the relationships that our psychologists propose between the human beings who observe nature and the human beings themselves. These relationships are not at all real; they are artificially created. What lives in the simplest farmers and in the most uneducated people of our world is that they seek deep within themselves—I say *seek*—deep within themselves for something that is not outside in nature. They search for something other than what they can find in nature, and you must speak to them about this, if the feeling they have as religious feeling is to rise up. Simple, uneducated human beings express it as it lives in their subconscious: "I am not made of this stuff out of which the world is made, and which I perceive with my senses. Tell me something about what I cannot perceive with my senses!" Such is the direct appeal that is directed to us if human beings are to make us their religious guide. We must tell them something about the real content of the suprasensible world.

All our theories of knowledge that say that sense-perceptions and sense-feelings are subjective, or more or less objective, and so on, matter very little to the great majority of people. People want to learn from us that something lives in the world, which, by its nature, does not belong to the sense world. Here it really comes down to the question: how do we meet this human need? We can do so only if we find the right path from doctrine to ritual.† I will give an introduction to this tomorrow. Today, I would like to hear what you have to say. I want to hear what your needs are.

Perhaps we will begin to formulate questions rather than produce answers. Certainly, it would be quite good if we were to formulate the main questions. For my part, while I am here with you, I would prefer to give you what can help you to exercise the religious element—but not the theological element—in your vocation as religious leaders. Thus, we will aim at the practice of religion, at the establishment of the religious aspect, and not so much at the theological questions. However, if you have theological questions that weigh upon you, we can also discuss those. Today I would ask that we at least formulate such questions as are of special concern for you.

(A participant recommends that Mr. Bock from Berlin should formulate the questions.)

Emil Bock: Yesterday evening, I gave an account of the concerns that we tried to clarify in inner preparation for this course in Berlin, and how we tried to differentiate various categories of questions there. In connection with what we have now heard, we can indeed now formulate one question that integrates three of the areas around which we had questions: namely, ritual or cultus; the sermon; and the question about the justification of the social element in the community or congregation. Yesterday evening, I tried to elucidate this with reference to church history. We actually found that for us it is a matter of clarifying the relationship between the Anthroposophical work of illuminating religious questions and purely religious practice. Thus, it is a question either of the relationship in the liturgy between the ritual and the sermon; or, encompassing this, what happens outside the ritual or cultus. That is, what is the relation of the religious service as a whole to the religious lecture activity or the relation of the ritual to the religious instruction for children? After all, whatever human beings have not yet brought to conscious awareness is achieved by symbolism. For us, then, the question is, to what degree must this become conscious at all? And if it must come to consciousness, how is it to be done and a balance wrought between the effect of symbols on that part of the human being which takes in the impulse itself, and on that part which simultaneously tries to attain consciousness concerning it? If we bear in mind the different natures of those before whom we will stand in the future, this again brings up several problems. Many of those in the congregation may not feel the need to bring religious impulses to consciousness, while many others will immediately and absolutely experience the need to become conscious of them.

Connected with this is another question: how can we actually reconcile the striving for religious life in community with the striving for an enlivening of the "I"? We have to take into account many people belonging to the middle class, for whom—as far as we can see—it will be a question of developing a proper independence of the individual—a connection to the "I"-forces—through religious practice. Yet with many others, we will have the task of regulating the striving of the "I" that has lost its way. This is what we found we experienced around the question of communal or communitarian forces insofar as we were able to gain some clarity for ourselves concerning brotherhood communities—Brethren—in the history of the church. This is one group of questions that was important to us yesterday evening.

We have three other areas of questions. The first is purely organizational. If we focus on developing ourselves to be able to do this work and assume the consequences that will ensue from this work into our own personal sphere of work, and if we find that it is, in the end, a matter of founding communities on the basis of a new principle, then the following questions arise: What preparatory work must we do? (It is clear that the practicalities will be different according to the situation of each of us.) Can we achieve this groundwork by giving lectures? How can we divide the work among us in a practical manner, and how can we arrange to do some of it together? Naturally we do not expect the work to be made easy for us. We do not expect simply to receive a position. We are quite prepared to create the field of work. Yet perhaps there are things to learn so that our work would be easier in a certain sense. In fact, there is a great deal that we would like to ask in the course of our discussions that is perhaps purely organizational.

The second area of questions, in addition to the organizational, has to do with our relationship to theological knowledge. There were, above all, two questions in this sphere. The first question has to do with the previous theological training of a person who will later work in such new communities, insofar as the training is connected with the university and we can learn from it. The second is a question of the new understanding of the Bible that presumes a theological background and, as technical training, goes in a way beyond a knowledge of the Anthroposophical worldview. There are also those among us who perhaps have a few practical questions. One or two of us are perhaps inclined toward a scientific occupation. It would be interesting for us all to see how this theological-scientific work can still perhaps be made fruitful for contemporary religious life.

The last of our six areas of questions is one that lends itself least to the formulation of a question. It is the question of the priestly qualities that we must expect of ourselves if we undertake this work. There is also a practical element closely related to this about which we should ask. This would be the question of the selection of the people who should take up this work. We need to know how we should make the selection, quite apart from the fact that, in the end, the decision will lie with self-judgment.

With this, I believe I have more or less covered what was said yesterday evening.

Rudolf Steiner: These are certainly the questions that must be asked at the turning point I have already mentioned. Our time together will be spent becoming clear about precisely these questions and with some things that form the preliminaries to them. For the moment, now that we have formulated the questions and before we discuss them, I would only like to point out that we live today in a time when just such questions must be assessed from the highest point of view—including the highest historical point of view. It is absolutely not the habit of spiritual scientists always to use the cliché "We live in a time of transition." Of course, every period of time is a time of transition from what existed earlier to what exists later. What is required of us is to look beyond what we consider to be a time of transition and look at what it is that is in transition. Something in our time is very powerfully in transition, and this is human consciousness itself, which is changing enormously. We are easily mistaken if we believe that consciousness as it is today is unchangeable.

It is very easy to tell ourselves that there are people who, because of their higher education, wish to become conscious of the content of the ritual. Other people conversely feel no need to bring the matter to consciousness, and so, do not strive to do so. You see, we live at the point in the evolution of humanity when it is characteristic that the number of people who want to have the ritual explained in a proper form is rapidly increasing. And we must take this into account. We may not develop the dogmatic prejudgment that believes you can explain it to one person but not to another. Whenever we presume that people at a certain level of education do not want to be enlightened about something, we will usually be wrong. The number of people who want to achieve a certain degree of consciousness about the symbolism and about what is living in the ritual is growing every day. The main question is a totally different one. It is how do we develop a ritual and a symbolic content if, at the same time, when people inform themselves consciously about the symbolic content, we do not want this content to become abstract or foreign to people's feelings? How do we maintain the full value and validity of a ritual and its symbolic content? This is the question that is especially interesting to us today.

One can—the example does not need to be precisely about the religious—point to Goethe's *Fairytale of the Green Snake and the Beautiful Lily,*[†] which came from a man of whom one can say, if one wishes to stress concepts, that he always *dreamed* such things. It is said that Schiller interpreted Goethe's dreams. In a certain way, Goethe was much more conscious of what lived in his fairytale than Schiller was. The nature of Goethe's consciousness was such that it could live within the images themselves. It was not the abstract consciousness that is experienced today as the only consciousness. Today people confuse the intellect with consciousness. They believe that what is thought pictorially is not as conscious as what is thought with the intellect. They confuse intellectual thinking with consciousness.

We will need to discuss the consciousness, unconsciousness, and superconsciousness of ritual and symbolism. This should certainly occupy us in the deepest way at the present time because, on the one hand, there is the Catholic Church with its very powerful ritual and its extraordinarily powerful, goal-oriented symbolism. What immense power lies in the Mass when it is celebrated the way it is in the Catholic Church—that is, when it is celebrated with consciousness on the part of the faithful who are present! Also the content of the Catholic priest's sermon is filled with symbolism and is permeated with will. [On the other hand,] we have the development of Protestantism over the last few centuries that has led away from ritual to the actual teaching of content, of doctrine. Doctrine has the tendency to work more deeply only when it is directed to the comprehension of the listeners or readers. For this reason, the Protestant churches face the danger of atomizing, of fragmenting; they face the danger that everyone can build their own individual church within their own hearts. Precisely because of this, it is impossible to form a community. This is one danger that must be met.

We must have the possibility of forming community—a community that is not based on outer arrangements or organizations, but is built on inner, soul nature. This means, we must build a bridge between the kind of ritual that can endure in the face of modern consciousness, and what leads over into deepened doctrinal teaching content as the Protestant creed does.

Doctrinal content individualizes; it analyzes or separates out the parts of the community, until one finally reaches the individual human being. The content of what is taught separates individual human beings according to their tendencies. Psychologists can see the conflicted natures of present-day human beings who are individualized—separated—right into and within their own individualities. Today we actually see human beings who strive to have not only their own individual creeds, but who have two or more creeds. These creeds then struggle with each other within their own souls. The countless conflicted natures of the present time are but the continuation of the tendency that individualizes, analyzes, and divides the community. The ritual, the symbol, is the synthesizing element that reunites what is separated. You can see this everywhere if you enter into it in a practical way. Therefore, this is the real question that lies at the basis of the community movement.

The question of Anthroposophical teaching or the Anthroposophical explanation of things and purely religious practice must be answered in a new way out of our own important time and moment. We are experiencing something tragic today, and it would be significant if a force would emerge from your community here that could lead humanity away from this tragedy. When, in addition to traditional, historical, and scientific education, you have what comes out of the whole of Anthroposophy as religious education, you can make an observation. When you examine the religious teachings that emerge out of Anthroposophy, the ideas that you attain and, as a consequence, the feelings that come about are such that they can lead only to a yearning to transform themselves into outer symbols, into images. These Anthroposophical ideas are often misjudged as being of the same nature as other ideas. Our usual ideas—whether from science or from social life—merely provide information and, in this sense, criticize and undermine everything. Anthroposophical ideas lead to a certain kind of devotion in the human being, to a certain kind of love. Just as our red blood can do nothing other than build us up, so Anthroposophical ideas can do nothing other than arouse our human feeling and will natures, so that they feel the deepest yearning to express these ideas in symbols, in images. The images in my *Outline of Esoteric Science*† are not merely artificially thought-out pictures. What it comes down to in the end is that we express ourselves pictorially, that is, in images.

In Dornach, in the center of the Goetheanum building—those who were there saw it, and naturally those who come later will see it finished—there is a sculpture, a Christ Group: Christ is shown with Lucifer and Ahriman, both of whom are defeated by Christ.† In the figure of Christ a synthesis of all that is sense-perceptible and suprasensible is presented before the eyes of all human beings. You see, one does not sculpt such a figure as this because we decided to place a statue there to decorate the place. Such is absolutely not the case; rather, when we form concepts out of Anthroposophy, eventually we have to come to an end with concepts, just as when we come to a pond and cannot go any farther or make progress, we swim. We come to a point where we can no longer form abstract concepts or ideas, but must proceed in images. The ideas themselves demand that we begin to express ourselves in pictures.

I have often told my audiences the following: There are certain theories of knowledge, especially among the Protestant theologians, which state that what we know must be clothed in purely logical forms—that we must look at things only with logic—otherwise, what we have is only myth. Especially such people as Bruhn† speak in this way. Bruhn agitated greatly against Anthroposophy, claiming that it builds myths, is creating a new mythology. But what happens when we challenge this charge with a counter-question? For instance, we can say, try just once to fathom the universe with your logic without using images. If the universe itself works not only logically but also artistically, then you, too, must also look at it artistically. When the universe evades your logical contemplation, then what? Furthermore, the human form similarly escapes merely logical rumination. In other words, if you truly take up Anthroposophical concepts, you will come to images, because nature does not work and create only according to the laws of nature, but also according to forms.

Thus we can say that Anthroposophy, developed in a living way today, takes into consideration the need that exists in the hearts of our contemporaries to get beyond intellectualism. Actually, every rational contemporary person participating consciously in evolution admits this. They understand that we must get away from intellectualism. Naturally, this is also the case in theology. However, most people do not yet understand that to pass from concept to image, which then becomes ritual in the sphere of religious practice, is just as justified and original as the logical element.

Most people imagine that we form pictures or images because we already have the concepts and we then clothe these concepts in symbols. To do so is to produce only straw symbols. Such is not the case [in Dornach]. In Dornach, no symbol is based on a concept; rather, at a certain stage, we move away from the idea, and then the image or picture is there as something original. It is there as image. One cannot say that one has led a concept over into the image. That would be straw symbolism.

This striving to overcome intellectualism exists today. On the one hand, this is a striving for a soul life, which, because of objectivity, passes over into what is image-like. On the other hand, there is no belief in the picture or image today. This becomes tragic. People believe that, if they are intelligent, they have to overcome the picture or image; they believe that they are conscious only when they have overcome the image. Such images as are found in Goethe's *Fairytale of the Green Snake and Beautiful Lily* are always stripped of their reality when someone attempts to explain or interpret them intellectually. This is the difference between my interpretation of Goethe's *Fairytale* and what other commentators do. They make annotations and explain the pictures intellectually.

Intellectual explanations are just as foreign to the real imagination as, for instance, the German language is to Chinese. If I want say something about the Chinese language in German, if I want to bring something Chinese to someone in German, I must lead them out of what is not Chinese so that they grasp what is Chinese as a whole and pass over into it. In exactly the same way must we prepare ourselves for what is of a truly imaginal nature. We must proceed so that the relevant images can arise and no explanation has to be added.

It is tragic that the deepest need for the image exists, but that belief in the image has actually died out. We do not believe that an image contains anything that cannot be explained in intellectual concepts. This must be understood first, if we are now to discuss the topic of the symbol and consciousness. We can actually successfully answer the question of a balance between subconsciousness and consciousness, which torments so many people today, only if we are clear about the need for the image and the lack of belief in the image's reality.

I would like for you to consider from now until tomorrow what I have said about the relationship of the intellectual concepts to true images or pictures. From this viewpoint, we will find that we can enter into the forming of community, because community building depends a great deal on the possibility of a ritual. Even the practical success of community building actually relies on the possibility of a ritual.

Those who have gotten to know India and Indian religions rightly raise one point. In India there are, naturally, very many sects. These sects have a quite strong community life that works deeply into the soul. It also exhibits itself as a practical community life and can include a great deal—from the perspective, of course, of the version appropriate to the East—that lies at the basis of brotherhood communities. This is, in many cases, based on the fact that the people in the East do not know what we call subjective, personal conviction in relation to their surrounding community. People in the East, when they participate in spiritual life at all, do not understand that one cannot have one's own opinion, for example, about a community or a doctrine; they absolutely do not understand this. As regards the concept, everyone can have his or her own opinion or thought. What one has in common with others is only the picture or image. The people of the East are aware only that the picture is the communal element. It is peculiar to the West that we have the tendency to value conviction, on being convinced, and that, because of this, an atomizing or fragmentation occurs. When we seek to be convinced, seek conviction, we come to atomization. This does not arise in community with others when we seek something other than conviction. Conviction must be able to be completely individual.

We must raise the issue that, on the one hand, the "I" is there as the culmination of the individual life and, on the other, Christ is the power and the being who unites himself with the innermost being not just of Christians: Christ, as power and being, must be expected to unite with *all* human beings. We must attain the possibility of a bridge between the totally individual "I," which wants to believe what it can, and community with Christ.

We should occupy ourselves quite intensively with the question of community building and, as Mr. Bock so rightly said, of the groundwork for it, as there are, naturally, things that will present quite other difficulties. First of all, we rely today almost completely on doing the preparatory work through instruction or teaching, so that we can find enough people who can develop an understanding for what is actually intended. Yet we face a totally splintered humanity. The simple fact that we present ourselves with the pretension to know something about something—which another perhaps would need a day to consider before making a judgment—is already almost enough for us to be immediately reprimanded. What works and weaves between human beings is extraordinarily difficult today. And this, of course, makes community building difficult.

Nevertheless, if you want to achieve something with the only thing you can be striving for by coming here, we will need to discuss most thoroughly the issue of building community. Above all, we need to consider the necessary preparatory work, which will have to consist essentially of our feeling ourselves to be, spiritually, community builders. What I will now say might not be immediately understandable, as it touches on one of the deepest issues of the present. The only way we can become community builders is, first of all, to attempt to dispense with teaching other people. People simply do not allow themselves to be taught today; this should not be our main task.

As small as the success of the Anthroposophical work I had to take on as my task is, this success does exist to a certain extent, even though in small circles. It is there. And this success exists because in the first place—as this work is taken up in our cultural centers— I have actually never wanted to teach anyone against their will. I have actually always acted according to a law of nature. I always told myself, the herring lays an infinite number of eggs in the sea. Very few of these eggs become herrings; a certain selection must take place. Those who know that whatever goes beyond the material continues to work further know too that even the unfertilized herring eggs serve a purpose in the world as a whole. They have a great effect in the etheric world, while the selection of the eggs, which are to become herrings, takes place on the physical plane. People who know this have no problem with the question, why are some herring eggs not fertilized? What is not fertilized has its great task in another world. Unfertilized eggs are not completely without significance. And it is basically the same in the case of teaching, too. When I have spoken to an audience of fifty or of five hundred people—I have spoken to even larger groups—I have never believed that I could teach half or even a quarter of them. Rather I assume that, with what I have to say, I would reach—on the first try—out of five hundred people, perhaps five who were predestined to receive the content. I would reach one out of fifty people and, out of five people, one-tenth of a person. That is the way it is, and one must expect it. What cannot take place through teaching occurs by selection. Human beings, in whom you have called forth a resonance, will come together. This selection is what we must seek today. Then we will make progress.

A certain resignation is necessary in order not to live out of the feeling of power that leads us to want to teach, to convince the others. We must absolutely have this resignation. That people so often do not have this is connected precisely with—I am speaking of those practicing religion—their theological educational background. This theological training is based fundamentally on the idea that we can teach everyone, and on the idea that we should not resort to selection. For this reason, we must find the ways and means of taking up, from the theological training, above all, a feeling relationship to spiritual content, to the content of the spiritual world.

You see, theology has also reached the point of placing *knowledge of God* higher than *life in God*, than the experience of the divine in the soul. This experiencing the divine within the soul is what gives us the power to have an effect upon the simplest, most unspoiled person. This experience of the divine within must actually be schooled. Modernity has worked against this. The more people strive to find abstract concepts for something that exists supersensibly, the more they work against the experience of the divine within, and the less they take suprasensible existence itself into their soul. We really need a living preparation and training for theological knowledge. Here something esoteric enters in: a law must be pointed out. First of all, as I mentioned before, when you want to teach someone something, you must not, as a sensible person, merely contemplate how you should bring a picture or some content—naturally, you must do this to the fullest extent—but you must also always know more than you say. I do not mean this in a bad sense at all. If you proceed from the standpoint of the modern professors, which is that you should appropriate for yourself only what you will communicate to the others, you will not achieve much with religious communications. You must have, when you speak about the Bible, for example, your own individual content in which you live, in addition to the exoteric content. The exoteric is nothing other than the expressed esoteric. There is no absolute boundary between exoteric and esoteric; the one flows seamlessly into the other. The esoteric content becomes exoteric when you express it.

Basically, the effectiveness of the Catholic priest is due to this practice of living in a content that is more or beyond what he speaks. This is what praying the breviary consists of. The priest seeks, through praying the breviary, to draw near to the divine in a manner that goes beyond that of the layperson. And the special content of the breviary—which goes beyond what one teaches—gives the priest at the same time the power to work effectively in the sermon and in other things. It is always interesting that Protestant ministers, who have served already a long time, come to me—it has happened quite often—and have said that they want something that is similar to the Catholic breviary. Please do not misunderstand me. I am not supporting Catholicism—least of all, Roman Catholicism. There are longtime pastors who have come to me and have asked, why is it that we cannot reach the souls the way the Catholic priests—who, of course, misuse this ability—do? This is due, essentially, to the fact that the Catholic priests seek an esoteric relationship to the spiritual world.

This is actually also what we are striving for in the endeavor to create a Threefold Social Organism.† Spiritual life, as we have it generally in common today—we are not speaking of the other spiritual life—is not a real spiritual life, but merely an intellectual life. People speak about the spirit; they have concepts, but concepts are not the living spirit. We must not have the spirit somehow merely in the form of concepts that sit in our heads; rather we must bring the spirit down onto Earth. The spirit must be brought into our institutions; the spirit must hold sway in what weaves and works between human beings. We can achieve this only if we have an independent spiritual life in which we do not work merely out of concepts of the spirit, but where we work out of the spirit itself.

Now, the church has long endeavored to retain this living spirit; the schools lost it long ago. But we must bring the spirit back into the schools and the rest of our institutions. The state cannot bring the spirit. Only what is activity of the individual priest and is, at the same time, community activity can bring the spirit in. The work of the priest must be such that the priest has, above all, a conscious connection with the spiritual world itself, and not just concepts about the spiritual world. And then we come, naturally, to the issue of selection, of the assessing of the qualities of the priest. Now, this judging of the qualities of a priest can be very easily misunderstood. First, more people have these qualities than is thought; they are just not developed or nurtured in the right way. Second, the selection is often a question of destiny. When we come to have a living spiritual life and the questions of destiny become enlivened again, priests will take their place more out of the community of human beings than out of self-examination, which bears a strongly egotistical character.

It is indeed true that we must appropriate a certain sense for what demands objectively that we do this or that.

Perhaps I might be allowed to relate an example that I have used in various places. I gave a lecture in Colmar on the "Bible and Wisdom."† Afterward, two Catholic priests came to me. You can imagine that Catholic priests have read none of my work, as it is forbidden for them to do so. And it is basically considered an anomaly when Catholic priests attend an Anthroposophical lecture. However, they were also probably harmless. They approached me guilelessly, as I had said nothing in the lecture that would have been repugnant to them. They said, "Actually, we cannot say anything [against what you said]. We, too, have purgatory, and also refer to a suprasensible life after purgatory." Now, precisely in this instance I had deemed it to be good to hold two lectures: "The Bible and Wisdom, I and II." In the first lecture I said nothing about reincarnation; thus, they did not notice anything that contradicted their Roman Catholic view. Therefore, they had nothing against *what* I had said, but the *how* was another thing. They felt they could not agree with this *how*. Their way was the right one because they spoke to and for everyone, whereas I spoke for only a few, prepared people—to people who already had a certain preparation. Then, after some back-and-forth between us, I said, "You see, it does not matter whether you or I are convinced that we speak to and for everyone. This conviction is understandable. We would perhaps not speak at all if we were not convinced that we formulate things and permeate what we bring with such substance that we are speaking for all human beings. It does not matter that we have the conviction that we speak for and to everyone, but what is important is whether everyone comes to you in the church. And so, I ask you, does everyone come to you in the church when you speak?" Of course, the priests could not say that everyone came. They had to admit that many do not. That is the objective fact. "I have spoken for those who do not go to you, and yet, who seek a path to Christ." The facts of the situation show us what task we have.

I wanted only to show a way in which we should accustom ourselves to allowing our personal tasks to be determined by destiny and objectivity. I wanted to show that we should not, as is the case [in the world] today, brood over our own personage—which basically is there only to fill the place which the divine cosmic powers have given to us—but we should attempt to observe signs out of which we can recognize where we should be placed. We can do this.

Again and again people come with the following soul question: What corresponds to my specific abilities? or How can I bring my abilities to bear in the world? This question is much, much less important than looking around ourselves objectively to see what needs to be done. When we get involved with what we notice there, we will see that we have many more abilities than we think. These abilities are not so very specific. As human beings we can do an extraordinary amount; we have quite universal soul qualities, but not so many specific ones. This brooding over our own selves and believing too strongly that we each have our specific abilities or talents that should be cultivated is basically a very subtle egotism. Those who wish to attain the qualities that we are talking about here must overcome this subtle egotism.

Now, I believe I have said, from my side, how I understand the issues. We can contemplate these things between now and tomorrow. If it is all right with you, I would like to recommend that we meet again at 11:00 a.m. And I ask you not to hold anything back. We want to deal as fully as possible with whatever you have on your mind.

Lecture 2

M Y dear friends! Of the two areas you spoke of yesterday, it seems to me that we must begin by treating the area that will provide the foundation for the entire work. Naturally, we must begin by preparing the real ground for this work, and in our time that can only be done by building community. In our discussions, then, we will better come to terms with what should develop upon this real foundation, if we talk first about community building itself.

In spite of the fact that community building can easily be underestimated, it is, without a doubt, on the one hand, the most difficult task you will have, and on the other, the most urgent. You can see this in the form that the Youth Movement has taken. The Youth Movement, as it exists today in the most varied forms, has a distinctly religious foundation. Thoughtful members of the Youth Movement always stress this religious foundation. And if you look impartially into this movement, you will notice something in it that is closely connected with community building.

Consider for a moment the following phenomenon this Youth Movement manifests. The movement arrived on the scene some time, even years, ago. How did it do so? It originated, at first, with young people explicitly striving to connect with one another. It appeared unmistakably under the slogan of association, of group building. But the significant phenomenon here is that in recent years the movement has transformed itself largely into its opposite. Precisely those who took this movement perhaps most seriously are now at the point of isolation, of becoming hermits. They stress the impossibility of associating with others. Why is that?

If one views things symptomatically, especially in Central, Southern, and Eastern Europe, it is perhaps one of the most significant social manifestations that the desire to become psychologically a hermit, and actually a certain fear of association, formed so quickly out of the striving for community in the Youth Movement. If you know the Youth Movement, you may discover some other aspects here and there; but, if you examine the matter impartially, you will find you have to characterize the relevant impulses in the way I have just done.

What lies at the bottom of all this? What underlies this situation is that it is clear that the Youth Movement contains a distinctly religious impulse, and that the religious community has not known how to retain and support these young people within it. Originally the Youth Movement arose from a rejection of the principle of authority, of patriarchal life—of looking up to the experience of one's elders. It was a blow to humanity's patriarchal principle of authority. The times had then changed to the point that one simply no longer believed in the fathers; one simply had no trust for the fathers deep within one's subconscious. But human beings need human beings, especially when it is a question of actions and effectiveness. People sought association with others, but they could do so only out of that spiritual life which today is anchored in human hearts as they live and are brought up in our ordinary schools, under traditional religious impulses, and so on. Religious yearning naturally stirs in young people precisely when outwardly something in religious life is not in order—but stirs only as an indeterminate, abstract feeling, as something nebulous. And, at the same time, connected with this religious desire, the yearning for community life also begins to stir. However, out of all that the youth could receive, out of all that is available, the possibility of building true community does not arise. What does arise—if I may express myself somewhat radically—is only the possibility of forming cliques. This is a characteristic of our time, that where there is a wish to build community, it does not occur; a true, inner sense for community building does not arise. What does arise is a sense for clique building. By "clique" I mean an accidental community—a coming together and a feeling of community with those who are nearest at hand. What brings people together, through an accident of place or of circumstances, leads to the forming of cliques. Yet all of such cliques, because they are not based on a truly spiritual foundation, bear the seed of their dissolution within them. Cliques dissolve; they are not lasting communities.

Communities can endure only on condition that they are founded on a firm, shared belief in community life. For those who know the history of social life, it is no surprise that what begins only in the formation of a clique cannot develop into real community life. To those who know this, it is no surprise that these young souls became hermitlike, experiencing in themselves the desire not to join with others—and yes, even in the end developing a certain fear of joining in. All those who once participated fully in the Youth Movement now go more or less their own way. And so, because the Youth Movement proceeded out of a shaking or overturning of the patriarchal principle of authority, it is clear that this recent histori-cal movement of young people does not bear the seeds for any real community building.

What you must seek in the first place is thus certainly community building. And in this regard, if you wish to achieve a goal that has truth and is filled with reality, there is nothing else to be done than to work in a practical manner out of the impulse of threefolding.[†] You will need to be aware of how you can work practically out of the threefold impulse. In your profession there is absolutely no need to campaign or agitate for threefolding in an abstract manner; yet it is quite possible, precisely in your profession, to work for it in a practical way. But you will succeed only if you seek the way to those to whom you wish to speak. You must find a real, effective path to the founding of communities.

Now, you do not need to think that, to do something like this, you must become a revolutionary in a radical sense. That is not neces-sary at all. For instance, it might happen, in the ordinary course of events, that you receive a position as a pastor or a preacher. On the other hand, it could also happen that you successfully direct outer, material circumstances in one place or another so that you are able to found a completely independent community or congregation. Yet such independent communities, as well as other communities, into which you intend to bring freedom of religious life must belong together. And this can be the case only when what you are striving for becomes a power, a force. Please do not misunderstand me; I am not talking about preaching the principle of pure power, but of one's preaching having a justified power, which comes about when you have a certain number of like-minded people. Anything less will not make an impression in the world. You must in fact be able to have priests from your actual circles spread out over a large territory. For this, one day you will have to expand your circle to at least ten times its current size. This will be your first task: to seek to create just such a large group of like-minded people. You will have to begin by doing so in the way that your own small group here has formed. Only when the same striving is to be seen in, relatively speaking, the most distant places, when a connection with you exists throughout a large territory, only then will you be able to proceed to the building of communities. This is true, whether you become a priest in the way that is recognized today, or in some other way.

You will have to work in such a way that your community members will be able to bond with you inwardly, in their hearts. By "bond" I do not mean that you trap or enchain them in any way. The point is that community members must receive, through you, the consciousness to live in a certain kind of brotherliness and sisterliness. Brotherly and sisterly feelings must be borne within the communities, which must recognize their priest as a self-evident leader and authority to whom they can turn with concrete questions. First of all, strange as it may seem at first, you must establish yourself within these communities as a self-evident authority on economic life. You do not need, in an incendiary way, to call these communities "brotherhoods" or the like. But members of the community must be able personally to recognize your authority, and to seek advice in economic matters and anything associated with economic life. When they ask their priest or pastor about something, they must be able to have the feeling that they are receiving a kind of directive from the spiritual world.

You see, if you observe life, you will find in seemingly insignificant symptoms things that will provide you with direction. For example, I was walking along a street in Berlin when I met a pastor I had known for a long time. He was carrying a suitcase. I wanted to be polite and ask him a question. Therefore, given the circumstances, it was natural that I asked him, "Are you going on a trip?" "No," he answered, "I am going to perform an official duty." Now, you might see this as terribly insignificant, but in the context of the whole event, I found his reply to be extraordinarily significant. The pastor in question was, in fact, more a theologian than a pastor in relation to his work. Inwardly, however, he was a very serious person. In his bag he was carrying the things he needed to perform a baptism, and yet he spoke and felt in a way that acknowledged he had someone standing before him who would understand the expression, "I am going to perform an official duty." This is somewhat the same as when a policeman seeks to arrest a thief; the policeman, too, goes to perform an official duty.

Any connection with official life or the like must disappear completely from the way in which pastors or priests do their work. Their whole way of feeling, as it then flows into how they speak, must be that of a person who, out of the free impulse of their human personality, acts out of his or her consciousness of God. They must be conscious of this fact: I am not performing this as an official duty, but naturally out of my innermost being, because the divine power has led me to do it.

One might consider this a secondary matter, yet precisely the fact that one sees such things as minor is perhaps what harms religious effectiveness most of all. We must begin to see such things as essential again. Only when we know ourselves to be permeated right into our subtlest feelings by the direct existence of the divine in the physical; when, as priests, we feel ourselves to be authoritative, in that we know that we carry divine life into what we do, and do not simply perform an official act as is ordinarily done today, but rather that we fulfill a mandate from God—only when we feel all of this can we convey to the members of our community the imponderable, spiritual element that must be conveyed.

This seems to be quite a long way from economic life. And yet the way things are today, we cannot consider that what we are striving for here in Stuttgart with the threefolding is relevant also in other areas of life. Here we are working on the threefold impulse out of the social organism as a whole. For your profession, however, it is a question of something else. Each of the three parts [of the Threefold Social Organism] is actually contained within your area of work. Even if they are not organized properly, they are there, and in your profession it is a matter of penetrating each of these three parts with religious-spiritual life. Although when it comes to the seeking of advice, complete freedom reigns within the communities, within which economic life also plays a role, the self-evident assumption, as it were, when it is a question of spiritual life flowing into the community, must be that in economic matters the decision rests with the priest. Such an agreement must exist, and for this, priests must, above all, live in heartfelt connection with the whole charitable, service-oriented life of their community. They must know how to reconcile social differences. We must strive for this in the communities. The priest must in fact be a consultant for the men and, in a certain way, also a helpful counselor for the women, helping them in their volunteer work. When it comes to organizing matters of economic life, economic aid, and economic collaboration in a higher sense, men and women must both feel unconditionally and as a matter of course that the priest is to have a say in it all. Especially in today's difficult economic life, religious communities cannot be founded if the priest does not take an interest—a participatory interest—in economic life.

It is true that to begin with we can present this only as an ideal. Yet in fact in one area or another we will more or less be able to approach this ideal. Naturally, if you strive for such an ideal, you will meet an infinite number of obstacles. You will experience rejection, but you must bring it about that members of your community attain the consciousness I have just characterized, and that by their own desire they discover the necessity of listening to the priest's incisive guidance in economic life.

I must say that for the priest who lives in a religious community, much of this—above all, much of what is in the rights or political sphere—must remain an ideal. Let me give a concrete example. Because religious life has increasingly lost its real footing or ground, things have arisen in social life that people today think are extraordinarily enlightened, but which in fact completely undermine religious life. Consider, for instance, today's view of marriage legislation. It is undoubtedly necessary that marriage laws to a certain extent must always conform to the Threefold Social Organism—irrespective of whether you take threefolding in the strict sense or more loosely due to other circumstances. For this, of course, we must feel clearly that marriage itself, as an institution, is in every way an image of the Threefold Social Organism. First, marriage is an economic community, and so it must become a part of the social organism inasmuch as it plays an economic role. Thus, we must look for a relationship between the economic community as presented by marriage and that presented by associations. Today we can do little more than think about this, yet the consciousness must arise in our communities that the economic side of the marriage must be supported by the actions of associations, of economic life.

Second, the rights relationship must clearly be felt as a separate element of its own. The state has to do with the rights relationship of a marriage only inasmuch as the contract of marriage is a matter of the law.

In contrast, within your religious community you as priests must claim the right to give the spiritual blessing upon a marriage in full freedom, out of your own decision, as your own special concern. You will have to strive for the ideal that the religious blessing of a marriage lies within the freedom of your religious decision, and that this decision will be absolutely respected, so that it will be viewed as the basis for something else. Namely, it will be the foundation of trust that exists within the community and on the basis of which the priest's decision is sought for a marriage in the first place. I know that such a thing as this is looked upon, even by many Protestants today, as no longer appropriate for our times. However, I can only say that the fact that such things are seen as out-of-date shows the defects of civilization that most inevitably undermine religious life.

Thus, you must bring to the members of your community the awareness of the fact that the actual inner, spiritual core of marriage has to do with religious life and that, throughout this area, the threefold impulse must be put into practice. This means that all three parts of a marriage must gradually find their form within social life†—that all three must be within it. With regard to threefolding, we should not imagine that we are automatically setting up a utopian program and that one should threefold things. We divide social life into these three parts best when we comprehend that all of life's institutions implicitly contain a threefold nature, and when we understand how to organize individual things so that the threefold impulse underlies them. Precisely within your profession perhaps, you do not need to place too much weight on representing the threefold impulse abstractly. We must only understand that life demands that threefolding occur—that is, that each of the three particular parts of the social organism is a truly concrete, existing reality.

Naturally you will meet with great resistance against this today. Yet precisely in such cases of resistance, you can develop, even if at first only in a way that has only an explanatory effect in your community, the relationship in which independent spiritual life—which, above all, contains the religious element—stands in relation to what must come to be. This can be done, not by giving well-intentioned speeches about mutual tolerance, but rather by placing before people, as their ideal, what the circumstances really require. Naturally, if you do this, you must expect that you will be met with the greatest resistance.

Third, you must have the possibility of really developing free spiritual life as it is meant to be in a Threefold Social Organism. Today, in society generally, we absolutely no longer have spiritual life. We have an intellectual life, but we have no spiritual life. We have, I might say, no dealings of the gods with human beings. We are not conscious of the fact that the working of the divine world should be present through us in everything that takes place outwardly in the physical world. Nor are we aware that bringing the spirit really and truly into the world—into actions that play a role in economic life, as well as in the rights and laws of the state, and in the education of the young, and likewise in the instruction of the old—must be a free deed performed by human beings participating in this spiritual life. This reality must be understood.

For this reason, you will have to fight for the full authority of your own independent will. This, too, is naturally a demand of our time: that the individual who gives a sermon does so under his or her own authority. You see, in this area we must simply look at the mighty collision of opposites reigning today.

When I go to a Catholic church and it comes time for the sermon, I see that the priest wears the stole. I know that when he is wearing the stole, the human being who stands there in the pulpit and preaches is absolutely not to be considered. The Catholic priest actually bears this in his consciousness. In reality he does not feel himself to be humanly responsible for any of his words, because from the moment he crosses the stole over his heart, it is the church that speaks. And, since the formal dogmatic decree of infallibility,[†] the pope in Rome determines *ex cathedra* everything proclaimed by the Catholic Church. Thus, [in the Catholic preacher] I have before me a human being who, in the moment [of the sermon], empties himself and does not for a moment think of representing his own opinion. He believes with absolute conviction that he can have a personal opinion that he keeps to himself and that may not agree at all with what he speaks from the pulpit. For him, his personal opinion does not come into consideration. In the moment when he crosses the stole over his heart, he is the representative of the church.

This is one extreme. Yet, it exists, and it will play a large role in the cultural movement about to be ushered in. As ruinous as we must consider this power, it is a power, an enormous power, that we cannot approach in any other way than to become fully conscious of it. You will not be able to fight it in any other way. With every step you take you will meet this power which is spreading in an immeasurable way while humanity sleeps and does not notice it.

On the other hand you have—if I may call it so—divine harmony, which is the task of our times and in which we must trust. This divine harmony, my dear friends, as it is in my book *The Philosophy of Freedom*† [also available under the title *Intuitive Thinking as a Spiritual Path*], has been totally misunderstood, yet it should be grasped today in the most eminent sense. In *The Philosophy of Freedom* the life of rights—legal life—is based on individual human beings working completely out of their own selves. One of the first, and indeed most profound, critics who wrote about my *Philosophy of Freedom*—in the English *Athenaeum*†—wrote simply that this whole view leads to a theoretical anarchism. This is, of course, the belief of many people today. Why? Because modern human beings lack real divinized social trust because they cannot grasp the most important feature of our time: namely, that, if we could really bring human beings to speak out of their inmost being, harmony would come about among them, not through their own will, but through divine world order. Discord arises because people do not speak out of their inner being. We cannot create harmony directly, but only indirectly, by bringing each human being to his or her innermost self. Then each person will do what benefits the other. As long as they have not found their own self, human beings act and speak at cross-purposes.

If we grasp that this phenomenon is a mystery of life, then we will say to ourselves, "I seek the source of my actions within myself and trust that the path that leads me into my innermost being also places me into the divine world-order in the outer world, and because of this, I can work in harmony with others." In this way, not only will trust be brought into our inner being but also trust in outer social harmony. There is no other way to bring human beings together. Therefore, if, in your profession, you wish to work socially—in a divine-social manner, in a spiritual-social manner—you must achieve the ability to work out of your inner being, which means that just because each of you has found yourself, you have the possibility of being an authority.

The Catholic preacher removes his individuality; he crosses the stole [over his heart] and is no longer himself: he is the church. The Catholic Church has the magical means—without trust [in the power of the individual]—of influencing social life powerfully through the effect of outer symbols on the soul. This method was necessary to found communities around the end of the second millennium before the Mystery of Golgotha. It was in its most ideal form in ancient Egypt, and in a roundabout way, which can be ascertained historically, it became the inner essence of the Catholic Church. The nature of the Catholic Church is such that still today it has the viewpoint of the inner makeup of the Egyptian priesthood and of social life as it was approximately two millennia before Christ. In the Catholic impulse what is old and past is working into our time.

In contrast to this is the need to stand today completely in our time and to feel ourselves as no more than bearers of that divine life which has become intellect within us. You must win freedom of speech for yourselves, so that no one can question the content of your sermon— so that there is no outer standard for the content of your sermon. You will not found communities in any other way than by making it a principle to gain freedom of the sermon.

With these few words I have sketched, as it were, the beginning of what must arise from one's own inner being and lead to community building. If you are able to actualize these things you will, in turn, also bring young people into the building of community, whereas on their own they have managed only to form cliques. I have the conviction and also the trust that if you realize these things, then, above all, young people will come together in such communities and something fruitful can come of it. Fifteen or twenty years ago, young people sought to join together in the so-called Youth Movement, but they were without a leader because no one believed in the fathers anymore—and so, they strove for community building without any actual inner impulse. The result was only the forming of a clique. Today their souls are hermits, yet such hermit souls would join together immediately if the possibility of a truly independent community appeared. This means, above all, that young people would come together in a community that has inner freedom.

It goes without saying that we also have difficulties with such things in our Anthroposophical Movement—because today the Anthroposophical Movement can be nothing other than a completely universal movement. It must apply to all areas of life. Indeed, as regards the Anthroposophical Movement, we are in a particularly difficult situation. On the one hand, a certain Anthroposophical truth must be communicated to the world; it must be given to the world because the world lacks the possibility of receiving spiritual content from the spiritual world. On the other hand, the striving to build communities, to some degree to form Anthroposophical communities, has arisen everywhere. Call them branches or what you will: there is a striving to found Anthroposophical branches. Yet because these Anthroposophical branches must be universal, they cannot really come to life. They oscillate between a religious element and a spiritual element oriented toward all branches of life. Therefore, naturally, they do not achieve a truly brotherly-sisterly attitude. They absolutely do not understand the social task that lies in the fact that, in small communities, we can found a concrete model that then could spread throughout humanity. Either they degenerate into merely disseminating the content of Anthroposophical teaching as doctrine, or they feel within themselves a resistance to uniting together, and so divide in their opinions and quarrel, and so on. Yet when we ask where the problem lies, it is not in the communities, but in the fact that today people cannot find an actual connection to religious life, even though they are able to penetrate the spiritual world cognitively. Anthroposophists do not find a religious life in any of the denominations existing today. Religious communities must be there first. But they can be there only if we earnestly provide everything that can lead to the founding of such communities. If the attitude that I have tried to characterize for you today permeates you, then the possibility of forming institutions will not prove so difficult if there are enough of you. Once you have ten times as many people [as you have now] preparing to take up the profession of priest throughout Germany, thus over a large territory, then you will be able to build community. Community building forms the foundation of your religious work. We must be clear about this aspect before we can go on to speak further about the ritual and the sermon.

Now I would like to ask you to say or ask anything in relation to your specific thoughts, wishes, and so on. You may have concerns about specific things that I mentioned, or you might feel that a question has not yet been discussed sufficiently, or you might have more practical questions.

A participant: Even though the practical aspects might simply emerge, it would perhaps be of great importance to hear about this or that practical aspect, since some of us are already engaged in practical situations. Therefore, I would ask that you say something about the possibilities for affiliations or connections. There are to begin with two possible opportunities: either through the church or through a connection to existing Anthroposophical communities. Above all, will it be possible later to find a connection through working out of the church? The fear that such a connection cannot be found holds some of us back, even though we could already now enter into the service of the church. What should we do? This perhaps already contains the question of what is practical. But the principal question is about the possibilities of affiliation. We are just not clear about where we can immediately connect in a practical manner. Are we wasting an opportunity by entering into service to the church now, in the hope that there will be a way to connect later? Would it not be better for us to do something else? We must, after all, connect with something somewhere.

Rudolf Steiner: The situation is such that it requires that the answer to this question must be multifaceted. The answer is not the same in every situation. In spite of the difficulties presented by the church, there are indeed still always opportunities to work out of the church itself—opportunities that one should perhaps not leave unused. Considering the specific circumstances here and there, if you want a position within the existing forms, you could say that, given the overall nature of a community, you yourself could found your own community there. You could then gradually lead it out of current ecclesiastical circumstances—whereas you would not be able to get members for your community if you wanted to simply gather them from outside the church.

On the other hand, there are certain areas where it will no longer be possible to work out of the church. Then, naturally, you will have to found free independent communities. I would just recommend that you do not, under any circumstances, try to join together with the Anthroposophical branches, etc., and that you not try to work out of Anthroposophy itself, because then the thread will break before you achieve anything. Anthroposophy as such will simply soon be opposed in unbelievable ways[†] and from all sides. Your actual strength—even if there are ten times as many of you as there are now—is not great enough to achieve peaceful community building within such a struggle. We do not live as yet in social conditions that would allow the building of religious communities out of Anthroposophy itself. The building of religious communities must be taken up independently, and then the association with the Anthroposophical Movement be sought. I can say positively that the Anthroposophical Movement will not fail to support this association. However, it would not be beneficial, so to speak, to build church communities out of Anthroposophical "communities."

You see, when we founded the Waldorf school[†]—it is not an exact example, but there is at least a similarity—we did not proceed to found a school that taught a worldview, that taught Anthroposophy. We sought merely to bring into the methods of education—the pedagogy and art of teaching—what Anthroposophy could contribute. I firmly held the view that Catholic children should be taught by Catholic priests, and Protestant children by Protestant ministers. However, it turned out that, because the main portion of the student body of the Waldorf school was made up of the children of the workers [of the Waldorf Astoria cigarette factory], many children would have had no religious instruction at all. Therefore it became necessary, as it were, to provide Anthroposophical religious instruction that was "free"[†]—that is, nondenominational or nonsectarian. Yet in all the details, namely in my own relationship to the matter, I insisted that this Anthroposophical religious instruction not fall within the organization of the school. Rather, such Anthroposophical religious instruction comes into the school from the outside, just as the Catholic and Protestant instruction does. Thus the [Waldorf] school as such does not give any religious instruction. It simply allows the Anthroposophical community to give Anthroposophical religious instruction to those children whose parents wish it, just as Protestant children receive Protestant religious instruction, and Catholic children receive Catholic religious instruction. In this area we must be serious about ensuring that the spiritual works only through the spiritual. As soon as people settle on a school system that would include the religious instruction within the curriculum of the school, they would probably achieve more to begin with than we do now, but later it would slowly disintegrate again. One must trust the spirit, so that one works out of oneself. Therefore, in the Anthroposophical Movement we stand before the great difficulty that when we found a branch, we do so in the outer world, where human beings always strive to work through outer means. But Anthroposophy cannot work through outer means. It can work only through what works on the human being as a spiritual substance. These two things— outer branch building and inner effectiveness—are always in conflict. It is a confusing struggle, and yet the moment that community building out of the religious spirit becomes possible, the struggle would become something healthy. Here, naturally, it is a question of really overcoming, as it were, higher discomforts, if I may put it so.

You see, when I speak to Swiss teachers about freeing spiritual life and freeing the nature of teaching, as a rule even the best of them responds, "Yes, in Switzerland we are actually quite free. We can do whatever we want in the school." But not one of them does anything other than what the state wants. Out of freedom they are basically as unfree as is possible. They just do not feel their lack of freedom; they feel the lack of freedom to be freedom because inwardly they have grown so together with it. We must learn to feel the lack of freedom again.

Once, at a meeting for the Threefold Movement, which I held in Switzerland, I could sense this in a quite remarkable manner—in a rather humorous manner, I might say. In the discussion one person became enormously, almost fanatically, heated, [saying] that in Germany everything was ordered by laws and police regulations. The people were ordered by law to be loyal, and to venerate the monarch with their loyalty. He raged terribly about this. I said to him, "Of course members of a republic might well rail in such a manner against the command of the monarch. Yet I remember that, when the German emperor[†] was in Switzerland a few years ago, people behaved toward him in an extremely devoted manner. Indeed, the image of devotion presented in Zürich by far surpassed what one was accustomed to in Germany." To which he responded, "Yes. That is precisely the difference between Germany and Switzerland. In Germany the people must do it because they are ordered to; we do it voluntarily." Such is the difference between free human beings and those who are not free.

Now, we must—indeed, all human beings must (this is quite international now)—actually learn what it means to be a free human being. For this reason I believe it is actually possible to connect, within the church, with that element wherein freedom is still possible, and thus found free communities out of the church itself.

I do understand the difficulty, but you must merely consider the real cultural conditions in Central Europe. A certain kind of community building occurred—we must really learn from history— when, after the promulgation of the dogma of infallibility, Old Catholicism came into being.[†] Now, when you look at the content of Old Catholicism, you must say that, with regard to its doctrine and the behavior of its priests, it is like the Protestant ministry. But Old Catholicism nevertheless has within it a ritual, which it has preserved in a simple, popular manner. We will still need to speak about this ritual. One may say that, precisely because it arose as a reaction, Old Catholicism already contains what could have led to the building of communities outside of the church. As you know, the Old Catholicism was taken up with great enthusiasm in Germany. Congregations formed here and there. But they could neither live nor die. Naturally, because such congregations could not be formed within the Roman Catholic Church, they had to be built independently. It would not have worked any other way. In Switzerland, where the Old Catholicism has survived much more than else-where[†]—because there are more Old Catholic congregations there— it is now clearly evident that these congregations continue to live a conservative life, but do not grow. These congregations remain the same or, more likely, decrease; they are in a descending evolution.

This is the difficulty today with the building of independent congregations or communities.

Therefore, you will need to collect as many people as you can in order to form independent communities. They should not be gathered from [among those who feel themselves a part of] the church, but from among those who [do not feel that way but] have not yet been able to make the decision to leave the church. You can bring these out, in order to form your free communities. If you handle things in this way, you can be quite certain that you will be able to achieve a connection with the Anthroposophical Movement. In spite of the terrible battles it has to fight, the Anthroposophical Movement will secure its validity and worth, though perhaps only by the sacrifices of many of those working within it. By great sacrifices it will attain validity, but it is hardly able to found a branch of religious life today. This is why I spoke today about the special features of your profession: namely, that the Anthroposophical Movement is hardly in a position to form communities in a specifically religious sense. What I am continually stressing here must become a reality for you: namely, the Anthroposophical Movement as such cannot found new religious communities, and so on. You must somehow build these communities out of yourselves, or form them, as far as you can, out of human beings who are still within the church purely out of their habitual bias. You could, however, perhaps reformulate the question more fully, so we could then speak about it more exactly.

Dr. Rittelmeyer†—who fell ill—would definitely have been able, because of how he related to his parishioners, to found a truly free community in Berlin. And once this community achieved a certain power and validity—and it was large enough—then no one would dare to bother the pastor. Is it actually your opinion that we should not have this last remnant of consideration for the church?

A participant: I believe that it will be especially difficult to work within the church, and I do not yet see clearly how much we can do in this regard now. We must still wait to do the actual work until we can all begin together. Would it be possible already to seek points of contact with the church? Yet, if we were already so far along, we would surely already be sent out.

Rudolf Steiner: As long as you do not already have a pastoral position, you cannot seek such connections. Naturally you must seek the preparation for religious work independently of the church—at least you must be inwardly independent. As long as you are studying, as it were, you cannot look for some kind of integration with the church. To begin with you can only look around to see where it would be possible to draw such communities out of the church. And if you find that this is absolutely impossible in Central Europe, free communities must be formed nevertheless, and the ways and means to do so must be found.

Now, there are two things I would be against when it comes to an absolutely free founding of a community or congregation. This is that one of you goes to X and the other goes to Y, and by holding sermons there for five, ten, or twenty people, you gradually create a community. The first difficulty I want to point out is that this method is, first of all, a slow one. You will see it is slow; it is the surest, but it is slow. The second difficulty is the question of resources. It is a fact that if community building were to be done in this way, it would have to be fully financed. It would have to be properly financed. Thus, the difficulties are that, first, a community would simply have to be founded by you and, second, the means of financing this community building would have to be found.

Now, I must say that, even if it has to be achieved with outer, material resources, this is naturally the best way to build community. However, no matter which method you use, you will need, on your part—I say this quite openly—great courage. Great courage will be called for. Naturally you yourself will have to join in the struggles that will follow. You will have to participate in dealing with the difficulties, even the difficulties of financial funding. It would, of course, be easiest and best if you could attain sufficiently extensive means so that you were completely independent and could then simply choose to gather together your community wherever you wished, even if it was made up out of the smallest groups of people. A community would then indeed come about. Community would form, but for it to do so you would naturally need the financial foundation, and this today poses really extraordinary difficulties. Immediately and most pervasively the established denominations would be there to hinder such a thing from developing. One cannot do such a thing on one's own; it must be organized as a large movement. You must found a community that is made up of all of those who take up this life goal. Then a financial foundation will have to be found for it.

Now, you can work this out for yourselves. If you numbered, let us say, two hundred people, that would be enough for this approach, because it is, as it were, a relatively safe approach and does not depend on speed. You can calculate how much you would need annually. As soon as you have the means to do it, you can do it. It is therefore the safest path. It is also the most obvious, and therefore the more natural one. However, given today's social and economic circumstances in Central Europe, raising such funds—and it can only be a matter of doing that—is terribly difficult. Nor can you do it anywhere else. Thus, it is absolutely out of the question to seek such funds in Eastern or Western Europe. In Central Europe, however, you could do it out of inner reasons, and precisely then you would be doing something truly great.

Werner Klein:[†] I must say that, until now, I have seen this last path as the only one we could take. Financing, of course, presents great difficulties, but we can overcome them. I believe, too, that we can—each one of us on the basis of our own forces—hold our heads above water by developing a field of work in a city, perhaps trying to earn enough money by giving lectures. We can form friendships with people, who then could help. But we could also take a job, since we are still living today in a time of shortened work hours. We could take a less meaningful position at the courthouse or somewhere else, where, out of necessity, we could support ourselves, in order still to have the time to do whatever else we want. I believe that we could hold our own this way. Yet, at the same time, we must also run a large-scale organization, and we must at least try to raise funds. Depending upon how much of this general yearning for something new and powerful lives in all of us in Germany, I believe that we will find something. It will depend on us. However, today, for the first time, I see a second way in connection with the church. I think we can cooperate there. The direct path of creating an independent community demands a totally different tactic. It calls for approaching the goal together and proceeding together toward a common point in time when we step forth as a greater movement, with each of us standing on our own. The tactic of the other path is that each of us begins to work on our own and attempts to create new communities out of the church. Neither of these paths will interfere with the other. When the time comes when those of us who have taken the surer, but more difficult path, are far enough along that we can—to put it bluntly—get going, then those of us who have until then taken the other path can join their work to ours and support us with real and positive fruits. If we manage to achieve success here or there in connection with the church, that is only to be welcomed and considered as a positive factor in itself. If we really want to create something socially in light of social-religious need today, it seems to me that the first, surer path is the best approach. In any case, we must try it. If we fail, then we can still take the other direction. When the other path is taken at the same time by those who already want to work to fill their time in the meantime, that is to be welcomed. If we want great things, we must strive for and attempt to do great deeds.

Rudolf Steiner: Here in Stuttgart we have some experience of precisely the difficulties that have to be faced on what was just described here as the safest and surest path. Of course, I am of the opinion that this course of action can be taken if enough effort is put into it, yet you must be aware of the difficulties that you will meet in every area. It takes exceptional goodwill to say that you can somehow take a job and can, in addition to that, work for the cause as we would want. However, it is an open secret that in the coming years students in German colleges will experience the most terrible financial difficulties. In this regard all kinds of impractical things have been proposed. A professor even came to me and told me that, because the students can no longer pay for the publication of their dissertations, one must think about setting up printing shops so that the students can print them themselves. Naturally, I do not have the slightest understanding for such a financial "inbreeding." I do not know how, if they are to print their own dissertations, students would be able to earn what it takes to do this. I found it to be more rational—and I pointed this out—to do away with the requirement of printing the dissertations during this time of need. Thus, every kind of impractical thing you can imagine is thought of. On the other hand, the matter is certainly very serious.

I think, for instance, it would be a wonderful idea if the *Der Kommende Tag*† [The Coming Day] would provide a financial foundation for at least a few students by, for example, every three months hiring a different group of students to work on its projects. After three months, they could go back and study at the universities. That would be a wonderful idea to put into practice, if one could do it. But in our businesses, as soon as we wanted to do so and hired a number of students, the union workers would revolt. They would tell us that it cannot be done. They would throw us out. And even if it was not a matter of getting thrown out, it would probably mean that no one was hired by the companies. Beyond this I do not see, even with today's shortened work hours, how you can really take a job in addition to the profession you have chosen, because this profession requires your full devotion in order to really satisfy its needs. I do not see a real possibility there.

You see, we are facing the fact that, because of difficult life circumstances, human beings are not as strong today as they actually should be. Therefore, I'm afraid that if each of you were dependent solely upon yourselves financially, it would lead at least to a mild form of neurasthenia or nervous exhaustion. It also seems to me to be fairly unlikely under today's circumstances that you could earn your support by giving lectures. You see, spiritual and cultural performance is paid according to the old currency value—we have just experienced this in a specific area—while food must be paid for according to the new currency value. When you are paid for cultural or spiritual work, you receive thirty Reich marks according to the old currency, but for food you have to pay out three hundred marks in the new currency. Thus, the matter would be difficult. On the other hand, it would be of real value to put your efforts into funding in the most comprehensive sense.

I also do not consider working together with the church, which seems more appealing to Mr. Klein than to some of you, as being hopeless. I think there are advantages to linking this work with the church…. [Here there followed sentences that referred to the financing, but which were not complete and not clear.]

You can do both. I think experience shows us today that if you first succeed in creating independent communities out of the church, you will find others to join you simply out of your actions. You will find others to join you [in this work]. People are not wrong when they say that there are many pastors in Protestant congregations who would gladly leave their position and need only an impetus to do so. If you succeed in drawing these people out of their congregations, then you will also find ministers to join you. They would be a good addition; they would help the movement to grow quickly. You would find reinforcements [for your work], while those who joined you would not have had the initiative to do what you did on their own. If the impetus would be given from without, you would find reinforcements.

Naturally it would be most desirable if you could somehow or other tackle the question of financing. I say intentionally "somehow or other" because if the financial problem is taken up properly, there is the likelihood for success. Starting [this effort], if it is done properly, is much more difficult than succeeding in it because today what is lacking, in the widest sense, is the ability of human beings to work together efficiently on the great tasks of life. Everywhere people become so stuck in their ruts that one cannot find coworkers who have enough vigor and initiative for the most important tasks.

I think that we should use our time together to the fullest, and since we now have come to the practical issues that should be handled first, I would ask that we continue by meeting at 7:00 p.m. this evening.

Discussion

Rudolf Steiner: I think it would be best if you would speak first about what we began to deal with earlier today. In this way, we will come to know each others' wishes and intentions. You must surely have some questions growing out of what I said.

Emil Bock: This afternoon the participants appointed me to report the results of our discussion. First of all, we thought about the different paths or methods and decided that all of them are possible. It became clear to us that it is a matter of gathering people, collecting money, deciding in which direction we want to organize, and deciding whether or not we want to strive to form a loose union. We agreed that each of us should take the initiative where we feel it is best to do so. In addition, we selected a location to which, as soon as the need exists, letters should be sent on a regular basis, so that we can organize the circulation of letters. Working publicly in the religious area could occur only within the church. What we might do afterward would have to wait until we have the people we need. As far as entering into this work goes, other people may join only if one of the participants of the current course speaks for them. The central location for managing the circular letters should be given to those of us who are from Berlin, and all the initiatives should be collected and sent out from there. We can begin to gather people together immediately. In preparation for an administrative position, the question is, who is to be selected? As for money, we would not want to collect money in the name of our group or union, because that would bring us to the attention of the public. We weighed the idea of whether it would be possible to make the administrative position a part of *Der Kommende Tag*. We also considered what other possibilities could present themselves.

Rudolf Steiner: Yes, so you think it is best to form a loose union of those who perhaps want to join this committee; to have a central location in Berlin for the collection of letters; and to collect money, at first, through *Der Kommende Tag*. We must make the last of these matters still more concrete. The question of the loose union should naturally also be discussed from the viewpoint of how fast you imagine it can proceed. Are they (the people sought) not most likely to be men and women who will be leaving school quite soon and entering life?

A participant: It varies.

Rudolf Steiner: Of course, it varies. In addition, the situation today is such that, above all, it is necessary when it comes to doing something like this not to lose any time. Undoubtedly the Movement for the Threefold Social Organism would have accomplished much more if time was not constantly being lost. And so, I think it is advisable here also that you do your best not to lose time. On the other hand, of course, one cannot rush such things. Have you formed an idea of how, in the event that you have begun collecting money on a large scale, you can go public after all? In a certain sense you seem to wish to avoid public life. Do you have special reasons for this? Let us try to discuss this question.

A participant: I just want to say that I have the feeling, after what I have experienced in the various cities, that there is no reason to avoid going public. Our lectures still have exclusively a spiritual scientific character. I am convinced that more people would join us immediately if the lectures were not just spiritual scientific lectures, but rather were religiously oriented.

Rudolf Steiner: I would gladly hear what you have against the openness. Your reasons are perhaps quite important.

A participant: We thought it would come to a culture war, and that we should wait before we found communities, and also even before we proclaim the idea itself. The minute we ask openly for money, it is reason enough for the greatest difficulties to rise up against us. Those are the reasons that prompted us to wait, including with regard to the founding of communities; for it has to do with the same problem.

A participant: We believe that we cannot step forward as actively working for the founding of communities.

Rudolf Steiner: Alright, then, wait with the founding of communities.

A participant: ... with going public.

Rudolf Steiner: But what are you going to do while you wait? The first task is to find ten times as many people as are here now. You can achieve this with your letter. I think, if the letter is done well, it will not be so very difficult to get ten times as many people to join you. Especially among theology students you will probably find ten times as many people. You found your way to one another relatively fast. Undoubtedly you will find people quickly among theology students. It all depends on how you try to finance the cause. This is naturally no easy matter, because it will only succeed if it too is done relatively fast. And naturally it is quite a good idea to first form a looser union and, through the use of correspondence, seek out those inclined toward this work. How many of you are there now?

A participant: Eighteen.

Rudolf Steiner: Eighteen students. Ten times that would be 180. As soon as you have 180 to 200 people, then it would certainly be a matter of beginning the work. The question is what can be done in order to act as quickly as possible? Naturally, working by means of an exemplary ritual—as good as that is in itself—is not very likely to be fast. Yet, the question is whether, while you collect people by correspondence, you could prepare a factual, very clear description of the main points. It could be printed. It does not have to be published, but it would need to be used by those collecting money, so they could give it to anyone who might be able to donate. How this could be done by *Der Kommende Tag* is difficult to imagine. *Der Kommende Tag* could indeed be administratively active in this work, but whether it could fund-raise on your behalf, while using its own name, is rather questionable. Did you mean *Der Kommende Tag* should take this on as *Der Kommende Tag*?

A participant: We saw only the advantage of the fact that they have many contacts and have administrative experience. It does not have to be *Der Kommende Tag* itself. We could appoint someone who then worked for *Der Kommende Tag* in a practical way.

Rudolf Steiner: I understand the situation. It is perhaps indeed not impractical to think of someone who is sympathetic toward this cause. One might think of Heisler[†] for precisely this task. One could indeed imagine that he, or someone in the same situation as he, could be considered the best for this position. But what do you think about a kind of quiet, objective, goal-oriented description that you would need to distribute so people could inform themselves about what they would be giving money for?

A participant: I believe personally that if we decide to fund-raise on a large scale, we will have to give up being hidden anyway.

Rudolf Steiner: It is possible that someone like Heisler could be entrusted with the fund-raising, and that we would not shy away from letting the work as such be made public. On the other hand, I believe that we could avoid letting your names and those of the others who join you become known. No one needs to know, when you have a priestly position here or there within the church, that you belong to this movement. There is no reason that you should be asked. The names of the participants of the loose union do not need to be made public, but only the idea and the cause as such.

With regard to Heisler the situation is such that it cannot harm him, because he will not be given a position in the church any longer anyway.

A participant: I am not thinking of a position.

Rudolf Steiner: You are not thinking of a position within the church?

A participant: No, I would not do that.

Rudolf Steiner: There are definitely candidates for the priesthood who are already so strongly compromised that they will have no problem with letting their names be known. Otherwise, the names of those in this loose union do not need to be made known. Of course, no one will deny belonging to it; you need to say it only if asked. This is what seems possible to me. Do you not think that, among the young people who have already taken a pastoral or ministerial position in a church, there will be some who will join your group?

A participant: It is a question as to how much of a relationship to Anthroposophy they have.

Rudolf Steiner: Yes, it is, of course, necessary that a certain core of persons is there who are Anthroposophists. However, it does not appear to me that all of them must be Anthroposophists. If among these there is a certain core of energetic personalities, then the whole thing can maintain an Anthroposophical character simply through the significance of these personalities—without shutting out those who are not Anthroposophists. You see, as a rule, the best Anthroposophists are those who were first opponents; or at least among the best are those who were opponents and have wrestled their way through slowly to Anthroposophy. We should not imagine that, with a short lecture, we can quickly bring to Anthroposophy those people who seek to find their way to a religious worldview in the modern sense. Many will resist it. Above all, it will not be easy to get beyond their belief that certain results of Anthroposophical research are out of the question because of their own dogma. Many will still believe that reincarnation is irreligious and not Christian. And yet, it is not to be wished that everyone who cannot yet accept this should be shut out, but the actual religious relationship should be held onto. Just as, at the time of the founding of Christianity, one could be a good Christian without knowing that the Earth is round

or that America exists; and just as Christianity was not shattered with
the discovery of America, so, too, can someone be a good Christian
without having access to the truth of reincarnation. For basically,
the essential thing with a Christian—I still want to speak about
this tomorrow—is his or her relationship to Christ Jesus himself, to
this totally objective being. That is the essential thing. A personal
relationship to Christ Jesus is the essential aspect of Christianity.
Any teaching or doctrine as such, which as a teaching is of course
assured to be true but is simply a cosmological doctrine, cannot be
the characteristic sign that a person is Christian. People are Christian
through their own personal relationship to Christ, just as Buddhists
are Buddhist through their relationship to Buddha. It is not through
any teaching or doctrine. You need the content of a doctrine—as we
will see—in the sermon, but you are not actually a Christian because
of a doctrine. No one, who does not have a positive relationship to
the suprasensible Christ-Being, can be a Christian today, in the sense
that we must understand it.

For this reason, for me, Adolf Harnack† is not a Christian. A
man who can say that Christ can be taken out of the Gospels and
that only the Father has a place in them† is not a Christian. For
him, there is no difference between Christ and Yahweh, the God
of the Old Testament. If you cross out Christ's name in Harnack's
book, *Das Wesen des Christentums* [The nature of Christianity],
and replace it with Yahweh, you would see that the meaning is not
changed. He simply sets Christ's belief in the Father in the place of
knowledge of the being of Jesus himself. He recognizes in the Christ
actually only a great teacher of the religion of the Father, which is,
however, actually a negation of Christianity and not the essence
or nature of Christianity. Therefore, I believe it is not necessary
to have the people swear, as it were, to the teaching of reincarnation or karma. These teachings are won only with great difficulty.
With time people will manage it. I just think that, because you
yourselves are Anthroposophists and because you will attract greater
numbers of Anthroposophists than of non-Anthroposophists, the
work will indeed have the necessary Anthroposophical character. The substance of Anthroposophy will see to it that it has an

Anthroposophical character, if it actually succeeds. And it must succeed, because it contains many conditions for success.

A participant: At the University of Münster many of the theologians wanted to gain independence. There already we would find theologians who would meet our needs. Whether many are Anthroposophists is the question.

Rudolf Steiner: I believe that in Münster Gideon Spicker[†] prepared the ground. He was a professor of philosophy at Münster. Do you know anything about him?

A participant: Only that the exams there were designed differently.

Another participant: It is exactly the same in Leipzig.

Rudolf Steiner: Thus, you will find a foundation prepared among the young theologians.

A participant: The theologians who want to be free of the church are mostly people who can no longer understand the doctrine of the Trinity and cannot acknowledge Christ as a suprasensible being; or they belong to the Community Movement.[†]

Rudolf Steiner: When there is a core of Anthroposophists, it is not troublesome if we also have such personalities in the loose union. Proof of this seems to be, for instance, that Mr. Rittelmeyer came to Anthroposophy immediately after he wrote this little piece about the personality of Jesus.[†] It was actually written from the point of view that you just characterized. It is written totally with the intent of presenting Jesus Christ as a powerful religious personality, and completely leaves out of the discussion the whole question of the suprasensible, of the symbol, and so on. It was absolutely what one could call enlightened Protestantism. Then he came to us and recognized relatively quickly that he needed to understand the Mystery of Golgotha and to wrestle through to a suprasensible understanding of its nature.

Thus, I believe that when people are serious students—they do not have to be strivers, but must be serious students—then it does not matter if they come out of Enlightened Protestantism. On the other hand, the best candidates you could wish for would actually be those young people—there are not many, mostly single individuals here and there—who have finished their Catholic theological studies and have broken away from the Catholic Church completely. They would be the best candidates you could wish for. One cannot deny that the Catholic theology, as theology, as theological content, has much that is sound in it. Those who have studied Catholic theology are well-schooled, and that stays with them. And then, if they have left the church—in the church, of course, they are held in iron shackles—then they are open to everything. I mention this—there are not many such people, but only isolated ones—only to stress the possibility. And then, too, the Enlightened Protestants are not to be underestimated.

A participant: … human beings, who strive for certainty in science, go so far that they can no longer acknowledge the suprasensible being of Christ, yet they long for it.…

Rudolf Steiner: This is how it was with Rittelmeyer. He could do nothing other than come to—of course, somewhat more power-fully and quite brilliantly—Weinel's conception† of the simple man from Nazareth. This was the personality of Christ according to Rittelmeyer, who wrestled his way very quickly to the suprasensible understanding of the Christ. Therefore, I believe, you do not need to shy away from drawing people to your cause.

A participant: The most difficult problem is the financing.

Rudolf Steiner: Yes, the question of financing remains difficult; and it will be, until we have the money. It is a fact that new difficulties will arise in the attempt to raise each new gift of 10,000 marks. These are difficulties that simply must be overcome. Many bitter experiences will certainly have to be overcome; you will have many bitter experiences. I think, however, that someone like Heisler is not at all the wrong person for this. On the one hand, he has become bitter because of his own destiny, yet on the other hand, he is convinced of the necessity that such a thing as this must happen. And he is already a respected older person—I'm sorry, but you are all younger than he is—which a person must be to take what comes when collecting money. It is not a comfortable thing.

Emil Bock: ... who find themselves in the position to do so, but who meanwhile are in another profession.

Rudolf Steiner: Yes, it is naturally a question of what such people will do. Mostly, they would enter into consideration with regard to fund-raising. However, it is not easy to bring the necessary enthusiasm to bear when one is not engaged in the work. Naturally, there might be a few individuals of this kind, but I think that they are already so overloaded with all kinds of work that they could hardly do more than dedicate themselves to a project like this as a sideline. I do not actually know of anyone who—without seeking the ministry himself or herself, even in such a free form—would be useful as an Anthroposophist here. Anthroposophists are not so interested in the renewal of the religious community, precisely because they experience in Anthroposophy—how shall I put it?—a kind of religious satisfaction. But there must be Anthroposophists who are also theologians, and you must look among them. They would certainly not be so rare since Rittelmeyer has been active. I think you will find many people among theologians, especially since Rittelmeyer published his book, which is a collection.[†] Whether all of them will be able to be of use for our cause is another question. But in any case they would improve the movement, I think.

Emil Bock: They would naturally have to change their course if they came to understand the idea.

Rudolf Steiner: Whether many of the students want to change course? Do you mean students from the *Bund für anthroposophische Hochschularbeit* [Association for Anthroposophical College Work]?[†]

A participant: Students who do not study theology because, while they certainly have a strong interest in it, have no interest in what is provided in the church today.

Rudolf Steiner: Do you think they can muster the active enthusiasm?

A participant: Yes, if they were given the possibility of being active in this sense.

Rudolf Steiner: It is certainly possible, after you have looked at these persons, to approach them and bring them along with you. I have noticed that the Association for Anthroposophical College Work, above all when it makes the effort to spread Anthroposophy in the individual branches of Anthroposophical college work, places natural scientific interests ahead of theology. On the other hand, we should interest the theologians themselves.

A participant: It is a question whether we can wait that long—until some of them have taken the special theological exams.

Rudolf Steiner: Do you think it would take too long?

A participant: I do not know how necessary it is.

Another participant: There are some among us who had not considered taking the exams in theology, but planned to use the preliminary studies in order to strive toward the goal and do what is to be taken up here.

Rudolf Steiner: Now it is a question of whether those of whom you are speaking—who have thought it through to the point that they would not take the theological exams, but would do something else— understand how necessary it is to turn to the priesthood. Naturally, this tendency is connected with a quite common cultural idea, isn't it? You see, the ideas that Spengler described in his *Decline of the West*† are sounder than one thinks. They are so well-founded that one can say that, if present cultural tendencies merely continued without a new impulse, what Spengler calculates would happen. We are in the midst of a complete decline—in a fully descending stream. On the other hand, you must not forget the corruption of the culture. The corruption of general spiritual life is not limited to the educated but is quite widespread. It is actually true that the majority of the people have been bitten by this, and the religious impulses that perhaps still existed among the less educated in the 1870s and 1880s have also already vanished today. Thus, we are in the midst of the stream of complete descent, and it will be hardly possible to come out of it, if religious life as such does not give rise to new impulses. And thus I believe, to be sure, that those who have studied theology and could work as priests should do that. It is quite necessary that those who have studied theology should work as priests, because we need this so much.

A participant: ... but then also within the church?

Rudolf Steiner: Within the church? I would like to stay just with what I said. You can remain within the church, if you gradually lead the members of the current church communities out of them. Thus, you can proceed to the founding of independent communities. I do not believe the church, as such, will reform itself in any manner or form; it cannot be renewed or regenerated. The church community is so corrupted that we can only reckon that one ... [the text here is full of gaps and cannot be understood] ... leads them out and founds something new with them ... [further gaps in the text]. I can say that it is not just my opinion about the possibility of reforming the church, but rather that it is objective knowledge that these church communities are doomed to destruction. The Catholic Church, naturally, is an exception, which must be thought of as absolutely not at all doomed to destruction,† because it works with widespread means and must thus be viewed as something quite different.

A participant: Some of us became philosophers, some scientists, after we broke off our unsatisfying theological studies. Should we do a doctorate and, after the doctoral exams, proceed to a theological study again? Or should one say that, after our preparatory training, we can begin immediately with the work in religion?

Rudolf Steiner: You see, that is precisely the question of what success we will have. In this connection one must not underestimate the nature of a transition. When the Waldorf school was founded I selected teachers based on nothing else than their personal characteristics; whatever training was to be given in pedagogy and didactics would be given a few weeks later. Such a thing must be possible in a transitional situation. I do not think that those who were frustrated with their theological studies and turned to philosophy, science, or something else have to strive for anything else than to bring the academic study formally to its conclusion. Though that is to be wished for, it is not absolutely necessary. It would be good if the academic study were completed, let us say, with a dissertation. On the other hand, we do not need to think for a moment that it is necessary for them to return to their theological studies. In this transitional period we must consider it to be absolutely right not to hold to the old exam process. This is undoubtedly true. When, for example, Mr. Husemann† completes his study and oral exams in chemistry, there is nothing to keep him from—if he wants to be a preacher—becoming a *preacher* of chemistry.

Know that the specialized theological studies—do not let this upset you—hinder the effectiveness of the pastor or priest in the community. It is a fact that the theology students learn too little about the world; they are actually much too unfamiliar with what their task is. They are given a position and are supposed to execute agendas†—such as I have described—in economic life. For this, a specialized study like theology—in which one becomes a thoroughly impractical human being—is therefore inappropriate. I have actually experienced that, for instance, there are excellent theology graduates who hardly know anymore what the Pythagorean theorem says. They are exceptions, but it does occur. However, disregarding standing fully in practical life—which one needs above all—we quite certainly cannot solve the world's problems by debating the validity of dogma and which theological faculties are to be cultivated. One could quite well imagine that among those of you who have not studied theology at all, there could be some with a certain religious genius. One could well imagine that.

What we naturally need is that, before you leave here, you find the person you want to have as secretary of your loose union. It would then be good if you would stay in contact with this person, precisely for the sake of *Der Kommende Tag*. You already have the central office in Berlin for letters.

A participant: We had thought of having another office in Tübingen, which is close to Stuttgart.

Rudolf Steiner: And this Tübingen central office, what tasks would it have?

A participant: The things that could be done in Stuttgart could be done through personal connections.

Rudolf Steiner: What other tasks would the Tübingen central office have? Looking for people? But then you are thinking of a separate office like the one Mr. Bock imagines would be connected with *Der Kommende Tag*, aren't you?

Emil Bock: First of all, we must take on the financing; we must work on it in different places. All kinds of things will have to be brought together at a central place, so the central office must have authority. We chose Berlin because most of us are located there.

Rudolf Steiner: So, you plan to have central offices in Berlin and Tübingen in order to find the suitable people (coworkers), and to have a person here in Stuttgart who would take steps for financing the work?

Now, I cannot in any way make a commitment on behalf of *Der Kommende Tag*, but it is my opinion that the matter could be handled in the way we have thought out. If it could happen that Heisler—naturally I do not wish, in any way, to control your choice for the position, so I mention Heisler only as an example—would be assigned to begin the process of financing, and if this could be done in conjunction with *Der Kommende Tag*, you would need immediately to think about properly designing the position for Heisler. Naturally I would have to bring this to *Der Kommende Tag* for discussion, so you would already know when you leave here what *Der Kommende Tag* would be able to do. Thus, I think many transitions from one thing to another lead us a little into uncertainty. It seems to me that it would not be bad to create a central office that would begin the work immediately. It cannot be done prematurely; I do respect all the reasons for not moving too fast. Yet, in reality, what we can do in two years or one year we can also do today. I cannot today commit to this on behalf of *Der Kommende Tag*, but it seems to me, if the plan actually is not to work under the name of *Der Kommende Tag* but rather only in connection with it, then you should actually do this immediately.

A participant: Do we have the material, financial resources? If we hire someone, we must have the salary for that person.

Rudolf Steiner: Yes, well, it is naturally the question of whether we can find a way around this, whether the concern regarding the salary would exist immediately for this person. Will you still be here the day after tomorrow? We could speak tomorrow, or the day after, about how we can solve this issue, so that such a person can be found immediately. It is obvious that one cannot take care of the financing for the person whose task it will be to take on the fund-raising so fast. We can speak about this yet tomorrow or the next day. But are you, in principle, inclined to begin immediately, if it is possible?

A participant: I would like, however, to ask whether we could decide now about who to hire for this position.

Rudolf Steiner: I wish only to say this: I always proceed from real, practical aspects. There are reasons that would probably allow the matter to be accomplished quite quickly, if precisely Dr. Heisler were to be a possibility. With him you would most likely be able to proceed faster than if it were a matter of selecting some other person arbitrarily.

Lecture 3

My dear friends! Today we will begin by continuing the reflections we began yesterday on the topic of community. After that, we will try to see whether we can make any further progress in dealing with the organizational and financial matters we also touched on yesterday. Yesterday I wanted to speak to you about the inner aspect of building community in the religious realm. Today I want to move on to the second area that you yourselves indicated as being of particular importance to you: that is, to the question of ritual.

It is certainly the case that we cannot bring about humanity's religious deepening without inaugurating a certain ritual, together with its so-called symbolism. I want to give you the reasons for this because you can work in a realm effectively only if you understand the requirements and forces involved.

You see, in recent times the whole development of the civilized part of humanity has taken on an intellectual form, one that brings concepts into consciousness only in their abstract form. And because this is so, a kind of fundamental feeling has arisen that a person can attain real knowledge only through this kind of abstraction. And this feeling has now progressed to the point where, in a certain way, we value only the abstract content of consciousness. Now you can understand why the abstract content of consciousness would have to be valued precisely during the time when humanity demands the primacy of the assertion of the value of the individual rather than of humanity as a whole. This is because the abstract content of consciousness places us before something quite universal. The feeling exists that, by means of an abstract understanding of the world, one could bring about a comprehensive understanding of the world in each individual.

How far, or to what, should our concepts extend? They should extend above all to what presents itself in our sense world as our perceptions, commenting on them in the most varied ways, and finding in them so-called natural or historical laws. But our intellectual content goes further than that to form hypotheses about what is not sense-perceptible. Partly such hypotheses extend to what is not perceptible in time or space; partly they extend to what is not perceptible for fundamental reasons. In time and space, for example, the Earth's beginning and end are not perceptible. Modern intellectualism, however, based on physical, geological theories has given us hypotheses about the end of the Earth. As for space we have hypotheses about the inner nature of the Sun or other cosmic bodies, the cosmic nebula, as they are called, and so on. We do not usually take into account that, when the Sun is said to be constituted in such and such a way, that this is merely a hypothesis. People believe that this hypothesis is a physical reality. Physicists would be quite amazed if they could see what really exists in that place where they project a kind of rarified gas as the Sun. In reality, there is nothing there that is even remotely comparable to our gases, or even to our ether. There is not just empty space where the Sun is but something that—compared to the intensity of *empty* space—we would have to designate as negative space. In fact, at the place in space where we speak of the Sun there is a hollowing out, a recess. It is not just space that is simply devoid of matter. It does not even have the intensity or substantiality of emptiness that we usually ascribe to space in the abstract. What is present there is less than space. In other words, in the Sun we move out of the physical element into the spiritual element. In reality we can speak of the Sun only in a spiritual sense.

I want to mention this today to draw to your attention to what extent intellectualism, which is justified in the area of natural science, has today taken hold of all areas. It even extends itself to the world of molecules and atoms, which is not perceptible in principle—for the simple reason that the warmth, the light, and the tones theoretically arise from the movements and processes constituted by molecules and atoms. In other words, perception is not transferable into the atomic world. People just hypothesize something into it that they suppose to be present there.

Intellectualism has thus spread itself over both the realms of time and space of the outer, spatial world and into what is in principle nonperceptible. It has also permeated all study of history and religious history. If you follow the whole field of Gospel literature and knowledge of the Gospels—above all, nineteenth-century biblical scholarship—you will become aware that all of this biblical science gradually slips over from a completely different kind of soul content into an intellectual understanding of the Bible, and of the Gospels. We can say that, at the end of the nineteenth century, biblical scholarship had gone so far that, because of intellectualism, nothing was left of the Gospels, even for the theologians. It is clearly characteristic that this intellectualism took on such forms as appear, for example, in the theologian Schmiedel.[†] In Schmiedel we see that conclusions are no longer drawn from what is in the Gospels concerning the nature of Christ's personality. Instead, a number of passages, in which something unfavorable is said about Christ Jesus, are sought out in the Gospels; for example, the passage is selected in which it says that he did not bother about his mother or siblings. And, from this limited number of negative comments collected from the Gospels about the personality of Christ Jesus, the conclusion is drawn that such comments must be true, because if someone wanted to make something up, he or she would not include such negative statements, but rather hymns of praise.

Here you see where intellectualism has hidden itself in order to have access to the Gospels at all. I say this because, from a theological point of view, the extravagant notions that nontheologians have managed to attain have become monstrous. One need consider only the fact that today psychiatric research into the Gospels[†] is widespread, and we have literary works that clearly state that what is in the Gospels cannot be understood. From a psychiatric point of view, of course, what the Gospels communicate must be designated as abnormal. From this point of view, it is accepted that the origin of Christianity lies in an illness of Christ Jesus, and that this illness has infected all Christians. The origin of Christianity is thus traced back to a mental illness to which Christ Jesus succumbed.

We can hardly say that any description is too strong if we want to point out that the whole of present so-called cultural life, which revolves around intellectualism, must actually lead to the undermining of precisely the Christian religious element, and does so with the greatest speed. That this fact is not sufficiently recognized is one of the great ravages of our time. If one could recognize it, one would have to say that it is the responsibility above all of those who take religious life seriously to see to it that religious life is rescued from intellectualism.

I do not want to become critical about the fact that during the last four centuries Protestantism itself has contributed a great deal toward religious life coming to this intellectualism. More and more we find a pagan element—perhaps in fact unconscious—in the ritual and symbolism. Now, what keeps people from sticking to the ritual and the symbolism does not lie in the feeling that there is something pagan there, but in the fact that people no longer have a sense for the forms of expression contained there. Just consider that the intellectual comprehension of the world gives people the illusion that they can, with the content that they have put into their souls, become clear about the whole world: that they can reduce everything to intellectual concepts. For this reason, intellectuals, when they have their intellectual concepts, feel that they possess the whole world. Because such people have given themselves up to the illusion that they have grasped the whole world, they feel themselves intellectually satisfied precisely because of this universal intellectual element. They believe they need nothing more to understand and sense the world. You can understand that precisely today intellectualism can take the upper hand because people now believe that they can fit the world into intellectual concepts. At the same time, because people are satisfied because they seem to have gotten the whole world into their "I," they lose their social connection with the rest of the world. The social element is atomized, split up into each individual. This situation exists throughout the Youth Movement today, because, through their intellectualism, young people simply separate themselves out into individual "atoms," each wanting his or her own religious creed. People are so absorbed with this that they are certain that the religious element cannot reach beyond their own skin. This shows that it is precisely this universal intellectual life that splits and atomizes the religious life and must therefore end in undermining religious life through the particular form modern science has taken. Here the most powerful force for the downfall of religious life exists among university theologians and other teachers of theology who have taken contemporary scientific thinking as adequate to understand the facts of religion as such.

Not even laypeople today do as much to undermine the religious life as modern theology does. It is actually a shame that attempts such as Overbeck's† have not made more progress. Overbeck's extraordinarily important book, *Über die Christlichkeit unserer heutigen Theology* [About the Christian nature of our theology today], proved that modern theology is unchristian. Overbeck was a church historian from Basel. He was a friend of Nietzsche and made a deep impression on him. Overbeck wanted to provide proof that modern theology is most unchristian, because it has completely separated Christianity from itself. He wanted to show that modern theology contributes most to the undermining of Christianity, because, through the universal power of suggestion that intellectualism exerts on modern education, it has become purely intellectualistic. Without grasping how modern theology, as it is practiced in the modern faculties, leads to the undermining of Christianity, you will not be able to bring the right impulse into what you are striving for.

What is absolutely important is that we learn to move toward another way of experiencing the world than the merely intellectual one. This other form involves what is pictorial or of an image-nature and which therefore can pass over into the ritual and symbolism.

When we founded the Waldorf school—as far as I can, I want to give you examples from our immediate, present life—it was important above all that the school arise out of the consciousness of the time and so to demonstrate to the world that, in founding our Waldorf school, we were not founding a school that taught a particular philosophy.[†] It is the worst slander against the Waldorf school when it is repeatedly said in the outer world (outside of the school)—this slander is already spreading to America—that the Waldorf school exists in order to teach children Anthroposophy. That is not its task! It is not a philosophy school. What we can gain through Anthroposophy can flow into the pedagogy and didactics. Only what Anthroposophy can penetrate should be included in the pedagogical process. This is why, from the very beginning, we have had the Catholic children receive religious instruction from a Catholic priest, and the Protestant children from a Protestant minister. It cannot be otherwise, until your work begins. Now of course, the Waldorf school arose, in the first place, for the children of the workers of the Waldorf Astoria cigarette factory. They formed the basis of the student body. Many of the children came from families that were Social Democrats, others from families that were dissenters. Thus, we were faced with the question: should these children grow up completely without religion? It was certainly a concern, wasn't it? But there were also voices among the parents, saying that they did not want their children to grow up without religion. Thus, just as we let the Catholic children have Catholic instruction and the Protestant children the Protestant, so did we have to provide a kind of Anthroposophical religious instruction for these other Social Democratic and dissenter children. In fact, I believe this class has the majority of the children; at least I think so. Is that true?

Ernst Uehli:[†] By far the majority.

Rudolf Steiner: So, by far the most children are receiving Anthroposophical religious instruction. Comparatively speaking, there are also relatively many Catholic children receiving Catholic instruction. The children who receive Protestant instruction are in the minority. We could not help it. We had absolutely no intention that the Protestant instructor should be ranked lowest. It was a sad day for our school when the Protestant religious instruction teacher told us that he was unable to make proper progress, because his children were gradually going over to the Anthroposophical religious instruction. It was his task to keep them in his class. We could not do anything about the fact that they went over to the Anthroposophical religious instruction. We do not have Anthroposophy as a subject or objective in our curriculum for the school. Just as in the case of the Catholic and Protestant instruction, the Anthroposophical religious instruction is also brought in from outside. We have tried to produce a method for it. Naturally, it is all in its beginning, for things that work with reality do not arise from one day to the next. They can come only out of practice, only out of extensive experience. Nevertheless, a beginning must be made. From this point of view, open, unbiased perception has shown us the need—and this is important in relation to our discussion yesterday—to add a ritual to our religious instruction— namely, the Sunday service, which two of your colleagues observed last Sunday. Of course, it too is absolutely only in its beginning stage. As of now, there is a ritual for such a Sunday service—every Sunday—and also a ritual for those children who have reached the age of fourteen and have completed elementary school,[†] and experience in this ritual above all what we think should be experienced through the ritual of confirmation. You must, however, regard all of this as being in its beginnings. Here the need to move to a way of working through ritual arose out of the circumstances themselves. Once you think through your task with real inner participation, you will also have to conclude that the ritual, the symbolism, must be added.

You see, religious life will disappear completely if it cannot represent a reality; it will fade away if it is to be something about which it can be said that everything can be expressed through intellectual thoughts. If this is the case, religious life absolutely cannot be preserved. Through religious experience something must happen; processes and events must exist, which, as such, as processes, have eternal significance not only for human beings but also for the cosmos.

Therefore, we must say to ourselves, everything that we take into our souls intellectually—all that modern science and scientific achievement acknowledges—dies when we die. The living concepts that we form in our soul in childhood, and which transform them- selves during our life, do not die, but the intellectual content—even though it extends our understanding of natural laws and has great ramifications—dies when we die.

Do not take this statement lightly. Intellectual soul content is, at best, only an image of the spiritual. Intellectual knowledge is subject to death just as the human body is, because it is obtained and conveyed entirely through the body. All soul life that is conveyed intellectually arises after birth and perishes with death. What is eternal in the soul is found first behind what is intellectual. No abstract concept, but only what we have experienced in life that is beyond the abstract concepts passes through the portal of death with us. Many present-day people will have to lead a long sleep-life after death, because they were fixed only in intellectuality between birth and death. Intellectuality grows dark after death. It will be only after a long time that intellectual people will be able to acquire a super-intellectual content (content beyond the intellectual), which they can then, in turn, work on for their next earthly life. It is a fact that human beings in their entire development lose much of their present lifetime because of their intellectual lives.

Our contemporaries see this as folly—our theologians, in any case, do—but it is certain, a result of solid spiritual scientific research. To the degree that our entire education today is based only on intel-lectualism, and because we are so proud of this intellectualism, we deprive human beings of any spiritual, eternal content. From various sides, then, we are inoculating humanity with this intellectualism that is subject to death.

My dear friends, it is absolutely correct to count statistically how many people in a population are illiterate, and how many can read and write, at a relatively early age. However, when education is based solely on intellectualism, as is the case in today's schools, this means the killing of our soul-spiritual nature and not the awakening of it. For the evolution of Earth this must be so; but on the other side, the balance must be provided for it. For this reason, in the pedagogy and didactic of our Waldorf school, we do not use an intellectual approach in the introduction and instruction of reading and writ-ing. There, too, in order not to destroy the children's eternal aspect, they learn and are taught through pictures and what is pictorial and artistic. The children learn to read and write through images. They receive their letters through pictures. They are given something abstract—our alphabet today is abstract—by means of something concrete and pictorial so that at least real soul life is not taken from them. The pedagogy and didactic of the Waldorf school always proceeds out of the Anthroposophical understanding of the whole of human life. And the great hatred that people already bring against this shows how much they feel that we are doing something here that has been extinguished in the outer world during the last three to four centuries—naturally, to the detriment of the life of modern humanity. We need hardly wonder that religious life is suppressed when we have a science that simply can no longer speak of the eternal at all. And the rest of the culture that has arisen shows to an even greater extent that science has become only a sparkling bauble, a glittering froth of thinking that has appeared everywhere in human culture.

In newer languages we do indeed have a word for what is "undying" or "immortal." Yet we have this word only out of our egotism—out of our wanting-to-have-ourselves-forever. We have a word for what is "undying" or "immortal," but we do not have a word for "unborn"— a workable word for being "not-yet-born." We must have a word for this, just as we have a word for "immortal." When we speak about the eternal nature of the soul, we consider only the end of life. Parallel to this comes the atomization, the splitting apart—the weaving of the intellectual elements into individual lives—the fragmentation, which today is even sought in the subconscious, for instance, as it is in the school of William James[†] in America, and so on. This atomization must be met—if one is serious about nurturing the religious element—with work through the image, through the rite, the ritual, in the best sense of the word. Just consider the significance of ritual, the meaning of ritual as such. Let me give you an example.

For this, I do not want to proceed in the same way as, but rather in opposite way to, the storm troops of iconoclasm who want to eradicate images or the attackers of ritual who want to eradicate ritual. I simply want to give an example to show what ritual means.

Consider the Mass. Strictly speaking, the Sacrifice of the Mass cannot be regarded as Roman Catholic. It may not be regarded as such, because it goes back to ancient, pre-Christian times. We can certainly say that the Mass was concealed in the rites of the Mysteries, and that it has been greatly transformed over time. The Mass in Roman Catholicism today is merely something that is partially transformed out of the Mysteries of Egypt and the Near East.

What was it at that time? What was the rite that finally passed over into the Mass? Actually, only those Catholics who are most in-the-know, the most "initiated," know the meaning of this rite, whereas the broad populace of the Catholics view it in image-form. What, then, lay at the foundation of the Sacrifice of the Mass?

It was an outer image of what we call initiation. This is absolutely the case. When you look at the basic parts of the Mass and disregard what has become connected with it—in part fully justified and in part based on misunderstanding—the Mass is an outer pictorial expression of initiation.

The four parts [of the Mass] are the Gospel reading, the offering, the transubstantiation, and the communion. These four parts form the essence of the Mass.

What does the Gospel reading mean? It means the sounding forth—the revelation—of the Word in the congregation. This is clearly based on the consciousness that the Word has a real content only when human beings experience the inspired Word that resounds out of the spiritual world and not when they simply investigate it intellectually. Without the consciousness that the suprasensible world embodies itself in the Word, the Gospel reading would not be a true, or real reading. Thus, in the first part of the Mass, we have the divinely enlightened proclamation of the doctrine. In the Gospel reading we have what the suprasensible world gives to human beings in the sense world.

What human beings can give in return out of themselves to the suprasensible world appears before us pictorially in the second part of the Mass: the offering. What human beings attempt to give in return, in the presentation of the sacrifice or the offering, is true prayer. The offering expresses symbolically the solemn inward feeling of consecration that human beings can feel inwardly for the suprasensible. This feeling is expressed through the symbolic deed of the offering as the response to the Gospel reading. This is the second part of the Mass.

The third part, the transubstantiation, consists of the symbolic presentation of the consciousness that develops within us when we feel the divine substance within us, when we feel the divine substance present within our own souls. For Christians, this transubstantiation is nothing other than the expression of the Pauline saying, "Not I, but Christ in me." We not only offer ourselves, but we become aware that the suprasensible lives within us. This is what presents itself to us in the image of the transubstantiation. And always it continues to be a beautiful and significant accompanying phenomenon of the transubstantiation that, while the *Sanctissimum* (the host and paten) are lifted up—above the chalice—the worshippers must actually close their eyes, and turn inward, so that they do not experience the transubstantiation through outer vision, but in their innermost consciousness. It is also significant that the *Sanctissimum* consists of the bread and paten, which has a lunar form. Indeed, the symbol of the sacrament enveloped in the *Sanctissimum* has the Sun and the Moon present pictorially within it. This points clearly to the fact that, in the time when the Mass was designed or formed, there was a consciousness of the connection of Christ with the Sun and of Yahweh with the Moon.

What the world received in Christianity, and what built on the lunar religion of Yahweh, is fully expressed in the host sitting on the Moon-form (the paten). It is truly a symbol for the flowing together of the mortal aspect of the human being with the immortal. The fourth part of the Mass is the communion. This expresses nothing other than the following: after growing together with the suprasensible, the human being allows his or her whole earthly nature to pour into the union with the suprasensible. This fourth part presents pictorially what a person who is to be initiated must experience in both the older and the newer Mysteries.

The first main part (the Gospel reading) consists of our learning to transform the cosmic knowledge and cosmic feeling that we receive as an abstraction, so that we can say with inner honesty, "In the beginning was the Word, and out of the Word everything has become that has become." I ask you, my dear friends, to consider for a moment how far modern Christianity has departed from a precise understanding of the Gospel of John. Think about the fact that in general today there exists the consciousness that actually considers only the Father God to be the creator of the world. The Father God—who, in addition, is confused with Yahweh, the Hebrew folk-god—is seen as the Creator-God, even though the Gospel says, "In the beginning was the Word.... All things were made by him; and without him was not anything made that was made." What we have in us which has come into being is the creative—the Word in the orthodox sense. Of the Father God we must actually have the idea that he exists through himself, subsists independently of everything, and that in the Son God, he gave the world that which signifies the creative essence of the world.

I say this only because those who are to be initiated have to raise their understanding to the point where the Word that is proclaimed sounds absolutely out of the suprasensible realm, while our everyday word sounds out of what is intellectual and transitory. This is the first act of initiation: that the person form the content of his or her soul into the Word as suprasensible revelation, as a real occurrence that proceeds out of the Angelic-All, the whole of the spiritual world. What arises out of the spiritual world and takes on the form of the Word in us is the first act of the ritual of the Mass. Even in discussing this consciously, we should be aware that it presents a proclamation of the suprasensible and *not* a proclamation of the sense world.

The second part of the Mass consists of the human being entering into a real relationship with the spiritual world through the offering. Once we are able to indicate the offering as the gift-in-return to the divine, only then actually do we have before us the many-sidedness that should be there. Modern Catholicism has let this become obscure. Modern Catholicism actually wants to receive everything from the Godhead and to give nothing back to the divine in return.

Now, we did not want our ritual of the Sunday Service in the Waldorf school to cause any great offense against contemporary prejudices. However, it was necessary that the person carrying out the offering question each child in the simplest way by asking whether he or she wants to strive toward the Spirit of God. We had to do this so that in the answer, "Yes, I will seek him, I will seek the Spirit of God"—at least verbally—each child could give an indication of the real relationship. Something should occur through each child being asked whether he or she will seek the Spirit of God. We must also have at least an indication or suggestion of the communion in our Sunday Service. The rest must come later.

In the third main part of the Mass, we become aware that the supra-sensible is not merely present, but that the human soul can unite with it. And in the fourth part of the Mass, the communion, the fourth act of initiation is presented. This consists in human beings permeating themselves totally with the suprasensible so that they feel themselves to be more of an outer sign, an outer world symbol. They must feel that they confirm—make true—the saying, "The human being is the image of the Godhead."

Consciousness of these connections has become so lost that they can be pointed out today only with great difficulty. We can say that we have presented before us in the Mass—which naturally cannot be simply adopted from Catholicism, but rather formed out of a contemporary sensibility—the deepest meaningful spiritual path of the human being. Therefore the important moments of life, such as the time of leaving school to go out into the world, should be accompanied by such ritualistic acts. We should also work similarly—through ritual, that is, through the image—with adults. An image or picture does not work just on the intellect; an image works on the whole human being. If I grasp something that is intellectual, I understand it only within myself, for myself alone. If I stand before a picture, an image, it goes into much deeper layers of my human nature than what is intellectual does. And when what happens through the ritual enters the members of a community, they experience together, in common, a suprasensible element. What teaching based on content atomizes and splits apart is synthesized and put back together through the ritual. What leads to a splitting, to an analyzing, in individual human beings when the content of teaching is reproduced in the form of intellectual ideas is reunited and synthesized when we try to speak pictorially.

You see, in modern times only *one* community has learned to speak pictorially, but it is a community that misuses this symbolism, this imaginatively ensouled speaking. I am speaking of the Jesuits. I must again and again point out how, in the Jesuit educational institutions, pupils are taught quite methodically—although in a way detrimental to humanity—to bring everything together in a picture, if anything is to be taught to human beings.

I shall give you a quite clear example, as I myself have experienced its immense significance—theoretically I must say—because I wanted to see for myself how the matter worked. It involved a famous Jesuit preacher ten years ago. He preached about the institution of the Easter confession. His intention was to reduce to absurdity what the opponents of Catholicism were saying: that the Easter confession is a papal institution and not that of the suprasensible. He wanted to reduce this to absurdity for his believers. I also witnessed this. If Klinckowström†—that was the preacher's name—had wanted to convey this to his audience in the abstract form that is usually used in Protestant sermons, he would have achieved absolutely nothing; he would not have accomplished even a little of what he had intended. He did it by summarizing the issue as follows: "Yes, my dear Christians, you see, when one says the pope instituted the Easter confession, it is really as if one were to say the following: imagine a cannon and the cannoneer beside it with the ignition cord in his hand. A little farther away stands an officer. What happens? The cannoneer holds the cord, and the officer gives the command. In that moment when the officer's command is given, the cannoneer pulls the firing cord, and through the [gun] powder in the cannon, it does what it is supposed to do—it fires." The whole congregation was united like one soul as this image was put before them graphically. He went on: "Now, imagine that someone would come and say that the cannoneer did all of that; through him everything happened. Yet he

pulled the firing cord only upon the order of the officer; and without the gunpowder, the officer could not have ordered and brought
about the shot. Those who say that the pope instituted the Easter
confession go much further than this, because what they are saying
would be the same as maintaining that, even though the cannoneer
only pulled the firing cord at the command of the officer, he discovered the gunpowder! It is just as thoroughly false when people say
that the pope is supposed to have instituted the Easter confession.
He was only a by-stander; he 'pulled the firing cord' as a representative of the suprasensible world."

Everything was, naturally, interspersed with the truth of what he
said. It is not the case that it worked because he had a special, fortunate
disposition. You can see for yourself that it is the method of teaching among the Jesuits to clothe everything in such pictures. There is
today even a Jesuit book[†] in which it is described in detail how one is
to move the forefinger when one speaks this or that word; and how
one is to move the hand when one says this or that. There are even
drawings. It is a methodical work that goes into the tiniest details.
It works through pictures, images. (Why was such a work brought
out? I have not looked into it. The Catholic Church must have
some purpose or intention with it, because it always has intentions.)
And here one must actually ask, why isn't the attempt made to take
what is designed to the detriment of human beings and to develop
it for the well-being of human beings? For it can also be developed
for their well-being; it can and must be designed for the welfare of
humanity. The strength must come from earnest soul-intentions to
transform the abstract into the pictorial. This pictorial element must
be experienced in the community. Through this element, the soul
of the community will be lifted up; the sense of community will
really be founded. Ritual is what will hold your community together.
Without ritual, you can only atomize, split apart, the community. If
you combat this only from a theoretical perspective, however, then
you are proceeding only out of prejudices and biases.

I wish to bring to your attention that a friend of our cause—an Old
Catholic priest who reads the Mass and other rituals in the German
language, or in the language of the country in which he is holding

it—did not want to bring the rituals in the peculiar translation in which they are often read today. He prompted me to bring some parts of the Catholic rituals used today into the original form that lay in them.[†] Through this we see how the spiritual world lives in these things, and we see what has become distorted since Jerome's time.

You do not need to believe, as is often said, that I am personally upset with Catholicism when I speak in this way about the Catholic Church. I want only to see things objectively and to make you aware that, without finding a transition to ritual, to speaking in symbols, it will be completely impossible to cultivate the religious life. You may understand quite well how to convince others, and how to work through intellectual presentation; however, you will achieve something in the religious area only if you can, in the right place in your talk, let your theoretical presentation culminate in a symbol. You yourself must experience the symbol as truth. For this reason, you must think only about such symbolic presentations that are truly connected with what is real in the world.

However, there are a number of difficulties with this, and I want to make you thoroughly aware of them. Assume, for instance, that someone today wants to imagine how the human being becomes physical on Earth. Despite all the achievements of natural science and what can be attained solely through the natural scientific thinking— about which we must be in awe—when you turn today to natural science and all the things it says about the female egg and the male sperm, and what it says about the development and growth of the fertilized egg, and so on, you do not receive ideas that help you grasp how a human being becomes a physical being. Instead, you get ideas that immediately, bit by bit, conceal the truth. You see, the human being—and also animals, and indeed the organic world altogether—is made up mostly of protein. Compare the constitution of protein with any mineral substance in the world. It is so different that naturally the researcher says—and rightly so—that the makeup of the protein is extremely complicated, and one cannot come to grips with it. One cannot find the bridge between some crystallized, inorganic material and what is present in the protein. But, you see, modern science does not know that when we have any inorganic form (a), which we can simply follow in a certain way—I will draw it symbolically—and if we compare it with the constitution of a protein (*b*), we have to begin with something apparently immensely complicated.

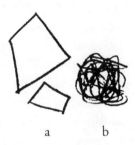

a   b

This complicated makeup is in all our food and in everything organic. It is then said, the inorganic element becomes more complicated in makeup in the organic; and only thereafter, for example, does the human body form itself out of this complicated consistency. This occurs through the splitting of the cells, through a particular configuration of the aggregate of tissue, and so forth. Yet this all is nothing but nonsense. What really happens is the complete destruction of all organic forms. The complicated nature of protein consists in the fact that all that is inorganic enters into chaos. In order to dissolve the form corresponding to the inorganic, and to lead the matter over into chaos, protein is always on its way into chaos.[†] The material that is most powerfully transferred into chaos is the fertilized egg cell. It is simply matter that is driven into chaos. Earthly natural lawfulness as a whole does not know what to do with the chaos; the laws of nature are excluded from it. To have become protein at any stage means to be excluded from Earth's laws of nature. What is the result? Natural lawfulness beyond the Earth—the constellation of the planets—the whole world beyond the Earth begins to work on this chaos to give it structure again. Because the protein passes over into chaos, the matter is, in turn, prepared to receive its constitution, not only from the earthly, but also from the whole universe, from the cosmos. And in this lies the formation of the human head, which is a replica of the vault of the heavens.

Humanity will have a true natural science only when we go beyond the earthly aspects. All natural science is used to having everything proceed from the inorganic. In natural science today we have something that leads everything into dying away. This is because natural science today allows only what one can research abstractly to be intellectually valid. In the moment that you have to think the transition—when what can be researched only in intellectual form passes over into chaos—you must cease to think, and you must begin to behold, to see. You must transition to another kind of knowledge. And there lies the difficulty. You see, intellectualism not only makes us into people who reject the pictorial element, it also even hinders us from coming out of the intellect and forming pictures ourselves. One cannot do it once one has become completely intellectually abstract; one simply cannot do it!

This modern intellectual culture has so great a power over human beings that they appear as if they were small girls and boys in the Waldorf school and wanted to learn to do embroidery and managed to bring various kinds of threads from above downward and from below upward; they can do this, but they cannot create actual pictures. They cannot do it. The entire soul activity of the modern culture, into which we have inserted ourselves, presses us so that no one can be flexible enough to understand that, in the protein, everything is simply excluded from natural scientific research, and that, because of this, matter is opened to conception from the side of the cosmos. This is also what points to the necessity to seek the renewal of religion precisely through Anthroposophy. It is for this reason that yesterday I stressed the following: obviously it is true that we must also enlist members from among today's ministers who, as Protestants, come toward us with honest hearts and, for this reason, reject what I have just discussed today. Yet the working core, on which everything should be built, must actually be made up of Anthroposophists. This is because Anthroposophy wants exactly what people seek everywhere, but in vain: Anthroposophy seeks to lead human beings to a real grasp of realities. If we have not freed ourselves from the natural scientific approach to the world—which has already taken hold of theologians—we will not be able to find symbolic pictures and so be able to really express ourselves in such pictures to the community of believers. And wherever you find this

Anthroposophical understanding of the world—which you can find everywhere in my lecture cycles—you must, in given places, let it simply pass into a picture, an image. When you read my *Outline of Esoteric Science,* in which I described the pre-stages of the Earth as Saturn, Sun, and Moon, you will see that I spoke of them only in pictures. When I say that something looks like when you sense a taste approaching you, a whole dozen of natural scientists—such as Dessoir, Oesterreich, and so on—cannot understand it; they cannot do anything with this image.

In your practical work as priests, Anthroposophy should inspire you, so that you first enter into working with the symbolic, the ritual, and what belongs to the ritual, and through this gain the possibility of community building. Otherwise, it will only be possible for you to speak to individual people. Building community can never be achieved through abstraction in life.

This is what I wanted to present today. Tomorrow I will take this further and will proceed to the actual content of the sermon. We will meet here again at 11:00 a.m. tomorrow, and I recommend that we continue today's conversation about other topics this evening at 7:00 p.m.

Now, I still wish to say something. Yesterday I made a proposal to the *Kommende Tag* that, through the *Kommende Tag*, a kind of bridge should be created to what you want to accomplish here. I presented as the most important aspect the fact that this cause should be financed, as it were. As we imagine our cause, it must indeed be financed. It must lead to the building of independent communities, even if these must be obtained mainly from the present church. I must say the following. I believe that, if the work is carried out properly, it could be possible that within three months we will be far enough along that the work of fund-raising could become self-sustaining. I believe that by then at least enough will have been done so that the work of fund-raising can carry itself and that, by that time, someone can be hired to begin the work. The *Kommende Tag* will declare itself prepared to take care of these three months, and I believe that you have indeed agreed to ask Dr. Heisler to take on this work. Things will begin to stand on solid ground if and when Dr. Heisler takes it on. I am firmly of the opinion that, when one is as far along with such a task—which has been started and is as far along as we now are—one should not wait too long. The circumstances are pressing, and we often do not notice how strong the forces are that pull us down. It can happen that we will simply miss the opportunity if we wait too long.

We would have advanced the threefold impulse much further today if people had understood the issue correctly in the spring of 1919. At that time, on the basis of my "Cultural Appeal,"[†] a cultural council was founded. People imagined, and rightly so, that people in positions of authority would also make the threefold cause their own. Care was taken and the cause was formulated in such a way that it would not give goose bumps to those in positions of authority, because we wanted to work in a real manner. Naturally, however, the people could not be kept connected with it or interested. It is a fact that they could not be held to the issue, and nothing helped. Because of this, you will have to rely on the youth, on younger people who feel that older people have become just that—old—and cannot do anymore. You must try not to lose any time. We should try to build the bridge, because I think that I am justified in feeling that, if it is done right, raising the money cannot become all that difficult. We will find people who have an understanding for precisely this cause. And I believe Dr. Heisler's eloquence will open many doors, if he limits himself in the next months to talking with individual people, in order to persuade them to open their wallet or write a check. Naturally we cannot win people with lectures; they will not give anything. We must approach people individually. Mr. Heisler must see his task as being that of using all of his time going to individuals. The only uncomfortable aspect is that a person might show you the door and usher you out; however, so far this happens only with words—other instances have not happened yet. You just have to accept it; nothing else can be done. The majority of people, however, do not show one to the door. I heard, for instance, that, of all those who were charged with raising money for the Swiss *Futurum AG*, only one was thrown out with words. Otherwise, people confine themselves to being extremely friendly and kind, and to finding the issue immensely interesting, but do not donate. Some of them write a letter later. You do not need to answer those. We must know that we will succeed with only a small percentage of the people we talk to, yet we must try. There is no other way than that we have to work selectively and have to try with many, in order to have success in a few instances.

Was there something else to discuss, or shall we take this topic further? Perhaps some of you have something to say about all of this. This evening we want to expand the discussion on all the three points that you named yesterday.

Gottfried Husemann: I think we would like to talk about how much we have to prepare ourselves now for a ministerial profession, that is, for speaking in a pictorial, imaginistic way. We cannot expect this preparation from the university.

Rudolf Steiner: Are you of the opinion that something can be done in this direction? Something positive? In these lessons I can give only guidelines; we cannot go into specifics. In order to go into detail, we would need a minimum of a fourteen-day course. We could, of course, think about holding such a course when, in the next few months, our group has grown in size. This course could be held for fourteen days and give, in its form, a course in what is called "symbolism" in educational institutions, but is actually nothing. Only among the faculty of the Catholic Church does symbolism still mean something. And perhaps even they do not yet see completely its inner makeup correctly.

You can see this inner makeup best from the facts. I have experienced that a large number of Catholic priests received a dressing-down by Rome. They are those who are teaching in a Gymnasium (an academic high school)—this happens often in Austria—or who teach in a university. They teach not only theology but also philosophy and other subjects, and they are mostly members of the order that was referred to later as modernists. Now, I spoke once with a man, who was quite important for his exegeses,[†] about how he came to receive a dressing-down from Rome because of the content of his talk.

Basically, the talk did not really call for a dressing-down, whereas—if one takes the viewpoint out of which the scolding came—you must say that Professor Bickell,[†] a Jesuit, went much, much further than an extreme liberal and yet is a *persona grata* in Rome. I told the man this, and he answered, "I am a Cistercian. Rome expects of the Cistercians that, if they no longer say what is prescribed by Rome, they might follow their own convictions and gradually depart from Catholicism. In the case of Jesuits like Bickell, it is known that they are loyal sons of Rome, even if they say such liberal things. They would not leave Rome; of this one is certain. The Jesuits are allowed their liberalism; they may base what they say on quite different things than the [Catholic] doctrine."

The Catholic Church itself does not lack this [flexibility], and thus it is more able to survive in its view. For example, I had a conversation about forty years ago with a Catholic theologian,[†] who was on the theological faculty in Vienna. He was so learned that people said, "He knows the whole world and three villages in addition." He was a very scholarly Cistercian. Even a Cistercian was able to speak about doctrine in the following manner. During the conversation we spoke about the dogma of the immaculate conception of Mary.[†] I said to him, "If we remain within Catholic logic, we can accept the immaculate conception of Mary." (That is not the dogma of the immaculate conception of Jesus that was always in the church. But the immaculate conception of St. Anne, which the Catholics maintain, going from the immaculate conception of Mary back to the immaculate conception of St. Anne. I said, "If we use the same logic, we must go further through all the generations preceding her." "Yes," he said, "there is no such thing—we cannot do that. Logic does not support it. We have to stop with Saint Anne. If we went further, we would eventually come to David, and we would be hard pressed to declare an immaculate conception of David."

There is no pure sense of truth in these words. When the man speaks outside of the church, he expresses a completely different formulation of the impulse toward the truth. We find this everywhere in the Catholic Church. Concepts are formed, not according to any kind of logic, but so they can settle into the wide masses. This makes

Catholicism so big. This can in no way be called good, but we must know about it. We must know what it is we have to deal with.

It is true, for instance, that a real standing-in-the-world—such that one stands in the world with pure thinking and not merely intellectual thinking—does sometimes exist in a certain manner with Catholic priests. Because of my destiny, I have been able to get to know many Catholic priests. Among these was the church historian at the University of Vienna.[†] He was an extraordinarily interesting person, but he was so extremely Catholic—to the most extreme degree that he admitted that he no longer goes out onto the street in the evening when it is dark and the lamps are not turned on completely. When I asked him why, he said, "At night, you see people indistinctly, with unclear outlines, and, in Vienna, you can also meet Freemasons. And you should see a Freemason only clearly outlined in sharp contours, because you can pass by him only if you can differentiate yourself clearly and sharply from him." You see, a person can be absolutely learned and be immersed in theology, and yet can still have the opinion that it means something if you pass by a Freemason without rejecting him or turning him away by way of sharp contours. Auras pass over into each other, and one cannot allow such a confused mixture of Catholic priest and Freemason to come about.

Ernst Uehli: The Catholic Church has worked quite intensively with legends, and I think it is true that the Catholic movement is supported to a great extent by legends. One could imagine that a future church community could come to the formation of new legends.

Rudolf Steiner: That is right. If you read specific lectures I have given in Dornach, you will find the attempt to express certain things, which can now be spoken of, in the form of a legend. I have held whole lectures in the form of a legend.[†] I will point out one of them. I once attempted to characterize the nature of the arts. You cannot enter into the nature of the arts with concepts; you must use pictures. Everything that you formulate abstractly remains external. My booklet *The Nature of the Arts* is presented wholly in pictures.[†] But again immediately one is misunderstood. When I had spoken about the arts out of the imagination, a quite old Theosophist came up to me and did not know what else to say than, "You have transformed the nine muses there." Nothing was further from my mind than to think of the nine muses. Everything had resulted from the necessity of the matter itself. It was far from my intention to warm up old stories again, but people could not imagine anything else but that it was an abstract treatment.

So, one must say that the use of pictures is again absolutely called for. For instance, we do not yet have an image for a very important issue. Think about the copious legends and stories about bulls in the beginning of the third millennium B.C.E. at the transition of the spring equinox into the constellation of Taurus. Think, for instance, about the legends of the Argonauts when, in the eighth century B.C.E., the Sun entered the constellation of Aries. Now the Sun stands in Pisces. The legend for this has yet to be created. We need to form legends in pictures. Although the Sun is already in Pisces, we do not have a legend for it. The imaginative element must still be developed. And there are a multitude of other things that live only abstractly today, but which should proceed out of cosmic events into the pictorial element. This must be worked on. By doing so we will again find the connection with the cosmos. Today the cosmos, or universe, can only be grasped intellectually. What is the cosmos for modern people? We could say, today's intellectual people think the entire cosmos is nothing more than solidified or frozen mathematics and mechanics. We must go beyond the merely mathematical and mechanical, and come to the imaginative, pictorial element and to legends.

We must just become aware that such research—like my late friend, Ludwig Laistner[†] presented on sagas, myths, and legends in his book, *Das Rätsel der Sphinx* [The riddle of the Sphinx]—can be quite helpful. I must stress that Ludwig Laistner understood nothing of spiritual science. I just want to say that, although Laistner traces all myths and sagas back to dreams, his book can help with this research. It is interesting to follow how he does not trace these legends back in the horrible way modern Protestant and Catholic researchers do. These researchers say, "The ancient peoples wrote fiction or poetry.

They transferred or placed the gods into the thunderstorm, and even into the battle of winter with the summer." As if the people had never known a peasant's mind and heart! No peasant soul (or *Gemut*) could ever write or create fiction. For these ancient peoples, to whom the writing is ascribed, writing and composing was as foreign as it is for the peasants or farmers. It was all imaginative. Ludwig Laistner brings everything back to dreams. Yet, it is interesting how he sees a connection of the inner experience of the human being in the Slavic saga of "Mittagsfrau" [Midday woman] and the saga of the Sphinx in Greece. It is for this reason that the book is titled *Das Rätsel der Sphinx*. Legends must flow out of life—today in full consciousness. This is immensely important.

Lecture 4

Rudolf Steiner: I think this should again be a kind of discussion time. I surmise that you will have quite a lot on your minds. Please feel free to express yourselves about everything.

Emil Bock: We are concerned about the issue of the ritual, because we cannot develop a new formulation of the ritual out of ourselves.

Rudolf Steiner: We will certainly need to develop some symbolic elements in this direction. This means that, in the ritual of which we have spoken, we must work on individual examples of ritual forms. The form of the ritual is such that one will come to it once one has the prerequisites for it. Naturally, it is absolutely important to accustom yourselves to creating pictorially what you are so used to considering intellectually. I think Mr. Uehli said some things today about the way the element of ritual is handled in the Waldorf school. Ritual is difficult to form, because for a long time people have limited all ritual to the traditional form. All ritual forms that exist today are actually ancient. Only here or there are they somewhat reshaped or rearranged. Furthermore, during a period when humanity has lost its ability to create pictorially, people also resist ritual in a certain sense. Perhaps it will help you understand the ritual if we add a few things to what we said this morning about a completely different ritual form.

You know that actually everywhere that real, inner community is sought, ritual plays a certain role. I remind you only of the fact that, as the somewhat questionable Salvation Army spread, even it sought to have a certain ritual. And we know, too, that the temperance movement has a kind of meager substitute for a ritual. Wherever a true community movement is to be the goal, some form of ritual is striven for.

Now, as you know, the modern Freemasonry movement is an extensive community. This Freemasonry movement also seeks to nurture the building of community through ritual. It shows what ritual must inevitably become when it passes over into a purely materialistic movement. For Freemasonry is the materialistic form of a spiritual movement.

You see, in their ritual acts and ritualistic symbols, Freemasonry essentially presents the mystery of the being of the human being. If you consider and study the actual being of the human being in connection with the world, the materialistically minded researcher today will say to you, The human being actually has the same muscle forms and bone forms as the higher animals, even the same number of these organic forms. The human being is a higher, fully developed animal—an animal that has been reshaped. More or less clearly spoken, that is what lies at the foundation of our knowledge today. This knowledge is immediately done away with when we consider how human beings integrate themselves into the entire cosmos in a totally different way than the animals do. The essential aspect of the animal—if we disregard isolated exceptions or variant forms—is that its spine is built in the horizontal. Please do not misunderstand what I mean. Naturally there are animals that can sit up, like the kangaroo, and appear to have their spines built at an angle to the horizontal. Similarly, certain birds—parrots—have more or less a vertical stance. But this is not a predisposition of, nor dependent on, the organic constitution. Nevertheless it is not within the structural nature of an animal to lift its spine out of the horizontal. The essential aspect of human beings, by contrast, is that the structure of the spine is vertical. The human spine is formed in the vertical. This is one of the essential characteristics by which the human being differs from the animal world. To see this you need only reflect on the fact that one cannot consider a being in the world as being separate from the rest of the world.

You see, it would not occur to anyone examining a compass to say that the needle points, by its own nature, in a certain direction. One would naturally say that the Earth has a magnetic north pole and a magnetic south pole. This means that the whole Earth directs the compass needle. In the case of organic nature, however, people like to explain everything in the organism out of the organism itself. They do not bring the human being into relation with the whole universe at all. Those who really understand the matter bring the organism into relationship to the whole universe. The situation there is such that systems of forces go through the entire universe.[†] One system of forces circles around the Earth [horizontally], and the other systems work so that, interspersed with the horizontal forces, they move in a radial direction. Human beings have their spines in the direction of the radial forces and integrate themselves totally differently in the universe than the animals, which have their spines—the most important line of their body—in the horizontal, parallel to the surface of the Earth. Many other things are based on this.

The human brain weighs thirteen hundred to fourteen hundred grams and would, if it exerted its full weight, crush the blood vessels beneath it. The brain is absolutely capable, because of its weight, of crushing the blood vessels. Why doesn't it? It doesn't because the brain is immersed in cerebrospinal fluid. The cerebrospinal fluid oscillates through the subarachnoid space that the spinal column builds within itself. This fluid flows up and down under the influence of the breathing. The whole brain swims in cerebrospinal fluid. Perhaps you know from physics that a body loses as much in weight as the weight of the volume of liquid it displaces. Thus, instead of pressing down with thirteen hundred or fourteen hundred grams, the brain presses on the blood vessels with twenty grams at most. The human brain is set up not to remain subject to its weight, but has an impetus to overcome its weight. This is possible only if the human being has a vertical spine. The animal's brain presses down with its full weight because the subarachnoid space passes horizontally into the brain. The circulation that is produced in this way proceeds in a totally different manner.

We must not look merely at the structure of the human being but must also look at how the human being is inserted in the universe.

If we do this, we may conclude that if we examine the exceptional position of the human being in the universe, several important lines above all arise. (This is drawn on the blackboard.)

First is the line parallel to the surface of the Earth: the horizontal. Second is what differentiates the human being from the animal: the line of the spine that stands in the vertical on the horizontal. Thus, we have drawn two figures: first, the horizontal or level, and second, the right angle. When we are aware of the significance of the horizontal that the animal basically creates, and the significance of the right angle for the placement of the human being in the universe, we can connect certain imaginations with the horizontal and the right angle, which by this means can become symbols.

Among its symbols, Freemasonry, which seeks to characterize the nature of the human being, has the level (the horizontal) and the square (the right angle). It also uses other symbols that reproduce through and through the forces of the universe—leading us to the following observation.

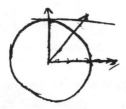

Imagine the Earth here. Human beings move, let us say, on the Earth—I will draw it in a radial movement. Human beings then have their direction in the vertical, and the way in which they connect with the center point of the Earth is a triangle. Freemasonry, in turn, has the triangle as a symbol in its ritual. Everything in Freemasonry—in the first degree—is thus taken from the configuration of the human being. There you see how symbolism is developed. Symbolism, where it is real, is not thought up arbitrarily. We arrive at symbolism only when we study it in reality. Symbolism is founded in the universe; it is there somewhere. This is true of the ritual, too.

Human beings are so constituted between birth and death that they have within themselves forces that constantly kill them. These are forces that harden them; they are the hardening forces that work to bring about the skeletal system. In their illness-causing nature, they can lead to sclerosis, gout, diabetes, and so forth. Human beings bear these forces within them as hardening forces. This is the one system of forces. The other system of forces that human beings have within themselves is what constantly rejuvenates them. This system of forces comes to expression particularly in pleurisy and fever illnesses—in all that burns the human being from within. In the Anthroposophical worldview, I have called the hardening forces Ahrimanic forces, and the forces that lead to fever, the warmth forces, Luciferic forces. Both of these forces must be held constantly in balance in the human being. If they are not held in balance, they lead the human body, soul, and spirit to some disastrous extreme. If the fever forces and the hardening forces, the salt-building forces, were not held constantly in balance physiologically, the human being would necessarily develop either a fever or sclerosis. If human beings develop only their intellectual or rational forces and tend toward intellectualism, they succumb to the Ahrimanic. If they develop only the fiery element—passions, the emotional—they succumb to the Luciferic. Thus the human being is always in the middle between two polarities and must maintain the balance. But think about how difficult it is to maintain the balance. The pendulum, which should always be in balance, always tends to swing out. There are these three tendencies in the human being: the balance tendency, the warmth tendency, and the hardening tendency. The human being must remain upright. Therefore, we may view the human as a being constantly seeking to maintain uprightness (verticality) against the forces that constantly endanger human life.

The third degree of Freemasonry presents this. A Freemason, initiated in the third degree, is presented symbolically with how the human being is threatened by three rebellious powers that approach and threaten life. This is done in various ways. The simplest form is this: the candidate is brought forth in a coffin and three murderers[†] who want to kill him slip up to him. In beholding this threefold danger, the candidate becomes conscious that the human being is in danger of death in every moment and must rise up.

Thus, couched in this symbolism, the human being experiences a kind of real ritualistic act; he experiences ceremonially something really important that is connected with life. It is really true that we must learn to know life, because it is from life that we receive the symbols. Freemasonry certainly has its shadow side in the fact that it uses these symbols, performs rituals—in Blue Masonry in the first three degrees, while, in the higher degrees, there are many other things—and this ceremonial element is drawn out of ancient traditions that are no longer understood. There no longer exists a connection with the origins, of which I wanted to provide a little sketch for you. The people see only the ceremony, and that is the dangerous thing, they remain stuck in the ceremony itself. They are not led into the ceremony in order, through it, to come to the spiritual.

There is another way that people still relatively late—indeed still in the eighteenth century—had a quite lively feeling for making world secrets present. For example, when you open up the illustrated books that were still widespread in the eighteenth century, which were meant to make human beings aware of much that could not be expressed in intellectual concepts, you will see a picture that appears again and again. You will find a man depicted with the head of a bull and a woman with the head of a lion.[†] The man with the head of a bull and the woman with the head of a lion stand beside one another. At first this is shocking for those who do not understand it. It is really true that we human beings are so constituted that, in form, we are most perfect in our physical body. There we are actually human. As you find presented in my *Outline of Esoteric Science*, the physical body goes back to the primordial beginning; it is the most perfect, or most complete member of the human being. The human etheric body is formed like the physical body. If you could take away the physical body from the etheric body, the etheric body would conform more to the astral body. This etheric body would then—probably to the displeasure of quite a lot of human beings—take on an animal form, as it would become the expression of the emotions and the passions. It (the astral body) is formed differently with different human beings.

When we look at the male head, the etheric head, as expression of what lives in the emotional nature, we have there as a type, as an average, something bull-like. In the female head, as soon as we examine the etheric head, we have something lion-like. These are average forms. You can feel this morally when you go into what comprises the nature of the woman, how she is the lion-like type. You can feel the bull with the man and the lion with the woman.

These things seem to be spoken of merely metaphorically, simply as images, but they are drawn out of the suprasensible nature [of the human being]. If the astral body is examined separated from the physical body, it takes on complicated plant-forms. And the "I" of the human being is a purely mineral, crystal-like formed being—formed completely geometrically. Thus, we can say that, with regard to form, the human being is in the physical body, human; in the etheric body, animal-like; in the astral, plant-like; and in the "I," mineral-like.[†] If we know all of these things, we think of how, in an earlier clairvoyant condition, the people really knew of the higher worlds and formed these pictures out of these higher worlds.

Now, I am telling you this just to point out how symbols arose and how they were passed on as tradition. Today it is possible to come to symbols only if we very lovingly steep ourselves in the world secrets. And only out of Anthroposophy can a ritual or symbolism actually grow today.

You see, it is quite necessary that we proceed from the basics. First, in a certain sense we must live again into the genius of language itself. Precisely where civilization is at its highest, our language has basically taken on a terrible outer, abstract form. We speak today without feeling in our speaking. Today's speaking is actually terribly inhuman, because we no longer live within our language. Take the

German word *Kopf* [head]. When we feel it, we feel immediately that it absolutely has to do with the round form, with being rounded off. In contrast, when we say the Latin word *testa*, that has to do with testing, with testifying, or with assessing. This proceeds, therefore, from out of a totally different foundation. And if you feel what lies in each of these words, you will then also feel the difference between the Latin and the German elements. The German language forms a word out of the sculptural element; the Latin (Roman) builds it out of mental information. The word *Fuß* [foot] is connected with *Furche* [furrow, groove, rut]; *pied* has to do with *placing*. This kind of thing is found everywhere in language, and we can feel everywhere how a special feeling for the world comes to light in the genius of language. Consider how strongly people in Goethe's time still felt the pictorial element of language. Recall the scene [in *Faust*] where the poodle appears on stage, runs behind Faust and Wagner, and Wagner says of the poodle, "Er zweifelt."† He means by this expression that the poodle is wagging its tail. With the word *zweifeln* [today it means to *doubt*], he is expressing the movement of the tail. When you look at what still lived as the picture-element then, and compare it with today's abstractions—how you had in the word *Zweifel* this wagging and swinging back-and-forth—you can really feel your way into the pictorial manner in which language worked.

This is the first element of the picture-nature of the soul life: when we live into the pictorial nature of the language. It is really true that we grow into the pictorial element of language, if only we want to do so. It is actually a very good training for the soul to grow into the picture-nature of the language. We speak so much in abstractions that the words mean nothing to us anymore. You see, where I come from a certain kind of lightning is called *Himmlatzer*.† I should like to know who does not feel the picture of this lightning in *Himmlatzer*; the word paints it. And thus it is thoroughly possible, when you really go into the dialect, to grow into the picture-nature. You should indeed train yourself to achieve the pictorial element of the language. It is sometimes almost impossible today to express what we need to because the picture-nature of the language is lost. We must, of course, disregard all artificially thought-up things (pictures).

It is the same for those who somehow get crackpot ideas, such as was the case with the *dun horse*,[†] which was walking with a friend and was talking energetically when it walked into a *"Tümpel"* [pond]. The horse thinks about this: *Tümpel?*—oh, temple! Naturally, you may not just think up crazy things by seeking such outer similarities. You must deepen yourselves inwardly into the picture-nature of the language. Then you will truly understand the word *"zwei"* [two]. Originally *"zwei"* was not thought of as putting together one and one, but rather breaking one into two pieces. The older forming of numbers was based on analysis (taking a thing apart) and not synthesis (putting things together). You can follow this, for example, when you look at the Arabic arithmetic that existed still in the twelfth post-Christian century.

An interesting little book by our friend Ernst Müller[†] about Abraham Ibn Ezra is out; I will give you the exact title tomorrow. The book is about numbers and is extraordinarily interesting for knowledge of how numbers were developed in earlier times. [When you follow this] you will find, without spinning any crazy ideas, the similarity between the word *"zwei"* and the word *"Zweifel."* It also leads us to the final syllable, "-el." In this manner you can find your way into the picture-nature of the language. This is the *ABCs* of pictorial imagining or ideation.

Another necessary thing is to find your way into the complicated way in which the human being is constituted. I have pointed out a few examples of this today. As I said, if you attain true knowledge in this way, images will begin to arise that are symbolic, and you will come to really grasp the evolution of life. Then you will come to the point of being able to have the ritual act before you imaginatively.

Take, for instance, the following: the Greeks were not yet able to fully separate concepts from objects. Similar to the way we perceive colors, the Greeks once perceived concepts *on* objects; for them, the concepts were perceived. If we take this as our starting point, we can really understand how much humanity has changed since the time of the ancient Greeks. Were we to portray, for example, an altar in an appropriate way to the Greeks, we would have to present it in bright colors. If we wanted to set up an altar that was more for modern human beings, it would have to be in rather more of a blue color; modern people are not so organized toward the lively, bright colors. The ancient Greeks did not have a perception of color in the sense that we have.†

When you approach a congregation or community with the ritual, you must make the ritual extremely simple. A complicated ritual would not satisfy human beings today. Thus, you must form it so that is extraordinarily simple. Above all, throughout the ritual, there must be an expression of the inner transformation of the human being. We could call this inner transformation of the human being the en-Christing of the human being, or the imbuing of the human being with Christ. Human beings are not born imbued with Christ beforehand by way of inheritance; they must find the Christ in themselves. This transformation, this "en-Christing" of the human being, can be expressed symbolically in a multitude of ways through simple, but effective, ritual acts.

Let me give you an example. If you were to form a verse or mantra, you would have it consist of seven lines. In the first three lines you would essentially express the nature of the human being when still under the influence of the conditions of inheritance, as born out of the Father-principle of the world. The fourth line, the middle one, would depict how the principles of inheritance are overcome by the soul principles. And the last three lines would describe how the human being becomes one who grasps the spiritual. Now, you could read such lines as these to the community so that you read the first three lines with a somewhat more abstract, colder voice; the middle line (fourth) with a somewhat warmer voice; and the last three lines in elevated speech, in an elevated tone. And in this you would have, in a simple form, a ritual act that would present the en-Christing and spiritualizing of the human being.

It is not a matter of explaining it afterward—that is precisely what should not be done. You should let it (the verse) be felt. The picture should be felt, and you should act accordingly. Thus, you see how it is possible to rise up to the ritualistic nature. Then, too, you must develop a feeling for how everything that has to do with thinking is similar to light, and everything having to do with love is similar to warmth. Just think what a powerful resource you have in the language, whenever you bring what you want to express that tends toward thinking together with the light. When you say, "May wisdom shine through the human being," you have said something real. You will feel how what has to do with thinking is actually gathered light that becomes thought. Likewise you must use images suggesting warmth when you speak of love. When you say, "A shared idea spreads warmth over a human community," you have the image of warmth within it. You have said something real. Thus, when you feel the inner wisdom of the language, you enter into the imaginal or picture-like, the world of images.

That is one way. I will give you more detailed examples sometime later when we come together again. You can even develop a modern ritual based on these things. I wanted only to indicate today the practical aspect of how we are led into this reality. It is, however, always a question of our emaciated souls. Please excuse the hard expression. We are not human beings at all; we have become so deadened by materialistic education. People feel everything as separated. They do not feel that their nerves catch the light, that their nerves glow through and through with the light. They believe that vibrations occur, yet thought forms out of the light. It is not just a picture. It is a reality when we say, "The human being is radiated through by thoughts."

People realize this much too little, and therefore they cannot achieve pictorial imagining or thinking. Yet I believe that if, for example, in order to visualize how it all takes its course in pictures, you read my *Outline of Esoteric Science* and immerse yourself in the way I describe the three metamorphoses (Saturn, Sun, and Moon), then you will come into pictorial imagining of your own accord. If you do not remain with the abstraction, or believe that I have constructed or simply thought out something, but rather if you feel that it is necessary that these things be represented in this way, then you have already achieved a kind of training for pictorial imagining and thinking. And everywhere there you have the opportunity of passing over into ritualistic acts. You must also develop out of what I have presented a feeling for the inner numerical arrangement in the universe.

Today we are often laughed at when we speak of the numbers seven or three in relation to the order of the universe. Yet these numbers are simply there to be found empirically in the universe. I should like to know who does not think of the number three when they think of the human being. The human being is simply a threefold being, and you come everywhere upon the number three when you think correctly about the human being. When, for instance, you speak to a group of older children and say, "May Light, your thinking, shine through you," you are not done speaking if you do not immediately add, "May Life, your feeling, stimulate you," or "penetrate you," and "May Fire, your will, strengthen you through and through." Things arrange themselves of their own accord, and this flows over into the ritual form. One must develop a feeling that something is incomplete if one says merely, "May Light, your thinking, shine through you." That is the same as if I were to place only a human head there. That cannot be. I cannot imagine anyone placing only a human head there. That cannot be; the rest must be added. Therefore, I must have the feeling that, if I say, "May Light, your thinking, shine through you," it is incomplete, and I must add, "May Life, your feeling, penetrate you," and "May Fire, your will, strengthen you through and through." If I take only the one of the sentences, it is the same as if I have only the human head. Thus, we come to the point of always thinking the rest in addition. Then we enter into the self-creative nature of the numerical organization of the world, and so there ensues from the issue itself the ritualistic form:

> May Light, your thinking, shine through you.
> May Life, your feeling, penetrate you.
> May Fire, your will, strengthen you through and through.

This underlies what Mr. Uehli will have told you today[†] about the Sunday or religious service in the Waldorf school. The ritual lies in the formulation; it is actually formed in this way throughout. It is difficult to understand when it manifests in life.

You see, if you were to take out, to separate out, a chapter out of my *Intuitive Thinking as a Spiritual Path*, it is almost as if you were to cut off an appendage from the human body. The book is intended as a whole, for it is a special form of thinking. It is not put together out of individual parts. It was allowed to grow of its own accord, and it can be developed further.

Paul Baumann:[†] Could you tell us something about the musical element in the ritual, Dr. Steiner?

Rudolf Steiner: The situation is this: we human beings are so placed in the world, that we are—I will draw it immediately on the blackboard (see plate 2, p. 181)—on the one side, a head organization.

This head organization is dependent upon the fact that the outer aspect of the world penetrates into it and is everywhere checked. Everything from the world penetrates into the head, is mirrored in the head, and what we perceive on the outside is what has been mirrored. This is what we usually have within during waking consciousness. And when you consider the structure of the human being—namely what the eye does, but also the other sense organs—then you find that everything there tends to be limited or blocked off in the back; something is reflected.

On the other hand, the human being also builds the skeletal system, the muscular system, and so on. With the head, we have actually the round, closed skull. Then we have the bones filled with bone marrow, the muscles, and so forth (see plate 2). The head is actually such that what works into it cannot penetrate through it, just as a mirror is impenetrable for the light, and so it mirrors or reflects. What we call, in the widest sense, the limb-metabolic system is different. There what comprises bone and muscle is taken in from the world. Therefore we can say, in the head organization everything is thrown back, but the limbs take in. Actually the processes of the limb-metabolic system are brought about from outside through the way and manner in which I am integrated in the world organism. Nothing is thrown back there. It is, as it were, organized through and through; it is taken in. And it stops—is backed up—namely in the lung. The lung is an organ that stops up. It is where the outer aspect of the world is fashioned into forms. A second, quite refined blockage is in the auditory organ. The auditory organ is actually a lung at a higher level. Whoever has a sense for it can see on the structure of the outer ear itself that it is not formed in the same way as the eye is. The eye is formed from outside inward. The auditory organ is closed off and encompasses the actual sense organ. All of the auditory organ that is visible is formed in such a manner that the human being is built out of two vortices. The one vortex is thrown back—it reflects; it goes back into itself. The other vortex builds an organism, develops the forms. It then approaches the other vortex, and they collide here (see plate 2), so that everything that comes in from outside is reflected here and yields ordinary memory—for example, the memory of images one has seen. In contrast, what builds up the human being is movement, absolute movement. It consists of vibration-forms that run their course in the human being. I have already told you about the cere- brospinal fluid. The human being is made up of about 92 percent water and only about 8 percent solid matter. The solid part merely integrates itself into the rest. The whole is movement. What orga- nizes the human being through movement is the Word. The human being is really, in the literal sense, Word become flesh. And this Word become flesh collides with what is reflected, so that we can say, we are first of all built according to the visual, which is, however, completely organized by what is thrown back or reflected. Then we are built according to the auditory, by what forms the human being, tone formed into words, which then is backed up in the hearing[†] and becomes audible tone.

Human beings become conscious of the outer world through the direct or transformed visible aspect. Because of what becomes tone within, what becomes the musical aspect, the human being is the being who rises up out of the sphere of the musical and is fertilized by the sphere of the optical, the visible, so that in fact the musical element is that which works further in us from out of the cosmos. We are built by music; our body is embodied music. This is so in the fullest sense. And the light works in here (see plate 2) and is reflected. This is the greatest difference between the ordinary memory that we have in regard to the outer world, where we have the visual aspect, and the musical memory. The musical memory is something totally different. This will seem wonderful to you; the musical memory arises in the opposite way, through the damming up or holding back of the tone flowing through. In musical memory, human beings throw their own nature back into themselves. Thus, what works in us as the musical element is our innermost nature.

Now think about the fact that we produce pictures in some way, be it visibly before people in the ritual or be it that we call forth images through our speaking. And then we imbue these images with a musical element, either with instrumental or vocalized music. It is no different than basically the two main world-principles being brought face-to-face with each other. What the human being is, as light-creation, is brought into connection with what the human being is as tone-creation. And the ritual becomes thereby … [gap in content] … polarity. Of course, this is already the case with the Word, and therefore the older rituals have not used the abstract speaking, but rather a declamatory aspect that has something that is song-like about it. And this declamatory element, which already played an important role in the old Mass because the Mass was sung, should absolutely represent the penetration of the light aspect with the tone. Thus, the musical element in the ritual is what most essentially spiritualizes the human being. It furthers the mystical element, whereas the rest furthers what is pantheistic—the pouring out of the human being into the universe.

Thereby we can, on the one hand, impel the human being to expand through all that is light- or thought-like. On the other hand, through the musical element, we can lead the human being into contracting into himself or herself—into taking in the suprasensible. And while, for instance, the nonmusical, the light element, in the ritual works to bring us a world-feeling, the musical works to deepen in us the "I"-feeling to the point of the divine. The ideal would be to work with the light element to a certain degree and then to let it pass over into the musical. Through this we would truly have brought the image of the makeup of the human being into the ritual.

Gottfried Husemann asked if the music up to this time—Bach,[†] for instance—could still be used. Would not the new ritual also call for a new kind of music?

Rudolf Steiner: If it becomes necessary to do something quickly, people will reenliven the old music. Yet it is absolutely true that human beings can no longer gain a completely inner relationship to these older forms. It is precisely the same as the fact that adults cannot develop the same life-forms that children do. It is absolutely necessary that music be fashioned out of feeling as it is today. One must naturally begin where one can. You will have already noticed that where we do eurythmy and work into the musical element, our friends have already discovered good musical forms out of the musical feeling of our time. This stems from the fact that human beings will more and more retrain and change their thinking in the musical field, just as in that of painting. There are clumsy attempts that we do not need to judge, but we must know that they are just clumsy attempts—also in music as, for instance, in Debussy[†] who projects himself into the individual tone, who lives in the individual tone. Yet it may not become a tone painting, or the pictorial in music. It is true that people will experience ever more what reveals itself like a mystery within the single tone, and then they will seek to analyze the individual tone. Perhaps they will have to expand the scale by inserting a few tones and yet enrich it mainly by experiencing the characteristic of the single tone. Through this, special musical possibilities will result. [To *Mr. Baumann*:] Also you hope, do you not, that one will already experience whole melodies within the single tone? It is indeed true that this can be done. Therein lies a possibility for training. In this the Anthroposophical musicians will have to come to meet other musicians. I am certainly of the firm belief that the Anthroposophical musicians will have a very great deal to do; precisely the Anthroposophical musicians will have an immense mission.

The old music had actually come to a deadend before Richard Wagner.[†] Wagner did not actually advance music. He expanded music by bringing it into a sidestream. We can find his music to be great and genius in nature, but it is a tributary. You will have to take up musical development before Wagner to find there precisely what can contribute much to the ritual. In the meantime, it will naturally be quite alright to use the older music. Basically, there are actually wonderful things to be found in both Protestant and the Catholic Church music. For the modern human being there will no longer be a totally inner relationship with the music. You will have to attempt to deepen yourself in the musical element itself.

Emil Bock asks a question about the Quaker movement.[†]

Rudolf Steiner: I have always had the feeling that the Quaker movement is something that comes specifically out of the Anglo-American element. In Central Europe there are no longer any more significant bases for the kind of community building that manifests in the Quaker movement. I do not yet know firsthand of any attempt to build community in this way, and so, naturally, cannot know whether there can be something within it that is fruit-bearing or not. I doubt, however, that anything similar to the Quaker movement can grow out of the Central European spirit. For you see, the Anglo-American actually experiences the religious in a thoroughly different form than the Central European does. The Central European experiences the religious, first and foremost, completely in thinking. This is the primary phenomenon. It is undoubtedly a mystical element that is illumined by intellectual light. This is everywhere within it, even where totally radical religious forms and sectarian efforts arise. You will find everywhere in Central Europe the mystical radiated through by intellectual light, thinking light, whereas the Anglo-American allows the religious element to be still immersed in the human instinctive nature. Of course, this exhibits itself in various ways, and it would be interesting somehow to examine out of which blood-mixture the Quakers recruit [their members]. You must go to the instinctive blood-nature; there you will find the foundation. You will surely find something like an instinctive tendency. Central Europe, however, never founds, out of an instinctive tendency, anything that builds community.

This is really an essential difference among the West, Central Europe, and the East. The West seeks the higher aspect more or less in subconsciousness; Central Europe seeks it in consciousness; and the East seeks it in superconsciousness. In the East people are absolutely always looking upward. The American looks to the Earth and expects everything from the Earth. The Russian—even more the Asian— always looks upward. The Central European looks straight ahead. It is indeed the case that, if we tried to imitate the actual Western element in the religious realm, we could enter dangerous paths. We may not do this in any realm. In natural science it has brought great harm, and in the religious realm it leads quite especially to rigidity and paralysis. We must work more with the soul than with the body.

Emil Bock: We have heard that there are already rituals in existence[†] that have been given on occasion: a baptism ritual, a funeral ritual, and part of a revised Mass. I want to ask if it would be possible for us to become acquainted with these rituals in order to live into them ourselves?

Rudolf Steiner: Certainly. These things would be considered as starting points. The funeral ritual came about because a member of our movement[†] wanted such a ritual. Of course, we had to connect with the existing funeral ritual, but, because that ritual was translated— naturally, not a dictionary translation, but a correct one—something resulted that was essentially different. I would ask to have these rituals back and would gladly base our course of study on them. I will simply ask our friend to copy them and send them to me. This is quite possible to do. The same is true of the Mass. In the first place, so far I have only made a translation of the Catholic Mass. Yet, it, too, has actually become something new. However, I translated only as far as the Offertory, so it is not yet finished. In the Old Catholic service the Mass is read in the language of the country. Our friend has gone so far as to read the translation of the Mass up to the Offertory in the Old Catholic service.

These things need time, and we have little time. Yet all of this can be made available to you. Only, it would naturally be necessary that, above all, a new baptism ritual be created. The old baptism ritual is not quite appropriate, because everywhere its goal was to baptize adults, and that baptism was then applied to children. If we want to baptize children today, we must find a new ritual. Also for this ritual there are already elements in existence that I can make available to you. The baptism rituals came out of baptisms for adults. When we baptize a child, we are speaking to one who is not yet conscious, and the ritual must correspond to this. The child knows nothing of the baptism ritual. We may not go so far as to oppose the baptism of children; we can keep that. However, much in the ritual must be redone and made new. John the Baptist's baptism consisted in immersion in water; the adults were immersed in water. You know that in this baptism the human beings can be brought to that point of consciousness at which their life appears before them in a tableau. Their life appears in a kind of tableau, and by means of this, they experience that they belong to a spiritual world. This is actually expressed in the baptismal ritual. But it cannot be done with children. For children we must have a ritual that expresses how the child is accepted and taken into our community, and the religious, suprasensible substance that lives in the community must stream over onto the child. This must be expressed in the baptism ritual, and it can also be done.

You see, until now there has been no reason in the Anthroposophical Movement to develop these things really concretely, simply because we actually wanted to avoid it. There are not a few instances where people wanted to introduce such things. I always refused, because from the very beginning on it would have killed the Anthroposophical Movement. One had to remain with what is half-way allowed.

Twenty years ago—today it is less so—the Catholic Church considered itself as having a monopoly on ritual. We would have been eliminated immediately, and for this reason there was little motivation to develop ritual in this direction. The rest, where of course ritual was developed, was interrupted by the World War.[†] We could no longer go any further with it, because if we had, we would have been handled as a secret society.

These are the reasons that the aspect of ritual in the Anthroposophical Movement was not developed. However, in your movement it will be possible, because it can be considered quite natural that ritual should be formed in a religious movement. Even though Protestantism has a certain horror of ritual, I believe that people can feel the need for ritual again.

A participant: The Catholics have more sacraments than the Protestants. Why is that? And what is the meaning and significance of the ritual act of Communion?

Rudolf Steiner: What exists in the Catholic dogma goes back to certain forms of more ancient knowledge. One imagines that the human being passes through seven stages between birth and death. The first stage is birth itself; the second one is what we call maturation or puberty; the third is the becoming conscious of one's inner nature around the twentieth year; the fourth is the feeling of not corresponding to, or fitting into, the world—of not being completely human. Then comes the gradual growing into the spiritual. These things then become somewhat shaky and undecided, but one envisioned the whole of human life, including the social, in seven stages; and one imagined that between birth and death the human being grows out of the spirit.

Today the Catholic Church does not recognize pre-existence. There exists only a thought of God, and this growing out of God's thought is presented in seven stages. Different forces must confront each of these seven stages. Birth is development or evolution, and maturation is an evolution. For every evolutionary form an involutionary form is set over against it: for birth, baptism; for puberty, confirmation. Each sacrament is the inversion of a stage of natural development. We can say that Catholic doctrine presents seven stages of development, and it places over against them the seven involutionary steps; and these are the seven sacraments. Four of these involutionary steps are earthly: baptism, confirmation, communion, and confession. These four are generally human, like the physical body, etheric body, astral body, and the "I." When you go up higher, you come to spirit self, life spirit, and spirit human. As the shining-in that takes place from out of the spiritual world, the last three sacraments are those that go into the social sphere: marriage, ordination, and the last anointing. The penetration of our world by the spiritual world is expressed by ordination. Thus, these are the seven sacraments, of which the last ones are marriage, ordination, and the last anointing. The sacraments are simply inverse processes for the natural processes that take place for the human being, and the ritual acts are arranged in accordance with these..

The idea of the seven sacraments is not arbitrary. It is much more arbitrary to limit these seven sacraments to two. This happened in a time when people no longer had a feeling for the inner numerical makeup of the world. These are the things, naturally, that make serious Catholic priests—namely those who are members of an order— despise Protestantism so much. They consider the whole of it to be a kind of rationalism—as something that no longer knows anything. There are real spiritual natures among the priests in the orders; the Jesuits are prepared and trained for this. Among the priests at Mont Cassino, I found Father Storkeman with whom I spoke about Dionysius the Areopagite. He showed me the altar where he usually read Mass, and told me about his feelings concerning the Mass. One saw that his feelings had nothing to do with the usual creed of the Catholic Church.

And at another time, in Venice, there was a patriarch who was a terrible fellow. Another, a younger cleric, preached; and I saw spiritually that he was really permeated with spirit. The sermon was also quite fine. Through the ceremony, the ritual, specific things become noticeable. I also saw a Mass read in the subterranean level [of a church] in Naples. With the transubstantiation I could see what lies behind the Catholic transubstantiation. It is indeed the case that when a real priest executes the transubstantiation, the host receives an aura. You may believe this or not—I can only tell you what I saw.

We do not need to avoid saying it: There is indeed an inner reality in the ritual; there is no doubt of that. We then see precisely the defects in Catholicism when we see what it once was and what has been lost in the rationalistic age. It is senseless that Protestantism has taken, out of the seven sacraments, only two. There is no reason for this.

Emil Bock: May we also ask what the laying on of hands was in early Christianity?

Rudolf Steiner: Here you must be aware that humanity has gone through an evolution and that certain spiritual forces, which existed in ancient humanity, receded more and more as the human being became more intellectual and developed freedom. In relation to natural life, certain forces receded. As a result, people do not understand many things that are recounted in biblical history—things that mean something quite different from what people connect with them today. For example, I draw your attention to how terrible and revolting the modern age sees something like the relationship of Socrates[†] to his pupils. People speak of a kind of homosexuality, whereas in reality it points to an aspect of the soul forces, by which, not through the word but through the presence of Socrates with his pupils, something was brought about. The presence of the human being meant something to them. It is a revolting and false representation when today the concept of homosexuality is used in connection with these matters in those times in Greece. And thus it is also with touching in the laying on of hands. The human hand is important essentially not only for feeling, but it also emits or radiates something. This emanation was stronger in earlier times. The hand can receive something that heals. I have often said in lectures that human life is a whole: childhood belongs together with the later ages of life. No one receives in later life the power to bless who was not able to pray during childhood. Those who never folded their hands in prayer during their youth can never bless with their hands. The laying on of hands was simply a process of consecration ... [gap in the notes] ... what is involved in the laying on of hands. This was something that was developed earlier, and we should contemplate the healing effect of the laying on of hands. Modern human beings are no longer in the same position; they are not urged to develop such a capacity in their youth. People developed such things in earlier times; it was once a reality. Yet this does not preclude the possibility of developing this ability again in a more spiritualized future. Would you not see this as desirable? The folding of the hands is a preparation for blessing. In like manner—in Old Catholicism, for instance—the following was taught: If you learn to kneel, then you learn to say in the proper manner: *"dominus vobiscum"* [The Lord be with you]. Do you think that is strange? You know how one says, *"dominus vobiscum."* This is learned through kneeling; otherwise it has no power.

A participant: It was said that the priests of ancient Egypt held positions of extraordinary leadership. We heard that the initiates led the people, that they worked through real thoughts. The question is how this would have to be modified today through the new [way of working].

Rudolf Steiner: Yes, it must become new, inasmuch as we may not return to that strongly unconscious, atavistic way, but we must become much more conscious and pay attention to the fact that all human beings must develop themselves into individuals. It is still the case today in Catholicism that the personality of the priest is completely suppressed. When the stole is crossed [over the heart] of the priest, the priest is only a figure or representative of the church; he is no longer a human being. We may not cultivate this. Precisely in the ancient Egyptian priesthood much depended upon the fact that actually, as long as the high priest lived, the others were only allowed to be figures or representatives. Only when the high priest died could another step in. There was always only the one. We must exclude all of this today.

A participant: What can you say about the priest's vestments?

Rudolf Steiner: Liturgical vestments arose so that one might imagine the color of a personal feeling in relation to reality. For example, one imagines a priest giving a blessing. This results in a particular coloring of the astral body, and the liturgical vestment is fashioned accordingly. Blessing produces an absorption of the individual personality in the suprasensible world, and from it the blessing streams onto the congregation. This leads to a blue inner vestment and a red outer garment. One simply makes a copy or image of the astral body. The same occurs in other acts—praying, and so forth. Imagine, for instance, that one has an outpouring of spirit. You can follow this quite exactly: the color of the astral body gives the color of the priest's vestment. The liturgical vestment is simply the coloring of the astral body. This could absolutely be duplicated. It is a question only of whether humanity is mature enough to validate such a thing...

I had a friend, who was an excellent Protestant pastor,[†] who had a great ideal. That is, he had many beautiful ideals, but among others, he wanted to do away with the Luther frock.[†] He wanted to go around like an ordinary dandy. It embarrassed him not to be able to go around like a dandy when he was a pastor. Therefore, it was quite painful for him not to be able to wear the modern aesthetic men's clothing, in which one is harnessed in two stovepipes. Today this hideousness is regarded as the only possible garment, and whatever else arises as new is as foolish. The greatest foolishness is our men's suits. Given a humanity that puts on a frock and sets a cylinder on top, it is clear that human beings of this kind cannot have an understanding of or sense for ritual vestments. Humanity must be reeducated. Perhaps when women also take up this profession, a way will soon be found to come to proper vestments for the rituals; women will certainly have to do something to attain the pastor's position. But men today want to do things like the Swiss lecturer, who found it proper, for example, while giving talks—of course, not sermons—to waltz a cigarette back and forth in his mouth as he spoke from the podium. This is the way he held his lectures.

You know, of course, that the ritual vestments were not restricted merely to the church. Judges also wore vestments. And if you expected judges today to put on old ritual vestments, they would rebel against it. Yes, even royalty went around in a kind of ritual vestment. And finally, you have in the universities the rector's cloak that is always passed on from one rector to the next. In this connection we need change only our aesthetic imaginations, and then it will work.

Lecture 5

STUTTGART, JUNE 15, 1921

My dear friends! Today I want to speak about the third area that you indicated: the actual content of the sermon. Naturally, all three areas are basically closely connected with each other. Concerning the nature of the ritual, I gave you a few indications of what we need today. We will need, of course, to complete these indications and try to make them concrete. But I have given at least a few suggestions about the nature of ritual. Today I would like to proceed from there to show you how the ritual connects, in turn, with the actual content of the sermon.

You see, the sermon calls on the capacity of human beings, the members of your congregation, to understand imaginatively. Obviously, the sermon must be given in such a way that what enters the human being through the capacity for imagination passes as quickly and as intensively as possible over into the soul or heart sphere of feeling, and, above all, also into the will. Yet, even though this is the case, we must work in a roundabout way through the sermon on the members of the congregation, by way of imaginations. In all our instruction we must affect all those we work with through their imaginative capacity.

Now, by its inner nature, this capacity for imagination contains something that is contradictory to human nature as a whole. Here we enter an area where, from the very beginning, modern science proves itself unable to understand these things. When making a statement like "the imaginative element contains something that contradicts the full nature of the human being," we find no understanding of this in our modern natural scientific worldview. And yet it is true. Whatever is received by the imagination tends to be taken in once and then is retained by the memory. You can easily see that this is contradictory to human nature.

When you look at the other extreme in the human being and consider purely bodily processes, you cannot say, I ate or drank yesterday; what I ate or drank is retained in my organism; therefore, I do not need to eat or drink again tomorrow. Eating and drinking must be repeated in a rhythmical manner. The performance of human actions must follow a rhythm. And basically, it is the actual nature of the human being to be integrated into rhythm in a certain way. In fact, it is a departure from human nature when something is taken in once and is then retained, is permanent. And this permanence is the characteristic of the imaginative element. In the extreme case, what is imaginative becomes boring if it is repeated too often. Connected to this as a theoretical idea is a fundamental sin against human nature, namely, not to want repetitions anymore. You can see this outwardly. Read a good translation of the discourses of the Buddha.[†] You will find that these contain countless repetitions; you move through nothing but repetitions. Foolishly, in the West, people have attended only to the thought content of Buddha's discourses and have omitted the repetitions, because they did not know that the Buddha had taken account of human nature.

Here we bump up against the point where, because of human nature itself, content as such must pass over into something that is taken in rhythmically. Formerly this was done naturally, completely out of instinctive knowledge, by inserting prayer as the rhythmical element into what was being taught. Prayer was inserted as the continuously repeated content of belief, in spite of the fact that every individual prayer has exactly the same content. When repetition enters, what is of an imaginative nature passes over into the will. Only in this way can we receive a content that has will-nature. With that fact, we already have the necessary inflow of instruction or teaching into the ritual. We must present our instruction in a form that, in a certain way, brings pictorial ideas, imaginations, to the members of the congregation or community. We must let what we are teaching pass over, in a certain way, into pictorial ideas or imaginations and arrange the main points in a kind of monumental way and let them be repeated as a formula. Without this we cannot take the content of our teaching beyond the level of theoretical ideas into the practical sphere of the will—which is what we must do. The more we persist in merely delivering the content of our teaching, the less we will come to a practical religious exercise.

That shows you directly how in something like the Buddha's discourses ritual is absolutely already contained. In these discourses we actually already have present how the will can be worked out of merely theoretical ideas. When we ask people to repeat the Lord's Prayer, we are working out of the purely theoretical into the practical religious aspect. But we will not be able to do this at all if we ourselves are not completely permeated by the suprasensible world-substance. And here I come to a particular characteristic of Christian teachings that you must pay attention to, if you want them to have an effect on the human beings at all.

You see, the greatest harm in modern religious work lies in the fact that we actually no longer take the Gospels seriously. I do not mean anything disparaging by this. I mean that people do not have the consciousness to seek a meaning in the Gospels that goes beyond the understanding of the sense world. Through Anthroposophy, in the most meaningful way, however, we gain the ability to penetrate the Gospels. As a result we can say that a subject matter that is beyond this earthly world flows through the Gospels. We must understand the Gospels; we must do everything we can to truly understand them. Today people only criticize the Gospels. In reality, they do not want to understand them, and their criticism comes mostly from the fact that they do not take the contents of the Gospels seriously, but rather take them superficially.

Here let me refer you to the third sentence of the Prologue of the Gospel of John, in which people usually hear the following words: "All things were made through the Word, and without the Word nothing was made that was made." How much is contained in this third sentence of John's Gospel! In reality, what it means is "All things that have come into being have come into being through the Word, and without the Word nothing has come into being that has come into being." That is what this sentence proclaims. It speaks forcefully of what has arisen in the world and is subject to becoming. Of what is subject to becoming, it says, first, that it is thing-like. Everything that we see as things that have arisen, all these have come into being and pass away. And second, concerning what has arisen and passes away, it is said that it is made through the Word—through the Logos.

This sentence would not mean anything if consciousness did not also produce a contradictory proposition—if underlying this sentence there would not also be the truth that in cosmic existence there is also something that is not subject to arising or passing away. That is, there are the eternal foundations that only transform but do not pass away. In modern education we have simply lost this polarity between what becomes—comes into being—and is found on the surface and the powers that lie in the depths—powers that, for instance, Plato called eternal ideas. We must assume that these eternal ideas do not pass away and that they underlie what comes into being and passes away. They do not exist in becoming and passing away in the ordinary sense; rather they subsist.

We must differentiate between existence and subsistence. What persists, or subsists, in relation to all things is the foundation or ground; it has to do with the Father. We must speak in so completely straightforward, ordinary, popular a way that we bring the Father God to the consciousness of the members of our communities as what is unconditionally eternal. This is not as difficult as you think. It is difficult only because today the world fights intensely against imaginations. I can assure you that the people who will understand most easily are farmers in rural areas. They understand the matter immediately. It is only the people who have been "mis-educated" through today's education who do not understand. They do not understand this.

We can learn a lot when we look at what is a last remnant of elemental spirituality that is present in the human beings who have not been "mis-educated." It is relatively easy to bring precisely the highest ideas to the human beings who have an elemental soul life. Only those who are "mis-educated" by today's schools will reject such ideas.

We must indeed grasp how, in a straightforward, popular way, we can bring people a conception of what is eternal in all things and of what is temporal (what comes into being and passes away). We must summon, in all possible direct and indirect ways, the imaginative idea that the Father God is the basis of all that endures; that Christ, as the creative Logos, is the foundation of all that arises and comes into being, and of what *becoming* itself is. For this reason, one must seek to understand the Father God as being *before* what has come into being, and to understand the Christ as being *in* what has come into being.

Such matters must be worked out again. If we do so, then we will come again to concepts that lie beyond merely natural scientific concepts. However, my dear friends, you must be able to speak about these things in the right way. You do not learn to do this by ruminating all kinds of logical thoughts. Logical thinking itself suffers from the one-sidedness that is always striving to grasp something only once. Brooding logically—when it remains only rumination—is the worst preparation for the sermon. If you want to give a sermon, it is not enough to prepare yourself with the didactic subject matter of the sermon. For the person giving a sermon, the only possible supplement to this preparation on the content is meditation itself.

Those who want to give a sermon must meditate before they do so, which means they must call into their consciousness something that will bring them into the inner realm of cognitive feeling, so that they feel God, the divine, within them. Those who do not prepare meditatively will not be able to allow the word to resound with the necessary nuance to summon an understanding of what they have to say. You will have to speak of immortality, the Fall, creation, salvation, and grace. But you must not speak of immortality, the Fall, creation, salvation, and grace with the consciousness you've absorbed from your modern natural scientific education. You must speak out of the consciousness that you have attained out of your feeling of the divine existence in your own inner being. Then your words will be given the nuance that you need to reach the hearts of those to whom you should bring the truths about immortality, the Fall, creation, salvation, and grace. Those who are to give a sermon must grasp this as deeply as possible. You cannot come to a deeper relationship to the content of the teaching if you do not prepare meditatively.

The collectedness that you first attain in meditation and that brings you to be alone with your whole being—even if only for a few moments—also prepares the proper inner mood for the Gospel reading. You must proceed from the fact that only a meditative life can prepare you, on the one hand, both for the reading of the Gospels and, on the other, for the special tone necessary for the sermon. The person who will give sermons must make this into a habit. Do not think that the understanding of ritual and the understanding of the correct nuance when giving a sermon come from intellectual considerations. It does not come from intellectually grasping the content of the Gospels. It comes through meditative deepening in the spirit and, at the same time, in the will that stimulates the human being—the whole human being. It always depends on this.

It is best when those who want to give sermons today become aware, by means of excellent examples, what inner soul battles must be fought when they want to press through what they have absorbed through their modern, outer education, including their outer theological education—that is, what has determined their whole way of thinking—to a real grasp of the imagination of the suprasensible that they wish to present.

It is really helpful for those who want to work in religious life to study, for instance, such personalities as Newman, the English cardinal.[†] He started from Anglicanism, involved himself semiconsciously in a modern philosophy, and then lapsed into Catholicism, to the point that he became—because such people are always awaited—a cardinal. It is interesting to observe the wrestling that such a person goes through. Newman's struggle started with his wanting to understand the Christian truths. However, he could not manage it. In the end, he found no way to understand the Christian truths with modern concepts. He was honest enough not to want to come merely to the "simple man of Nazareth," as Weinel did.[†] Newman, on the other hand, yearned for the suprasensible. He could not accomplish this until he realized that Christianity began not with scholars and scientifically educated people, but rather with fishermen of Galilee, who understood nothing of what they spoke about.[†] They spoke without logic, for they were not imbued with logical understanding. This means that actually everything that theology is—what works so hard to be logical, what even arrives at negation in logic-permeated critiques—first arose out of the simple words of fishermen from Galilee. Out of this realization, Newman reaches the conclusion: if there is logic, it can only be born out of the un-logical—out of a simple way in which Christianity lived among the human beings who were around Christ Jesus in Galilee.

And from this he arrives at a special view of Christianity's evolution or development[†] from what was experienced religiously into what was more thought up. And now, accompanying this realization, because he is stuck in the reality of the unfolding of the religious experience, he is forced to accept the whole Catholic Church. Why is he stuck? He is stuck because he denies the possibility that today, through observation and contemplation, one can pass through the logic into the superlogical. Thus, he could, stuck as it were between Scylla and Charybdis, face the danger, on the one hand, under the influence of the Scylla of succumbing to a rationalistic interpretation; or, on the other, of succumbing to the Charybdis of killing the rationalistic way of thinking. But at the same time he must also accept the whole tradition and so fall back into Catholicism. Everyone who thinks this way actually reverts to Catholicism. You need only think about those people who cannot participate in what is in keeping with our times today and enter into the suprasensible. Scheler,[†] for example, who is characteristic of this in our German education, reverted back to Catholicism. When people seek the suprasensible and reject the path that Anthroposophy seeks to take, they revert to Catholicism.

Today there is no other possible way to negotiate between the Scylla of rationalism and the Charybdis of irrationalism than to take the Anthroposophical path—even to take up Anthroposophy as the element that can bear religious life—in order to attain suprasensible truths. On this path one will also find—and this is necessary for you, for it builds community—a popular, simple form for what we cannot yet do within Anthroposophy, because something else must first be there. To present suprasensible truths in Anthroposophy, we have to express ourselves too much in modern educational forms, because we are speaking to those who are a part of the modern education. However, when you are a larger group, it will certainly be possible for you to find a simple form in which to speak to people so that the high concepts of the suprasensible become concrete once more.

I will mention only the following. Do not disdain to speak to people like this: look at the stone; look at the quartz crystal. Look at a mineral object so formed, and you will be able to say to yourself: how is this mineral made? It is formed out of the Earth. You have no reason to think anything other than that it is formed out of the Earth. It is a piece of the Earth. The Earth can create such forms; it is a piece of the Earth. But look at plants; look at what you always see around you. Can you imagine that the Earth alone brings forth the plants? No. The seeds that the Earth bears within it must wait until spring comes, until the rays of the Sun penetrate into the Earth from outside. And when the Sun's rays lose their strength, the Earth also loses its strength to bring forth plants. Look at plant growth, and you will notice that when it wants somehow to survive through the winter, it takes in a lignifying element, a mineral element; it becomes a tree that, in turn, loses in its wood the shooting, sprouting force. It takes into itself something of the mineral. The Earth could never bring forth plants out of itself; to do so, what surrounds the Earth is necessary. One must rise to the ability to bring people to a proper consciousness that the Earth would be only a body of stone, if it had only its own forces. The Earth would never possess or be permeated with vegetation if it did not form a unity with the cosmos—if cosmic forces did not play into and work upon the Earth. The Earth would not have a plant kingdom without heavenly space.

If in ancient Egypt one could teach slaves such truths as, for example, the transition from the force of the Sun to the force of Sirius, then we need not doubt that we can speak to the simplest human beings about the Earth owing its vegetation to the cosmos beyond the Earth. In this way, by bringing people to a feeling for what the Earth receives in terms of forces from heavenly space, we detach them from their inclination for the purely earthly.

What I mean, then, is that we must work to guide the eye of the soul to the whole of cosmic space. We can already begin to do this through the observation of what is in the plant world, which everyone can understand. In this, we can receive a great help when we realize how all of nature is actually without guilt, and how impossible it is to speak of guilt or sin in the mineral and plant kingdoms. And if we work through these concepts of guilt and sin successfully, and also present concretely nature's guiltlessness and the capacity of human beings to become guilty, then we can work out what it is that leads us to understand that something that does not exist in space enters the world with human beings. If we have first understood that the plant owes its existence to space and is guiltless, then we have a way to make clear to ourselves that what makes human beings guilty cannot in any way come from space. It then becomes necessary for all of us to seek the essential soul nature of the human being outside of space. We must seek a path that goes beyond space. You see, if we find a way to go beyond space, we will certainly find our way even further.

You can see how difficult it is for modern educated people to get beyond space from the fact that the cleverest people of the nineteenth century fought against immortality from the viewpoint that souls have no room in the cosmos.† They could not extend their concept of the soul beyond spatiality. The concept of the soul must move beyond spatiality. Once we have achieved this, we can next direct people's attention to the animal world and attempt to enliven the concept that we receive from it, one which takes hold of not only our imaginative life, but also takes deep hold of our souls, hearts, and minds (*Gemüt*).

We find that minerals and plants cannot become guilty and, therefore, also cannot suffer. The human being must suffer and can, however, become guilty. When we direct our gaze to the animal world, we see that they, like the plants, cannot become guilty, but they must suffer. If we can then gradually learn to grasp repeated earthly lives, not as theory but as a clear comprehension, and if we can come to feel, not in a trivial, but in a practical way, that there is a cosmically lawful connection between guilt and suffering, we become aware of a great world tragedy. We come to understand and feel these truths and to realize that we do not see this lawful connection because we direct our attention to guiltless nature and seek to place the human being into the unity of nature. The world tragedy consists of the fact that we have thereby bound the animal world to us. The animals must suffer with us, in spite of their not becoming guilty. Thus we come to the tragic thought that animals are there because of human beings; they must suffer with us, even though they cannot commit error. Enter into this concept with your feeling. Feel this reality, that the animal world suffers evil, even though it cannot do evil.

When we can, in this way, develop living ideas of evil and wickedness that are at the same time feelings or feeling-ideas, we can make a connection with the world. We must but feel the tragedy in world-existence that consists in the animals around us suffering with us to become aware that there are responsibilities that go beyond the realm of rights and the law. This is a point by which you can lead people completely beyond the immediate sense world. For in the immediate sense world you find nothing but the concepts of rights that regulate the outer, sense relationships between human being and human being. Our responsibility to redeem the animals emerges out of a totally different world. But, in our present existence, we cannot assume this responsibility at all. We can do nothing in this present existence to redeem the animals that suffer because of us. We can redeem them only when we look forward to the end-condition of the Earth—a condition in which natural laws do not hinder us from intervening in the redemption of the animal world and from removing the suffering from it. Thus, we must move forward to grasp an end-condition of the Earth, into which physics has no right to speak. Thus, we expand what lives in us to a grasp of our cosmic connection.

This is the way we must speak to people today, because if we speak in terms of old religious ideas, people will object that, viewed from the perspective of natural science, everything we say is impossible. We must, however, find a way against which natural science can say nothing. This is there then—this suffering without guilt of the animal world. This is a direct transition to the possibility of knowing about super-earthly responsibilities—or better, about responsibilities beyond the earthly, of duties that can be fulfilled only when the Earth has come to the end of its present physical condition. We will be able to lead people to an understanding of this Earth condition by objectively overcoming natural scientific thinking.

We cannot do this, however, if in our sermons we appeal only to human egotism. This egotism has arisen gradually in humanity and has made religious conviction so difficult. Today our best sermons appeal basically to human egotism, which happens because we speak only of immortality and not of being unborn—of being not-yet-born.

Anthroposophy makes the nature of immortality clear. It becomes clear through knowledge, yet how do the modern preachers speak about immortality? They shake human beings' egotistical needs out of their sleep. They speak to our deepest emotional egotism. Preachers would not reach people's hearts at all if the following desire did not rise up to meet them: the desire that we do not want to perish at death or cease to exist. Of course, the human being does not cease to exist at death. But knowledge of immortality must not simply proceed from this desire. Preachers speak to desire and fear, and stimulate them in people. Even if they are unaware of it, they still do it because it is a habit. You cannot approach life before conception in the same way. You cannot speak about life before birth from an egotistical standpoint. When you speak about it, people are indifferent, because it does not mean anything to them in their innermost being. Because they experience this present existence, it does not interest them whether or not they lived before. You must instill interest in life before birth in human beings. You can do this only if you can infuse people with the idea that, with their earthly existence, they were given a mission to fulfill—that is, that they are coworkers in the divine world order—and that this world order could not attain its goal without the sense world. Here an important thing is that the Deity let human beings go. It must be understood completely that human beings experience freedom, but they could not experience it if they did not descend into a physical body. We must describe the human being as having been sent down by God. Without being clear about pre-existence, you will never create a sermon that takes hold of the whole human being, and not just the desiring human being. This is the great harm done by sermons today: that they appeal, on the one hand, to desires and, on the other, to fears and that they do not present the human being as an image of the Deity, who lets human beings go so that they may work in earthly existence.

You see, the Word that resounds over to us out of ancient times and plays such an important role in the Catholic Church—the *Gloria*—is inserted between the Gospel reading and the offertory in the Mass. *"Gloria in excelsis Deo"*—"Glory be to God in the highest and peace on Earth and goodwill toward men." Today, in the Greek-German dictionary, the first translation given is "honor," instead of "glory." Now, this translation would be thoroughly misleading, because the idea of "honor" does not lie at the basis of the Greek concept (*Doxa*), which should be translated as "glory." The idea expressed in the Greek *exusiai* is much closer: namely, the idea of "shining outward," "revealing oneself." The verse then actually means, "The divine reveals itself in the heights, and on Earth its mirror image is the peace of human beings who are of good will." We must come to a new concept of *Gloria*; then we will again understand these things.

Consider, for a moment, how terribly blasphemous against the divine it actually is when what the Gospel tells of the one born blind is translated as follows:[†] "Why was this one born blind? Did he sin, or his parents?" And the answer: "Neither did he sin nor his parents, but that the work of God shall be revealed in him." Is it not blasphemous that the one born blind is supposed to have been healed so that one could see God's work in it? Although one always translates it so that the works of God are revealed through him, the truth lies in the fact that, in a pre-existing life, this man brought blindness upon himself in order that, within him, the God should be revealed.

We must exclude this false idea, which appears so frequently. Then we can make it understandable that human beings stand there as an image of God and they are there to allow the Godhead to work in them. We cannot reach this understanding if we base our hopes only on life-after-death and not on life-before-birth. We must grasp in a radical way that here on Earth we are living the continuation of a pre-earthly life; that we are not merely at the beginning of a post-existent life-after-death; and that, if we speak only of immortality after death and not pre-existence before birth, human souls will not find their way to selflessness. Your sermons must be aglow with these ideas. If they are, then it will be possible for you to reconnect human consciousness to the suprasensible. And then the rest will come of itself.

You see, to help people attain a concept like creation, you must call forth a consciousness of the following in them: If you consider mineral nature as we view it today, the law of the conservation of matter and energy holds sway in it. Thus, the world that we see there appears to be eternal. But then we become aware that this world is only earthly space, and minerals alone come about out of this earthly space; and plants come from space beyond the Earth; and animals come from a pre-earthly condition, for naturally earthly natural law could not make an animal into a human being. When you become aware that natural laws themselves began on Earth— whereas today we merely extend natural laws forward and backward into infinity—then you will be able to understand that the concept of creation includes within it the origin of natural laws. Thus, in this way, we can attain a conception of creation.

I want to draw something to your attention now that will provide proof of the fact that, actually, you can always find a certain understanding among simple souls when you speak of the highest things. During my youth, if you went to an Austrian farmer who was not formally educated but had learned only to read and write in the village school, and spoke to him about nature in the sense that is taught in school, he would just stare at you. He could not reconcile this idea of nature with what he knew. You could not tell him in the usual way that you observe that nature brings forth plants and animals, and that it is beautiful; it appears in the light, and so on. You might as well have spoken to him in Chinese. There was a poet who wrote in the Austrian dialect† and who used the word *"d'Naduar"* for nature. When the farmer, who had learned only to read and write, and who had no sense for the concept of nature as it exists in modern science, spoke of nature he had a different conception of nature than we do. "Nature" for him was the masculine seed; and without this connotation, he could not understand the word "nature." His understanding of nature went somewhat as follows: What lives without guilt in nature is also in him, but it is drowned out by what in him can become guilty. He saw nature as a part of himself and as something connected with birth. But he also had the idea that something else, something other than nature, enters the human being at birth. Therefore, he called the masculine seed "nature"—the natural aspect that has to do with being born. For him, there was a mysterious connection between our being born and what it is to be a work of nature.

As in the case of this striking idea, so you can also find, if you seek it, a way of connecting with concepts that the simplest souls can grasp. This is true also for the concept of creation. The concept of creation can be made thoroughly understandable, but you must really have the goodwill to try to go beyond what modern education offers. As you do so, you will gradually be able to bring people to understand that the creation of the human being precedes the creation of nature. The human being came into the world in a time when nature was not yet working—when heredity, reproduction, and so on did not exist yet. You go back to a condition before our present world existed as an outer structure, before heredity and reproduction existed, when the Fall of spiritual beings who then later took the human beings with them could occur. You go back to a condition in the period before nature, when the Fall into sin was not yet a possibility for the human being.

You can come to these things, and you must come to them if you want to find a content for your sermon. It is not enough to present ideas of the Fall, salvation, and so on, to people theoretically. You must be able to present such concepts in all possible variations. You must count on the fact that they will gradually enter into people's souls. You will learn that if you rely only on formal understanding— only on doctrinal content and not on varying the repeated expressions of it—you will not be able to hold the community together. If you vary the way you say it, then you can hold the community together. In this way you will also bring people to understand "grace."[†] You will bring them to the point of being able to develop, at least in their consciousness, concepts of guiltlessness and of the not-evil ... [gap in the notes], the freedom ... [again a gap], and of the fact that, though we can become inwardly good human beings by all of our efforts, we can find a connection to the world with the good only when grace is working: when grace comes toward us.

I can give only indications of all of this, because there is not enough time to go into it thoroughly. However, in short, there are ways to get beyond today's education into a fully human system of ideas, one that has access to the suprasensible world. For all of this, it is absolutely necessary that you allow yourself to be enriched by Anthroposophy in a certain sense. People can understand what you say to them—they will understand absolutely—if you find the tone by first immersing yourselves in meditation.

In modern times, sermons and preaching have become too abstract. They are not living. I say this to you only for you to contemplate. I do not want to force it upon you like a dogma. I can only tell you: the worst kind of sermon is one in which you remain with abstractions and then become unctuous. To believe that you speak to the soul by simply presenting abstractions in an inward manner is poison for the soul. When you speak of the "simple man of Nazareth," without taking into account the suprasensible nature of Christ and base every-thing that is Christian only on his humanity, and when you want to teach this to people, while at the same time taking on an untruthful tone in your soul, then you poison their minds and souls. Then you live in untruthfulness in relation to what the sermon should imbue with warmth.

What should be transmitted through the sermon in an appropriate manner is the connectedness of the person giving the sermon with the suprasensible content and impulse of the world, and the suprasensible content and impulse can never be communicated through abstrac-tions. The person giving the sermon must, with heartfelt humility, be permeated with the knowledge that the use of logical reason alone is itself already sin; and must know that the activity of natural science in modern times kills the religious element and that it is through reli-gion that we must redeem the world from the natural scientific view. Priests must know that it is a part of their religious task to overcome natural science, and that it is a commandment of Christ Jesus himself to overcome natural science. They must know that Christ Jesus lives among us for this reason, and that, when we unite ourselves with him, we express his mission of overcoming natural science.

We must be clear that human beings must work in the world and, therefore, must sin by understanding the world through the senses. We must see that this sin is necessary. We must also see that, because rhythm exists in the world, the pendulum must swing to the other side—to the side of redemption from natural science. Then we will see, in an unprejudiced way, that natural science has to exist. We will not be able to eradicate it, because we must recognize the necessity for human beings to become acquainted with Ahriman, but at the same time we must also be clear that the pendulum must swing to the other side. Yet we must also be aware of the rhythm: that these two aspects can work together only if they are in balance with one another.

Here I must bring your attention to something that might surprise you, but which must enter your consciousness if you wish to find the necessary tone for your future sermons.

You see, today we actually live in a consciousness that is a kind of continuation of the ancient Persian cosmic consciousness concerning Ahriman and Ahura Mazda. This consciousness sees in Ahriman the evil god who resists Ahura Mazda, and sees in Ahura Mazda the good god who destroys the work of Ahriman. What people do not know is that the ancient Persians knew that you cannot follow either Ahriman or Ahura Mazda alone, but rather must follow what comes out of their working together. This working together revealed itself in a figure like Mithras. Ahura Mazda is a Luciferic being who, when we devote ourselves to him, makes us "world-less." He wants to tear us loose from heaviness, gravity, and wants us to burn up in the light. Human beings must find their way between the light and the heaviness, or gravity: between Lucifer and Ahriman. For this reason, we must be able not to think in some kind of dualism, but rather to think in a trinity. We must have the possibility to say, today, the Persian dualism of Ahura Mazda and Ahriman is Lucifer and Ahriman, and Christ stands in the middle between these two. Christ is the one who brings about the balance.

Now the whole of religious development up to now—above all, the development of theology—has established a terrible comparison:

it has brought the Christ figure as close as possible to that of Lucifer. When we experience how Christ is spoken of today, it is almost a resurrection of the ancient Persian god, Ahura Mazda. Human beings still think only in duality: evil in opposition to the good. The problem of the world cannot be solved through a duality, but only through a trinity. For as soon as we have duality, we have the battle between light and darkness. This battle cannot end with one conquering the other. It can end only with the harmonizing of both. This harmonization is what we must bring into the Christ concept. It is not for nothing that Christ sat with tax collectors and sinners.

You see, dear friends, the world we live in has come because it was originally formed by influences that worked their way into the pattern we experience today in the echoes or repercussions of ethnicity, individual peoples, and the like. Examine and contemplate this world and how it comes from the element of birth, and then contemplate the mission of Christ. The mission of Christ is to conquer this element that clings to nature: to plant love for all humanity in general over against life in the tribe or ethnic group. What was present from the beginning of the Earth—all that has to do with Adam—all that should be wiped out through Christ. What was appropriate for individual peoples, folk egotism, should be conquered through Christ, through universal humanity. But redemption does not consist of working against nature in as real or concrete a way as nature itself is. It consists in our taking up all that clings to nature and bringing about a balance between the purely spiritual and the natural.

The concept of Christ between Ahura Mazda and Ahriman—between Lucifer and Ahriman—has not yet been developed in its purity. The concept of Christ must be conceived of as what brings us to a harmonizing of the opposing poles. Universal humanity—the love for one's fellow human beings—is something different from what grows out of families, peoples, ethnic groups or races, the nation, and so on. Yet the one should not eradicate the other; ethnic groups and individuals must be harmonized. Human beings will comprehend the mission of Christ only when they know, that the Father God is connected only with the eternal, and not with what comes into and passes out of being. The Christ impulse entered time, because he is connected with what comes into and passes out of being. Christ transforms the temporal into the eternal.

We must learn again to take literally what the Gospels say: "Heaven and Earth will pass away, but my Word will not pass away."† Let us translate this into words that can be spoken today. The plants that the widths of space—heaven in the outer, spatial sense—call forth on Earth and the minerals that the Earth itself calls forth will all pass away. That is, the whole earthly world will pass away. But when the plants, stones, and Earth are gone, what came to Earth in Christ will live: what is in the Word lives on. If we take Christ into our word, then after the end of the Earth's existence what is living in us through Christ will continue to live temporally, in accordance with the words of Paul: "Not I, but Christ in me."†

We must bring ourselves to believe that the laws of nature are not eternal. The Earth will come to an end, and what will then exist can do so because a creative working will carry it on when the Earth passes away. Stones and plants will pass away, but what is in us may not pass away; it must be carried beyond the end of the Earth. This can happen only if Christ is in us. Only the animals will come with us—whom we must then redeem. The animals are on Earth because, at the moment when the possibility of sinfulness pierced the world, the animals were at a stage of development when it was inevitable they would be seized by what was good only for humanity. There could be no suffering in the world before the possibility of sin entered the world. Minerals and plants as such do not need to suffer, but they pass away, they cease to exist. The animals were in a stage of development in which they were swept along, through the human beings, into suffering. They must be released and redeemed from this when this stage of evolution is over—when the Earth is no longer there. Just as today our laws of nature hold sway, so then laws will hold sway that we experience today only within ourselves. But we cannot understand this if we do not know that the human being was there before the Earth was.

We must open the way for people for an understanding of these things. It must sound into our sermons. You do not need to think that you have to say to your congregations exactly what I have said today. Your words need not be similar. But you must understand what I have said; then it will live in your sermons, even when you deliver them in the simplest manner. For there is not only the ponderable understanding of what your mouth utters and your ears hear; there is also the imponderable, which works from human being to human being without being physically uttered.

Unfortunately, my dear friends, I could give you only these few indications; nevertheless I hope that you heard in my words much that seeks expression in humanity today. Without this will, we will not advance. It is not a matter of arousing our intellect; rather we must arouse the whole human being.

Discussion

Rudolf Steiner: So, now that you are full of plans, let us begin.

Emil Bock: We sat together this afternoon to try to determine what we can contribute toward clarifying what we ourselves must do. In relation to this work, the fundamental question arose as to what extent we should work openly. Insofar as there is clarity among us, we see that not everything can be handled in the same way. We must consider how we do so as a question of method or procedure. In each specific case each individual must know what he or she may do. We now have a concrete goal before us, and that is the prospect of a course. We intend to gather at least a hundred people for this course. After the course, we must take a big step into the public arena, and this we will do. We have even discussed the question of how to join our loose organization, and we have drafted a text for those who wish to participate. We have not prepared an entry process for individual people, but rather a joining in on the request for a course. This would be the most practical way to draw people. The text reads as follows:

> The undersigned feels the desire to work together toward the awakening of a new religious life to overcome the present forces of decline, and hopes to attain this goal in a new synthesis of ritual and Christian teaching, and hereby registers for a course in religion to be led by Dr. Steiner, and commits to a strictly discreet handling of communications here received.

Representative   Name / Address

Rudolf Steiner: When would you want to hold the course?

Emil Bock: We decided to have it in September, if possible. I have been charged with the task of asking for an approximate schedule.

Rudolf Steiner: With respect to my being available in Switzerland, it would be good to schedule the course at the same time as other events are scheduled to take place here. I have only a certain number of days that I can be away from Switzerland. It is a complicated situation. It would certainly be good if the course could be planned to take place at the same time as other events. We could consider September. [To *Ernst Uehli*:] When are the events planned in Stuttgart?[†]

Ernst Uehli: They begin the last few days of August and extend into September.

Rudolf Steiner: How much time would your events require?

Ernst Uehli: Ten days.

Rudolf Steiner: The course must have fourteen days. Perhaps we could have two lectures a day.

Ernst Uehli: A different event is planned for each day.

Rudolf Steiner: But not by me. Naturally, I can dedicate myself completely to this course, except when I am obliged to give lectures [in the Congress]. If I receive no other requests or demands, this could work.

Ernst Uehli: Yes, I hope there will be no such requests. As I said, we want to begin at the end of August, if it is possible for people to come then. Is there an event in Dornach immediately afterward?

Rudolf Steiner: I checked, and the last day of events in Dornach will be on August 27th. A eurythmy performance, therefore, will not be possible on August 28th. We must of course have a rehearsal for Goethe's birthday program. We cannot have a eurythmy performance for Goethe's birthday that has not been rehearsed. August 28th will not work if you want to have the eurythmy performance. We could begin with the general work; but it seems to me that the time is a little too short for you. It is now the 15th of June. It could be possible to do it, because there are still two-and-a-half months from now until September 1st. Also, it does not have to happen before September 1st. Do you think you will be ready by September 1st?

Emil Bock: We hope to have a hundred people by then.

Rudolf Steiner: We may assume that you would be able to gather more people, if you took more than two-and-a-half months.

Emil Bock: We also have to consider people studying in the universities.

Rudolf Steiner: Do you mean this is a difficulty?

Emil Bock: It presents us with certain possibilities. Naturally, it is just a different set of possibilities.

Rudolf Steiner: If you are not in a position to be ready by September 1st, beginning in the fall will be problematic. If you can only get people after the universities open, then again we will have to wait, probably until the second half of October and into November, I think. Is that not correct?

Emil Bock: Then it is better to wait, because trying to get people when the semester has not yet begun is not possible for the most part. Would we be allowed to ask for a course if we were fewer in number?

Rudolf Steiner: Yes, certainly. I will say that it would be most wonderful if we could hold that course in Dornach—if it would work and be financially manageable. That would be the best. It is naturally easier to give samples of ritual, and so on, there. Also we would be more able to shape the course in Dornach. Last fall we successfully held the college course [*Hochschulkurs*]† in Dornach. We tried to get the entente countries to pay for the participants, so that the members of the audience from Germany were our guests. Naturally, this would also have to happen with this course. Then it would only be a matter yet of seeking in some way to raise the money to cover travel costs. I think that to travel from Berlin to Basel would not cost much more than to travel from Berlin to Stuttgart. Accommodations in Dornach would also have to be arranged, but that can be decided later; it does not have to be handled now. I think that it would naturally be acceptable to some of you if we could hold the course in Dornach. In principle, you would not rule out this possibility, would you? The difficulty, my dear friends, lies in the fact that we could indeed suggest to the entente countries that they support a general course of study, as it is an international event; however, the question is whether many people from the entente countries are prepared to support only German theologians. We must, of course, tell them what the support money is for. That is the question. I almost believe that they would give their support, but whether they have it in their hearts to support only German theologians…?

For, and this might interest you—though I did not stress it especially in my talks—what I said to you is only valid for German theologians. The question is only ripe for decision in the Central European nations. Even in Switzerland it would be useless to pose the question, and all the more so in France and England. Actually, it would be of no use in the entente countries as such; you would be refused immediately. No one would understand that such a thing could be done.

A participant: I thought that perhaps we could expect help from Holland. I also know Dutch theologians who are friendly to our cause—young theologians. Would Holland not be a possibility?

Rudolf Steiner: Yes, of all places, Holland would enter most into consideration. I can well believe that we have some friends among the theologians there. But they will not exactly be the ones with the purse. I do not doubt that among Dutch theologians there are individuals who could understand the question. However, on the whole, no one has the heart for it. On the other hand, I think that the course can be financed from here. To raise the money from here to hold the course in Dornach would be invaluable.

A participant: How is the matter seen in Sweden and Norway?

Rudolf Steiner: I hardly think that you will find any understanding there. In Sweden and Norway there is an intense consciousness that reform can grow out of the church itself. In Sweden people gave me a direct promise to negotiate concerning this or that. The people there have the idea that they can actually reform the church, and where this idea is still deeply rooted, it works very strongly. However, the idea is not so deeply rooted here in Germany.

A participant: To begin with, we are not acting officially against the church. The people in Sweden can safely assume that our work involves a movement that will be on a neutral basis with the church.

Rudolf Steiner: They would, however, ask you: What do you actually intend to do? Do you want to build independent congregations or work out of the church? The minute you say that you want to found independent congregations, it will become very questionable for them. Holland is still the country that best enters into consideration. People in France and England do not understand it. In Switzerland it is totally out of the question. I think, however, that we will be able to get what we need from Germany. How we will do this financing cannot yet be discussed. We can do this just as soon as you are in a position of authority. We want to try. As I said, I doubt it can be done in foreign countries.

You have no idea how terribly conservative Switzerland is. Thus, there were almost no Swiss students at the Easter Course.† And Swiss theologians are simply naïve. I do not believe, however, that what happened to me recently, just before I left, would happen to you. Two theology students from Basel came to me and asked me if I would like to respond to Heinzelmann[†] and present a second paper against him at the seminary. I cannot get involved giving responses. However, they were not in any way really committed to the idea; it did not matter to them. They also thought that I should give independent lectures. Then they began to speak about the issue itself—and that was really quite naïve. One said, "I recently read Luther's talks. If things were like that again, then things would be fine. Someone just needs to speak like Luther spoke." Yes, there is a great deal of naiveté among the Swiss theologians. Do you not have colleagues in Switzerland? No? The Swiss are intensely conservative.[†] They will be a strong hindrance to the progress of Europe.

In spite of that—which has nothing to do with our holding the course—I think it would be wonderful to hold the course in Dornach. We could schedule it in connection with other courses, so you could hear other lectures as well. But you must see to it that you get some more people.

Emil Bock: Do we have to wait until we have a hundred people?

Rudolf Steiner: I have nothing against there being fewer people than that. I am not thinking the way you think I am. I think that however many people you can get in two months—when it is not vacation, but when the universities are in session—will be fine. It might not even be eighty people—perhaps only sixty.

Then we would do the course with sixty. We would have the course transcribed by a stenographer, and those who come later would be obliged to read it. Therefore, you must include in your formulation of the pledge of commitment the requirement that those who come after the course is over must read the course. We can do it that way. But I believe you have misunderstood me: I did not say that a particular number of people must attend the course.

Emil Bock: It came from us that we have to add two hundred people.

Rudolf Steiner: I actually meant that you ought to have that number of people if you want to do something *practical*.

Emil Bock: There must be two hundred people who are prepared to be active.

Rudolf Steiner: I can hold the course for however many people you can bring together in two-and-a-half months.

Emil Bock: Would the course in Dornach be held at the same time as the college courses?

Rudolf Steiner: We have not yet scheduled a college course. We will hold an art course and a series of events from August 20th to 27th.† Most of the people attending will be English, but naturally we do not want to limit it to the English. After that, we are supposed to come back here to Stuttgart. That would be during the first fourteen days of September. It would be possible to hold the course here in Stuttgart during that time.

Emil Bock: And the second half of September would not be possible?

Rudolf Steiner: No, because I must return to Switzerland then. Of course, if we could arrange to hold the course in Switzerland, we could well consider the second half of September. But I cannot yet say for sure today. It is extremely difficult to procure the financial resources for what is needed.

Emil Bock: Perhaps by then we would already have Dr. Heisler's initial success in fund-raising.

Rudolf Steiner: Consider that, if the course were to cost you ten thousand Reich marks here, that is very little. We could do it in Dornach for ten thousand Swiss francs. But [due to the exchange rate] the ten thousand Swiss francs would cost one hundred thousand marks.

We can collect ten thousand Swiss francs in Switzerland much more easily than you can raise one hundred thousand marks here in Germany.

Emil Bock: However, it would not be a matter of paying for all of us. Many of us could perhaps pay for ourselves. If we could stay in some of the sheds, that would be perfectly good enough for us.

Rudolf Steiner: We have accommodations. However, you would need to pay four Swiss francs per person per day. For one hundred people, that would be four hundred Swiss francs per day for fourteen days. It would come to a total of fifty-six hundred Swiss francs. Perhaps six thousand Swiss francs would be needed. That would be sixty thousand marks if raised here in Germany. It is quite possible that we can get it there in Switzerland.

A participant: As far as the time is concerned, the end of September would be much better. Many students are then on their way to college.

Rudolf Steiner: This is a question we cannot yet answer. I think that it would certainly be easier to hold it in Dornach. It could also be held here in Stuttgart, but it would have to be in the first half of September, and there would then have to be a break of six weeks before I could come again.

Emil Bock: It would be worth a lot if we knew which dates we should plan for. We have discussed all the possible ways to get people to join us. According to our discussions up to this point, we are considering finding theologians by turning to pastors who are close to Anthroposophy. We would do this by sending circular letters to all possible places. We have also discussed all the possible ways of approaching people in the universities, similar movements that want to reform the ritual, and also certain Youth movements. People have already declared that they are willing and ready to do certain things.

We attempted to divide up the German universities among us, and saw that there are a few universities that we are unable to reach. We have planned to make specific travel arrangements for a small number of us to travel to any such university city. Then we want to share with one another our experiences of the work of publicity or promotion. We will do this through the circular letter.

And here we want at least to suggest that we put together a brochure†
that will give a brief orientation of what this work is all about, especially for those who could become our coworkers. We felt it would
be practical for the brochure to contain three articles. These would
be as follows: The first would orient people with regard to the overall
cultural situation. It would be titled "Intellectualism and Religious
Life." The second would be about the ritual. And the third would be
about communicating and imparting religious teaching. We have, to
begin with, assigned at least three members of our group to each article,
so that the best of the submitted contributions could be put together.

Then study groups should also be formed everywhere for the
purpose of studying copies of the lectures we have heard here. We
have decided it would be good if Ernst Uehli would have each one
of us sign a statement that we will use these copies properly and that
they will be for our use only. We decided that, for the expanding
group, I will personally take on the responsibility of getting the signatures of the new participants. When the signatures are collected, they
can be given to Mr. Uehli. It would be of great benefit to our group if
we could receive from Dr. Steiner the content of the rituals that have
been developed so far. When something appeared to be of value, even
if it was not directly related to the course, but only indirectly related
to the course, we could then send them to the various participants
from our central office.

In order to prepare for the founding, and to support the activity
of publicity and promotion, the idea also arose that we should hold
concurrent lectures that do not publicize our work, but rather seek
to bring about an understanding that a renewal of religion out of
Anthroposophy is possible. All kinds of suggestions came up. For
example, it was suggested that one of us could travel with the Haas-
Berkow-Truppe [Troupe]† and then, after their performances, hold
lectures on the relationship of Anthroposophy to the renewal of religion. We could hold lectures wherever we were.

And then I have a request that a certain general misunderstanding could be taken care of. Perhaps it is too much to expect. The
misunderstanding is that it is generally thought that the relationship of Anthroposophy to religious practice is not as positive as

we have found it to be here now. We have found again and again that people, in Anthroposophical groups and elsewhere, think that Anthroposophy has a fairly negative relationship to religious practice. If these people could know about the main ideas that we have spoken of here, some of them would be amazed. For this reason, we want to ask you, Dr. Steiner, to hold a public lecture in the near future if possible about Anthroposophy and the renewal of religion. And then if it were possible, this lecture would be printed immediately afterward and be made available to the public. By this means, the positive stance that Anthroposophy has to religion would be known publicly, and it would prepare the foundation for our work in every respect.

Rudolf Steiner: Do you think it would be especially good if I were to give the lecture? We must naturally consider how it will work best. From this point of view, it would undoubtedly be much better if such a lecture were given—and given well—by someone who is already involved in religious work. That would be better than if I gave it. I have nothing personal against giving the lecture myself. I would say what I have to say, but it would make a big difference if at the present time Mr. Rittelmeyer would give such a lecture. I would gladly speak with him about it; and I think he would be quite helpful.

Ernst Uehli: That coincides with an idea I had in connection with the congress.[†] I had the intention, if possible, to put a lecture by Dr. Rittelmeyer into the program. However, he is not well.

Rudolf Steiner: Dr. Rittelmeyer is not well, and there is really not another person to be found—at least I cannot think of another at the moment. It would actually be good if someone active in religious work would give the lecture.

Emil Bock: We discussed this and concluded that doing that would only increase the number of opinions that have existed up until now by one more. The theologians who are close to us are not unified in their opinion, and there is, as far as I know, always the Heisler-Geyer opposition there.

Rudolf Steiner: I do not know about it.

Emil Bock: Pastor Geyer† says that Anthroposophy is absolutely not a religion. It is only science and can as such, like any worldview, only enrich religion. On the other side, there is a written piece by Dr. Heisler,† which is at least understood to say that Anthroposophy should replace religion. In our discussions we were aware that this antithesis was always there. If Dr. Rittelmeyer joins in as a third opinion, people will all the more really not believe it. We were of the opinion that it does not have to be a lecture, but rather could be a pamphlet. The request for the lecture itself was supposed to mitigate our presumptuous request for a pamphlet.

Rudolf Steiner: You see, it must absolutely be remembered that in the culture as a whole it is necessary that the origin and source of Anthroposophy be seen to lie in scientific considerations. This is the first thing we must remember. Thus, we cannot say that Anthroposophy can replace religion directly, or that Anthroposophy, as such, is only a renewal of religion. What I have stressed with you is that one needs Anthroposophy for a renewal of religion and that we should seek a specific religious stream that can need Anthroposophy. This must be emphasized.

Hermann Heisler: The antithesis arose because Geyer said, "If I accepted everything that Dr. Steiner says, religious life would have absolutely no meaning for me." I responded with, "That is wrong, because Anthroposophy is certainly not a religion, yet it necessarily becomes religion, when it is understood correctly, and builds religion." When theology is correct, it strives toward religion; it does not matter what theology I have; the same is true with regard to Anthroposophy.

Rudolf Steiner: You see, in the case of Geyer we have to take into account the fact that, above all, he does not want to come into conflict with officials of his church. Geyer's standpoint is not that he absolutely does not expect, for himself, essentially religious impulses

from Anthroposophy. On the contrary, he has received many religious impulses from Anthroposophy—and doubtless he has also
received impulses for his sermons. However, he had to say what he
said, because if he does not draw this line of separation, he would be
thrown out of the church. His church does not want a new content to
show itself in their religious work. Therefore he says that his concern
is only about God, and not about the world. Yet, in reality—please
excuse me—that is nothing but foolishness. God concerns himself
greatly with the world; he created it. I do not know how people can
concern themselves—please excuse the analogy—with the wood-
worker without concerning themselves with the woodworking. It is
simply absurd, but one must commit absurdities if one does not want
to be thrown out of the church.

A participant: Pastor Geyer held a lecture, and it was quite obviously
an attack against Pastor Heisler. If still another minister comes out
with something, it will only give the impression that it is only another
opinion. What is important is that something is said that will really
stand.

Rudolf Steiner: Take the tenor of how these things are being said. If a
real difficulty exists, I will indeed do it myself. However, look at the
tenor. It is as follows: One says that Anthroposophy appears to be
claiming to be founding a religion. This cannot be, because never can
a content, such as Anthroposophy brings, found a religion. Gogarten,
for instance, says, "Yes, Anthroposophy wants to found religions."†
In those circles no one would wonder, if I myself would explain that
Anthroposophy can bring a renewal of religion. That changes nothing. Rather the whole discussion gets started up anew. If, however,
Dr. Rittelmeyer would give the lecture—he is basically already
pushed out of the church, and yet is still within it because he is so
greatly loved by his large congregation—if he were to do this from his
own standpoint as a representative of the Protestant Church—which
he feels himself to be—I think that it could really work.

    You could try even something somewhat more daring. I think that
Dr. Rittelmeyer would help if it were a matter of writing a brochure.

He can write. You could also think about uniting both ideas concerning this task: that I do the one part and someone else does the other. Perhaps that would not be so terrible. Now the question is whether someone else besides Dr. Rittelmeyer could write this. Did no one else besides Rittelmeyer [from the theological side] write in the *Lebenswerk* [Life work]?[†]

Ernst Uehli: No one besides Geyer.[†]

Rudolf Steiner: Geyer wrote in that. And we actually have no other Protestant theologians, except Rittelmeyer and Geyer.

A participant: There are a few, but they are no longer in the public to the same extent. Schairer[†] is an example.

Rudolf Steiner: Yes, yes. Schairer created a tremendous to-do. He held a lecture that was full of warmth for Anthroposophy, but he could not finish it all in the same evening, and so he was going to finish it the following evening. However, after that first evening, he received a dressing-down. The next day, when he continued his lecture, he spoke against Anthroposophy. That is a brilliant example.

Hermann Heisler: I do not have the list here. Reverend Klein[†] would be a possibility, and then there is the elderly minister in der Pfalz (The Palatinate-Rhineland-Palatinate)....

Rudolf Steiner: Do you mean Sauter?[†] An elderly gentleman like that cannot do this.

Hermann Heisler: Jundt in Mannheim[†]....

Rudolf Steiner: You can do it. Do you not have the courage to step forward to do it? Please do not misunderstand me. I have nothing against my writing such a brochure, but I believe that it would not work as powerfully as it would if it would come from a person who seeks the renewal of religion—from a religious standpoint. People will say about me, "Yes, sure, he wants Anthroposophy, and he wants to renew all areas of life." For I have already given very many lectures on the renewal of religion. They simply have not been printed. In Berlin I gave lectures that speak to this topic: "the Bible and Wisdom,"[†] for instance. I need only to refresh and renew what I have often said about these things. I do not know, but you seem to think that people believe that Anthroposophy does not seek to be a religion. Neither Bruhn nor Gogarten,[†] however, believe it. All those who write from the Protestant side do not proceed from the premise that Anthroposophy does not want to renew religion. They fight against Anthroposophy precisely because they are of the opinion that it does want to do it.

A participant: Rittelmeyer could do the brochure.

Rudolf Steiner: He would be able to write it.

Emil Bock: We also thought about the prejudices, precisely in relation to religious questions, present among members of the Anthroposophical Society.

Rudolf Steiner: Among the members?

Emil Bock: There are certain prejudices present.

Rudolf Steiner: Why do you say this?

Emil Bock: One never finds the right attitude toward those who are theologians.

Rudolf Steiner: That rests solely upon the fact that the kind of theologian, which you represent, has not yet appeared. You surely do not expect Anthroposophists to have a much different judgment than you yourselves concerning the majority of the theologians. Anthroposophists take the position that you have taken, which is justified. Even more than was the case up to this point, in order to protect Anthroposophy we will have to seek out absurdity in all areas and to set ourselves intensely against it.

I can assure you that theologians achieve as much in relation to absurdity as in relation to the lie. Professor Traub,[†] for instance, is an example of absurdity. He says that I maintain in my *Outline of Esoteric Science* that the spiritual beings move like tables and chairs. He wrote that! When he was called upon to give an authoritative judgment, Dr. Traub wrote that I maintained that spiritual beings moved in devachan like tables and chairs do in the physical world. Because he will not admit that he wrote this while he was in a condition in which, for him, tables and chairs move, I can assume nothing other than that it is an absurdity. You find these absurdities everywhere. Read Gogarten, and so on, with attention to logical absurdities!

And then, too, these people lie. They are so terrible in relation to untruthfulness that it is monstrous. It is really true. Read in what totally roguish manner a Protestant church newspaper (*Stuttgarter Evangelische Sonntagsblatt* [Stuttgart Evangelical Sunday paper],[†] which invented the whole matter about Bernard of Clairvaux) took up Rittelmeyer's response to the story and took advantage of it. One must pay close attention to what untruths they came to. They are capable of doing the following. I believe I am presenting this correctly. Dr. Rittelmeyer responded to the claim made in the Sunday News that I, out of gratitude for his having written *The Life and Work of Rudolf Steiner*, called him the reincarnation of Bernard of Clairvaux.[†] He responded by expressing his amazement that someone would claim something so untrue in the Sunday News. In the News this became that Rittelmeyer was amazed that I called him the reincarnation of Bernard of Clairvaux. They turned it around to say that he was amazed that I did this. They are such shrewd liars. It is all so cleverly done that one cannot expect, because theology is so unclear, that people appreciate the untruthfulness of it. It is not a matter of a person somehow rejecting religion as such. There are people among us who do such things, but it is not in any case relevant. The reality is only that, because of various events, it has been made impossible for us to cultivate what has to do with ritual any further.[†] Before the war [WWI] we cultivated it to a certain extent. In Seiling's brochure,[†] which is also untruthful, you find that stated. And we did do it. We can even speak of having experience of it. It is true.

Since I have been working in Anthroposophical circles, there have been at most eight or ten people leave their church. That is a very small number. We have eight thousand members—not followers— and eight or ten people are naturally very few in comparison. The number of people who have left their church is limited to these few. They left for various reasons. Recently someone wrote to me and asked if I would advise him to leave the church. I advise no one to leave the church—also not Catholics. I do not advise Catholics to do this because, according to the Catholic Church's current view, they do not have the right to leave. I am being serious. Given the dogma of infallibility, Catholics do not have the right to leave the Catholic Church, because a decision was made *ex cathedra* that Catholics cannot leave the church. Catholics are simply within the church, even if they claim to have left it. Since the institution of the dogma of infallibility such things are possible. It seems to be a strange theory, but it is absolutely correct in the eyes of Catholicism. As a Catholic, one cannot leave the Catholic Church.

Hermann Heisler: Aren't the Catholics automatically excluded if they do not follow the requirement of the Easter Confession?

Rudolf Steiner: That is not stated anywhere. The Catholic Church has also never asserted it.

Hermann Heisler: Catholics have told me about it. Catholics say that it is taught in the catechism.

Rudolf Steiner: Yes, it may indeed be taught, yet you know that many things are taught and said. I recall only the conversation between a parish priest who serves in the world and a priest of the Jesuit order. The Jesuit said, "Under no circumstances may a Catholic priest read newspapers, because they are godless today." The priest, who is out in the world and freer in his views, replied, "How should we then preach?

We must know something of the world when we preach, and we can do that only if we read the newspapers. And yet you preach about everything." The Jesuit reiterated, "I do not read newspapers." The parish priest then said, "But you know what is going on in the world." Jesuit repeated, "I read no newspapers." To which the parish priest finally asked, "Yes, well, how do you do it then?" And the Jesuit said, "I let someone read it to me." The Jesuit follows the requirement or commandment in the strictest manner. Yet, you see, Dr. Heisler, I do not know how a person is supposed to be excommunicated. Assume that a Catholic has not bothered with the church for years. Do you believe that, if I wanted to go to confession tomorrow, they would turn me away? I do not know how an excommunication would come about.

The most curious thing happened to Franz Brentano,† the philosopher. Brentano not only left the Catholic Church—he was an ordained priest—he converted to Protestantism and also married. Yet, the Catholic Church declared that he could not be called to a professorship in the university because he was still a priest. He was no longer looked upon as a Catholic—indeed, he was excommunicated, and he converted to Protestantism—but he was not allowed to become a professor, which he once was, in the University of Vienna. Brentano was professor of philosophy in the university, having been called there in 1873. Then he wanted to marry, but he could not, because Austrian law forbade the marriage of priests. Thus, an Austrian citizen who is a priest may not marry. Brentano became a Saxon citizen and a Protestant and married a Jewish woman. Therefore, he had to give up his professorship. They promised him that they would call him later, but they never did, because the Catholic Church protested. The Church explained, "He is a Protestant; yet, at the same time, his ordination is not taken away from him. And a priest who behaves in such a manner may not become a professor in Austria." Then Minister Conrad took heart and went to Emperor Franz Joseph to deal with it that way. The emperor looked at the situation and said, "Yes, it is a devilish thing. Is the Jewish woman at least '*sauber*'? "*Sauber*" means "pretty."† This she was not. Therefore, Conrad could not truthfully say that she was pretty. The emperor then said, "Then nothing can come of it."

In conclusion, if you believe that I should write such a brochure, there is nothing to stop me from doing it, but it would perhaps be good if someone from the other side (from that of religious work) would write it.

Emil Bock: Rittelmeyer has now written about Anthroposophy and the renewal of religion,[†] but I don't know if that is relevant, since he does not know what we have heard here.

Rudolf Steiner: But tell me, do you not believe that it is not at all necessary for a renowned practitioner of religion to write this? Do you not believe that, for instance, one of you, out of the circle of younger people, could write such a piece—something that works purely out of its inner goodness and soundness? Would it not be better if precisely someone who seeks religious renewal were to write it, rather than someone who is known for writing from the standpoint of Anthroposophy? It would work even if the person who writes it does not want to become a priest. I do not know why a younger person could not do it. It just must be done well. Think about it. Now, I will never refuse to do it; I would, of course, do it.

Emil Bock: I ended my report with the fact that a central office would be set up in Berlin. It would be worthwhile for us, first of all, to stay in constant contact with Dr. Steiner from there—if possible, at least temporarily.

Rudolf Steiner: That will work quite well.

Emil Bock: Next, we have something that reaches into Dr. Heisler's domain. We tried to draft a fund-raising flyer,[†] but have not yet finished it. I would now ask Dr. Heisler to report on the fund-raising plans.

Hermann Heisler: We were aware that we should begin according to a plan—that we should begin by going to places where we have acquaintances. We will enlist these acquaintances from among the

Anthroposophists. It is not good to approach the branches officially, but rather we should seek out from among Anthroposophists several people from whom it would seem appropriate to obtain addresses of people to approach in order to raise money. We are convinced that a great number of our members will support our cause. Therefore, it would be better, to begin with, to turn to others. We are certain about members of the Anthroposophical Society; we do not need to cultivate them just now. The person in question should bring the people he or she has collected together into a committee of representatives. These people will receive directions, and then they will work on from there.

Rudolf Steiner: I would indeed advise that you do not go to the branches officially, but rather on a personal basis, and that you put much effort into getting members to give you addresses of nonmembers. I would very much advise this. You will find that there are quite a lot of people who do not want to become official members, but who care a great deal about doing something in this direction.

Unfortunately, it is a little too late for a totally fruitful collecting of money. This will, of course, not hinder you from achieving a great deal in spite of it. It is quite remarkable how strong two or two-and-a-half years ago the striving was, precisely in Germany, for people who had money available to give it to such causes. A large number of wealthy people at that time said, "We absolutely do not want the state to take our money from us." Keyserling's cause† lives solely from such money. Quite a lot of such people gave to his cause at that time.

Hermann Heisler: Is not this picture still relevant?

Rudolf Steiner: It is no longer as true as two years ago, but you can still find it.

Hermann Heisler: Business people have quite a lot of money in their cash boxes. For them, spending their money is a real art now, and so perhaps they will give it easily.

Rudolf Steiner: In addition, there were no taxes before; now the stupid taxation enters in. I do not doubt that you will raise money for this work. The situation is different for the *Kommende Tag* to receive money. You are more likely to get money for such a cause as yours.

Hermann Heisler: Then I also considered Austria. I plan to begin in Baden. I would go first to Freiburg where I have something specific in mind. Then I would like to go up north and travel down along the Rhine as far as Cologne. I think this will take a good month. If this effort is to be fruitful, it must happen quickly. It is urgent, and it is impossible to do it all myself. If the course is to begin already at the beginning of September, then I have hardly one month to do this. August will be very bad. It is not a practical time. September and October again will be better, but I can promise little from August. Therefore, I thought that if the question of time becomes urgent, I would ask Rudolf Meyer† to take over the fund-raising in Hannover, and the gentlemen in Berlin to work there. If I have the time—which I doubt—I will make short visits to the cities in southern Germany. Otherwise, that must wait until later.

It would follow that we would take a break in August. Then it would be possible for me to take a trip to Saxony, and perhaps also to Lake Constance and Konstanz. It does not make sense to plan further ahead than that, because the plans for further work must arise out of practical experience. Dr. Steiner, would you like to say something about all of this?

Rudolf Steiner: While I am here I will think about this issue, and then we can still talk it over.

Hermann Heisler: I would like to go to the Executive Council and ask that they call together the appropriate people. Then it is a question of what should be done first with the money. I was of the opinion that we should open a checking account in my name, and then we would invest it with the *Kommende Tag*, where we hope to receive quite a high rate of interest. There is a certain lack of clarity concerning the favor that the *Kommende Tag* wants to do for us. In addition to my salary, there would be travel expenses for the people who help (Mr. Meyer, etc.), postage, printing, and all the other expenses. Then the course itself also comes under consideration. We hope that the *Kommende Tag* will support us for the first three months.

Rudolf Steiner: I have engaged the *Kommende Tag* only for your position. You must cover any additional expenses out of the money you bring in. I thought the *Kommende Tag* would bridge the gap but that, under the circumstances, it would then be reimbursed for travel expenses later. You must enter into a much more thorough agreement with the *Kommende Tag* than I have. I had to be satisfied with getting this much.

Hermann Heisler: Yet, I hope....

Rudolf Steiner: Whoever says *A*, once in a while will also say *B*, if it is begun correctly.

Hermann Heisler: We thought that would be the first effort: to have people everywhere to whom we can turn. Then we would take up the production of and sending out of a circular, and the obvious further work. After this whole work is accomplished comes the course. After the course, the main thing is the spiritual work.

Rudolf Steiner: However, if it is not to turn out badly, the spiritual activity must begin immediately by the taking on of pastoral positions or by founding communities. One may not represent this cause theoretically; it must be taken up practically.

Hermann Heisler: It would perhaps also be good if one would let the religious element flow into lectures.

Rudolf Steiner: I am of the opinion that it would succeed if all the young theologians, who now join this loose union, set to work directly to enter into the office of the priesthood—to enter into practical religious work. I do not know that it is much use to propagate ideas and campaign for ideas. I believe it is more likely that to do so would weaken the impetus.

Emil Bock: We were not clear whether we should immediately put a ritual in place, or whether we should prepare for it through our work.

Rudolf Steiner: You see, as soon as you think of founding a community, of beginning pastoral care, you must begin to practice real pastoral care with the ritual.

A participant: Some people are perhaps old enough to be able to prepare themselves. In any case, many are not; those should then come after the others.

Rudolf Steiner: Yes, that, too, is correct. But most of you are younger theologians. More particularly, some of you who are here will enter into pastoral positions before too long. I do not know that you should aim to wait until your studies are completely finished. You can found independent communities quite well with only three semesters behind you, if you just try really to penetrate into matters—though, of course, the course will help you penetrate into them more deeply. You must, however, under all circumstances, believe that you could already exercise pastoral care better than others who may have eight semesters behind them. If you do not really believe this, you will have too little impetus and drive. You cannot let that happen.

A participant: There is always the danger that the academic degree will not be attained.

Rudolf Steiner: But in other fields many [students] have enrolled somewhere, and later they went after a doctorate. That would be possible here.

A participant: Perhaps they would not admit us.

Rudolf Steiner: That is a question. Naturally, it is certainly necessary to attain an academic degree because, otherwise, people would form the prejudicial judgment that only the "broken lives" (those who could do nothing else) do something like this—which must not happen. Even if you first build communities for a time and then, after a few years, complete your degree, it can be done. There have always been people who stayed registered, and then later took their oral exam.

A participant: If giving pastoral care is enough, then it (the degree) has no significance.

Rudolf Steiner: Do you think it is difficult to get a doctorate?

A participant: Six semesters are necessary.

Rudolf Steiner: Somehow it has always been possible. For example, twenty years ago Mr. Posadzy[†] came to me and said, "I want to get a doctorate in philosophy. Could you look through my dissertation? I want to write about Herder."[†] He had written a good dissertation. He only committed the grave error of quoting from my *Christianity as Mystical Fact*.[†] And he was told, "No, if you quote Steiner, we will not accept your dissertation." He did not want to delete the reference, and so he came back to me. I told him to go to Gideon Spicker, under whom he gained a *doctor cum laude* degree. You can always do it somewhere. Of course, you can no longer do it under Gideon Spicker in Münster, because he is no longer living. Previously, people could get their doctorate under Spicker's successor. He is actually a blustery type, but not the worst. His name is Braun.[†]

Emil Bock: The one who wrote about Schelling?

Rudolf Steiner: Yes. There is also one of your colleagues who wants to get his doctorate in Basel—Altemüller.[†] He also is part of your circle.

Hermann Heisler: Lauer, Doldinger …

Rudolf Steiner: They are theologians. I am convinced that among other students are those who take the reverse course.—[To *Gottfried Husemann*:] You studied chemistry, did you not?—Once there is a movement, there will be philosophers who transfer to religious practice. This Mrs. Plincke†—isn't she interested also? Many people will undoubtedly come around to theology.

A participant: I would like to ask how we could get the lectures, "Bibel und Weisheit" [Bible and wisdom].†

Rudolf Steiner: I will check into that when I go to Berlin. There were still copies on hand. Frau Dr. Steiner will know. I will see if there are copies.

A participant: Perhaps there are also other texts?

Rudolf Steiner: I will have the lectures looked at. I have spoken many times about the relationship to religion. It is extraordinarily difficult—especially because of the large amount of literature produced by theologians—to come to a conclusion with people. When one refutes something, they twist it around to say something else. One is never done with them. It is much easier to write something than to speak about it with people. For their own purposes, such people cannot be truthful. This leads them to speak untruths in other areas also. They find it totally appropriate to speak untruths. For example, in the article in which Traub† did what I mentioned before, he was so brazen as to write that he could no longer remember my "Cultural Appeal" and also that he had not read it carefully, but he could only say that he has seldom seen something so pompous. You can find that in the essay that he wrote as a supposed authority. His essay is full of such things. It contains the "wonderful" statement: "Anthroposophy calls itself a secret science: however, what is secret is not a science." He calls this a self-contained contradiction—an oxymoron. Above all, "esoteric science" is not secret, but even if it were, that would not preclude its being a science. "Secret" and "science" are two things that have nothing to do with each other. Such literature is terrible. It teems with such statements. One of our members[†] took the trouble to pull together all of the concrete untruths in Frohmeyer's booklet.[†] I believe there were 183.

Let us meet again at 8:00 a.m. tomorrow.

Lecture 6

STUTTGART, JUNE 16, 1921

My dear friends, I want to add to some things we have discussed. Later, it will be possible to bring something concrete about what you have to teach, as well as about the ritual. Today I wish to say something about how, first, you can find the way, the inner path, that holds teaching together with the ritual; and then, second, how you can find the path that leads over to modern science, which is completely lacking in ritualistic thinking. You need only to understand the matter correctly, but precisely this understanding is so far removed for modern consciousness. I will give an example through which you will see that today what is material—what human beings perceive through their senses and then combine with the intellect to come to the so-called laws of nature and history—is placed alongside what is called spiritual.

We must always bear in mind that an outer dimming of consciousness entered the Western evolution. (In another way it was necessary for the development of civilization.) This dulling down occurred in connection with the relationship between what is bodily-physical, on the one hand, and soul-spiritual, on the other. This occurred as a consequence of the well-known Eighth Ecumenical Council of 869[†] which established the dogma that the threefoldness that existed until that time—namely, that the human being consisted of body, soul, and spirit—was to be replaced with the duality that the human being is made up of body and soul alone. This dogma was formulated as follows: "The Christian must believe that the human being consists of only body and soul; and the soul has some spiritual characteristics." Thus, the trichotomy was replaced by a dualism, and a few spiritual characteristics were assigned to the soul. Modern philosophy, which claims to be an unbiased science and to draw only from experience, repeats what has come as dogma since the year 869. Philosophy speaks only of body and soul, and does not know that, in doing so, it is only complying with the decision of the Council of 869. The effects of the council have penetrated right into the worldly philosophy. This is something you must be thoroughly familiar with, if you want to look at the fact that the actual trinity in the human being was covered up in the ninth century, and that since then difficulties in the interpretation of the world have increased.

In other words it was as a consequence of this that the situation came about in which what is bodily-physical was gradually so separated from the spiritual that human beings were impelled to look upon the bodily-physical as if it were absolutely void of spirit, spiritless, and to speak of the soul-spiritual as something totally abstract. Just try to become clear about what people today think or imagine when you place the three aspects of the trinity—the soul forces of thinking, feeling, and willing—before them. Look at modern textbooks on psychology and see what nonsense is written about thinking, feeling, and willing. And look at what was accomplished in this regard by—as was rightly said—*Philosophen von seines Verlegers Gnaden* [Philosophers by the grace of his publisher], namely, Wilhelm Wundt,[†] who certainly started from a psychology of will, but nowhere revealed that he had any idea of the essential nature of the will.

It is entirely the case that those who are really able to study the soul see in the structuring of the soul nature into thinking, feeling, and willing a structuring like that which exists in the human being when one distinguishes youth, mature adulthood, and old age. These three characterizations refer to three different conditions of the one spiritual nature.

What exists in thinking or representation is an inheritance of our pre-existence, of our life before conception. The spiritual aspect that we may call the thinking in our soul may be characterized as what is aged, as what has grown old. It needed the period between death and a new birth in order to develop. The oldest aspect of our spirit is thinking. Feeling is in the middle, and willing differs from thinking in that it is spirit that is only in its childhood. When we consider human beings spiritually, when we describe them from the point of view of soul, we must say that they bring with them into life something aged that simply involves itself. They then develop themselves gradually into the middle stage, into feeling, and then they evolve the will that only at the end of life becomes so strong that it can lead to the dissolving of the body. For it is the will that essentially, in the end, when it is fully strengthened, brings about the disintegration of the body. The will is that aspect of the human being that presses constantly toward disintegration; it is what works to break down or dissolve. Spiritually, it is nothing other than a youthful form of thinking, which, when we age physically, begins to develop itself further. It can develop itself further still when we pass out of earthly life into the life between death and a new birth.

In this way, we come gradually to see into the interrelationship of our soul and the bodily natures within one another. We can do the same with our spiritual nature, so that we can come to see spirit, soul, and body within one another. Whoever studies this knows that at the moment of awakening, when we wake up from sleep, the spirit is most active so as to penetrate the body. It is then that the spirit manifests itself the most outwardly, because it is penetrating the body. It is while they are awakening that human beings show the most powerful spiritual activity in relation to the physical. It is then that they overcome the physical most powerfully. On the other hand, it is while going to sleep that they show the greatest flight from the activity of the physical. We do not grasp the nature of the human being if we do not consider this activity of the spiritual.

What we must strive for is to see the spirit, soul, and body penetrating each other again. We must see spirit, soul, and body working in each other; we must not see matter without spirit, nor see spirit without matter. We should see that which is creative—what is productive, what even forms matter out of itself. We should see the unified working of spirit and matter everywhere. When we look at our pre-existence, at life before conception, our spirit is working in the cosmos. And Anthroposophy teaches us gradually to interpret phenomena that are outside in nature, in such a way that they are also revelations of human existence as it is on the other side of the threshold, beyond earthly, physical existence.

I am telling you all of this only in order to point out a phenomenon that one can see everywhere today in which people, on the basis of church dogma, try to fight "scientifically"—as they put it—against Anthroposophy.

You see, as the Mystery of Golgotha was taking place, a working together of matter and spirit existed everywhere in the Middle East, Greece, and on into Northern Africa and Italy, in what was then called science or *Mathesis.*† Matter separate from spirit was not known then. One saw the spirit working everywhere. Augustine encountered this, but did not understand it. We understand his great struggle only when we learn that Augustine went through decadent Manichaeism.† The view that Augustine could no longer understand, and which was present at that time in the Middle East, North Africa, Greece, Italy, Sicily, and indeed even farther afield, is what people then later usually designated as *Gnosis.*

Anthroposophy absolutely does not seek to be a renewal of Gnosis. Gnosis is the last phase of the old atavistic science, whereas Anthroposophy represents the first phase of a fully conscious science. It is calumny when the two are thrown together. Since I began by mentioning this, I may be allowed to say that Gnosis was the first attempt to understand the Mystery of Golgotha. Gnosis was a deep spiritual science—even if of an instinctive, atavistic kind—that tried to understand the Mystery of Golgotha at that time. Gnosis, which was widespread at the time, was then completely eradicated. It was destroyed so completely that only little in a positive way remains—only a few writings that say very little. The form of Christianity that had gradually become quite Roman and had permeated Christianity with Roman ideas about the state saw to it that anything still remaining of the initial understanding of a spiritualized Christianity in Gnosis was completely eradicated. When theologians today speak about Gnosis, they know of it only from its opponents. Harnack and others expressed their doubts[†] about what Hilgenfeld[†] and other opponents of Gnosis proposed.

Imagine that all Anthroposophical literature were destroyed. Then there would come for future generations only the writings of General von Gleich,[†] and so on, and those of theologians who oppose Anthroposophy. If future generations were then to try to reconstruct it from these people's quotes, what we would have of Anthroposophy would be the same thing as what theologians today have of Gnosis. You must be quite clear what untruths theologians have loosed into the world. What happens today is just as thoroughly untruthful. The falsehood is not seen, because people always say that the holy people could not do such things; it simply could not happen. However, there it is, even though one believes that it cannot be. One absolutely does not imagine that such immorality can exist.

You will find the necessary enthusiasm only if you can summon up moral indignation with regard to what is presented in this historical research. The effect of this on world evolution, however, is that the understanding of the interweaving and interworking of spirit and matter have been completely lost. Because of this, nothing of what existed is left but only an outer, totally abstract verbal understanding.

Today, my dear friends, the Lord's Prayer is taught in the congregations in the form presented in Matthew's Gospel: "…but deliver us from evil;[†] for thine is the kingdom, the power, and the glory forever. Amen." No modern theologian who teaches the Lord's Prayer understands its closing sentence. Because of the way the theologians handled Gnosis, spiritualized Christianity, the understanding of this last sentence has been covered with nonsense (actually garbage). What does it mean?

The closing of the Lord's Prayer was linked in the Mysteries from which it was taken with a specific symbol—with guiding over one's whole consciousness into symbolic contemplation. It was said, when one selects a symbol for the "kingdom," it is this (see plate 3, p. 182). The boundary is the symbol for the kingdom. The kingdom encompasses a certain area. However, it only makes sense to speak of the "kingdom" when we picture this area within its boundary, when we picture the extent to which the kingdom, the area, reaches.

Such a kingdom, however, has a meaning not just when it is a limited area, but when a force streams through it, when it is permeated with a force. The force must sit in the center-point and radiate through the kingdom. Thus you have something that spreads out through the area of the kingdom. The force that rays out from the center-point is the "power." The radiating force that rules the kingdom is the "power."

All of this would, however, take place in the interior, within the "kingdom." If only this were present, this kingdom with the power would stand there closed up within itself. It would exist only for itself. It is there for others in the world, for other beings, only when what rays out reaches the edge or surface, and rays out from there into the surroundings: so that what rays out into the world is a radiance found on the surface: a "glory." The raying out from within is the power. The power that sits fast on the surface and shines outward from there is the glory. When you look at this picture—which leads completely into *Mathesis*—in a clear or graphic imagination of what can be thought with the concepts of kingdom, power, and glory, then you have this guiding-over-into *Mathesis* or contemplative representation, imagination. Then you seek to find in the outer reality what you have in soul-spiritual contemplation. You look at what you have grasped in *Mathesis*; you seek it in the external world; and you find it in the Sun, because that is the image of it. And instead of ending the Lord's Prayer with the words used in Protestantism ("...for thine is the kingdom, the power, and the glory"), you can also close it with the words: "... for thine is the Sun."

Every being was viewed as a trinity. Those who still know something of the true Gnostic knowledge know that the closing of the Lord's Prayer was prayed simply in such a way that the members of the solar trinity were expressed in words. The Gnostics were aware that, when one closes the Lord's Prayer, after having made the seven petitions and referred to oneself, one actually says the following: "deliver us from the evil, for you, who live in the Sun, you are the one who makes this possible." Everywhere there was a consciousness that external nature is not unspiritual. There was a consciousness that it was permeated with spirit everywhere. They found the means to make the spirit in nature present to themselves, because they had the working and effects of this trinity everywhere.

Look at the objective facts, and read all the accusations that are made—even if they are untrue—when people want to prove that Anthroposophy is supposed to be a renewal of Gnosis. Everywhere people take great pains to place Gnosis in a bad light, and then to say, "Whoever is a Gnostic today leads humanity back into the fog again." What is theology trying to do? It is trying to distract people from what existed before the Council of Constantinople (of 869), and from what existed especially strongly before Emperor Justinian closed the last of the Greek schools of philosophy† in the sixth century. This then caused the last of the philosophers to flee, under the leadership of Damascius, Simplicius, and five others, to Asia. They found refuge in Gondishapur,† where philosophers still could work; but this work was then also completely wiped out.

It is absolutely necessary today that the opposition between a merely abstract verbal science—which counts as science today—and the view of reality as permeated with spirit be overcome. People must return to this view of reality permeated with spirit. Without this view, founding a religion, a way of a religious working, is absolutely impossible.

And if you want to speak out of ritual, you must gradually advance to an understanding of the outer world. You must be able to see the power, the kingdom, and the glory objectified in the Sun. You find this expressed in many instances throughout almost the whole Gospel. You need only understand it as being expressed in a language in which the Word flows consciously over into what is created, formed in the world out of the spirit. You will really understand the Gospel only if you imbue yourself with this consciousness.

Now, if we focus on this, we can then see how far modern science—in spite of its believing itself to be wholly realistic—is from the true reality. For you see, what happened was that, after the debris had buried the understanding of reality—as happened to the understanding that the Sun is contained in the closing words of the Lord's Prayer—and after it had gone so far that everyone who connects the concept of the Sun with the Christ is deemed unchristian—the time came when people no longer understood how the experiences of the soul relate to reality.

In the ninth century after Christ, a person like John Scotus Eriugena† could still find harmony between what the soul experienced and what was outside in the physical, sense-perceptible world. But during this time there also arose gradually other views, in which people thought up concepts and began to brood over the question of whether their concepts had anything at all to do with reality. Then came the time of the Scholastics, of Albertus Magnus and Thomas Aquinas,† who had a last resonance of the old consciousness. They felt something of the fact that concepts and ideas have meaning only when they can be found outside in the world as reality. With them the realism of early Scholasticism was realized. The others, who had lost the consciousness of the harmony of ideas with reality, developed Nominalism. They were the forerunners of modern theology. They held those to be heretics who spoke of a connection or harmony of the Sun with the kingdom, power, and glory. The great quarrel between Nominalism and Realism† flowed from the decree of the Council of 869, which spread darkness over the view that the human being consists of body, soul, and spirit. Today we have come so far that we see a polemic unfolding when it is pointed out that the words in the Lord's Prayer, "thine is the kingdom, the power, and the glory forever. Amen," inwardly, soul-spiritually signify Christ, while outwardly what is meant is what corresponds to him in the outer environment: namely, the Sun. What this means is that, if we want to summarize the trinity of the kingdom, the power, and the glory outwardly, we say, "for thine is the Sun"; and if we want to contemplate what is inner and soul-spiritual, we address the Father God, who persists and subsists, and say, "for thine is the Son, Christ Jesus. He is with you."

The Protestant Church has become quite unconscious of these things. It knows nothing of them, and does not know why it knows nothing, because it does not inform itself about the nature of such things. The Catholic Church has preserved the tradition and knows a great deal about it; especially in the Jesuit Order, a lot is known. However, the Jesuits comply with religious politics as follows: "It is said that if people were to realize again that besides the body and soul, the spirit is also at work, they would then not be far from the path toward the suprasensible. We must prevent the people from knowing anything about the spirit."

From this you see that, precisely in Jesuitism, in which an outstanding scientific capability is fostered, a scientific politics is complied with and, indeed, in the following way. They say to themselves that the world today demands science in the sense of what is called science since the time of Galileo and Copernicus. The Catholic Church resisted this science until 1829. Only then were the Catholics allowed—*ex cathedra*—to believe that the Earth revolves around the Sun. Since then, Catholicism follows a different politics. Namely, its politics is now to carry the politics of Gailiean and Copernican natural science into the most extreme materialism. For this reason, you will find everywhere in the Jesuit-inspired literature the position that science should occupy itself only with what is sense-perceptible. Science should remain with what is spatial and temporal, and it cannot rise to what goes beyond what is spatial and temporal. By this means, they seek to force humanity to stop at a science that speaks only of the spatial-temporal aspect of the world. The rest is referred to the realm of faith, which encompasses only what is decreed by the infallible pope, or his advisory council. Thus, Jesuitism practices in the most extreme manner a strict separation between what should be the domain of science and what should be *believed*. The Jesuits shine in the realm of materialistic science. Indeed, no one has gone so far in taking up materialism as the Jesuit scientists have. Jesuits educate their students to become especially smart researchers in the materialistic scientific field and shine there. The Jesuits do this in order to make all the greater impression when they say, Science should never hold forth on what Christ gave the pope as his right as the representative of spiritual doctrine. Expressed dogmatically: Christians must see the head of the Catholic Church as the owner of divine teaching. By this dogma, science was evermore firmly attached to the outer realm of matter, preventing the spiritualization of science.

You see, my dear friends, there was a Strauß, a Renan, a Büchner, a Bölsche; and there was a Haeckel, who in his heart was not a materialist, and only through the sheer quantity of his works appears to be so. There have been many materialists, but they were like orphans. They were no match for what was accomplished in materialism in the way I have just described. The actual creators of materialism in the area of science were the theologians of the last four centuries. In the church it was difficult to resist the scientific materialism that was breaking in.

Think for a moment about how little a person such as Oetinger[†] was understood. He said, "All material manifestations are the last manifestations of the spirit."[†] By this, he meant that what is present outside in the creation comes originally from the spirit. He meant that, in that the spirit creates, it comes to an end, to its most outward expression, and thereby creates material manifestations. You find this wonderful presentation intermixed with nebulous mysticism, but projecting into it are such nuggets of a spiritualized worldview. You must be clear, when you read the works of such people as Oetinger, that you cannot accept everything, but that you must let yourself be stimulated by much that you find there. You must see the concepts that appear like bolts of lightning from a fully spiritualized worldview.

This is what I wanted to say in order to characterize a little for you the relationship of the development of theology and of science. Just as the universities arose out of the foundations created by theologians, so too our modern science—even though it manifests itself in a worldly fashion—is the result of the development of theology. We must always remember that in the founding of materialism people like Strauß, Büchner, and so on are orphans compared to what the theologians accomplished.

On the other side, another element worked its way into the scientific movement, and that element came from the East. You see, in the southern parts of Europe people turned away from the early stream of spiritual life since the middle of the fourth century after Christ to the time when Justinian executed the final act: closing down the Academy of Athens and driving out the seven main Athenian philosophers, who were actually a kind of international society.[†] Among them were Damascius, Simplicius, and other philosophers. They took with them the last remnants of Aristotelian knowledge, which was itself already in a kind of decadence as compared with

Gnosis. This Aristotelian knowledge was implanted in the spiritual wave that then traveled, by way of Arabia, to Spain; and we see how in the eleventh, twelfth, and thirteenth centuries a wave surged from there to the West. From this came what exerted a strong influence on minds such as Roger Bacon[†] and is clearly perceptible in Spinoza's philosophy, which, in turn, had such a great influence on Goethe.[†]

Through the flowing together of feeling- or heart-Christianity —which lived on as true Christianity in contrast to theological Christianity—and the force that came from those involved in the migration of the peoples, one stream of Christianity spread. This Christianity did not deliver an outer science of the world like the other stream, which arose because the Aristotelian knowledge was brought via the Arabs to Spain, and which from there had such a great influence on Spinoza. Within this knowledge that influenced Spinoza was contained what has influenced modern science for centuries. From the beginning modern natural science proceeded out of a kind of protest ... [gap in text], which is always called "to lose God." It can only lose, but never stop, God. There arose the new science devoid of God; and in relation to nature, it is a true science, one however that cannot go beyond certain boundaries. And yet, at the same time, it furthered the education of the human being toward freedom. Today we have reached the point at which the spiritualization must be sought out of science itself. Science must be led out of a merely anthropological science—which knows nothing more about the human being than the bodily aspect, which can produce only empty words about the soul, and which knows absolutely nothing about the spirit—to an Anthroposophical science, through which matter imbued with spirit will be recognized, especially with regard to the human being.

If we do this, we can bring about the moment when science and religious life meet in such a way that people will again find the spirit in all material things and overcome the view that there could be a material thing anywhere that would not lead one to the spirit. If you permeate yourself with this consciousness, if it gains such power in you that, when you deliver a sermon, you speak out of this consciousness, then you will find precisely in your area of work the possibility of seeking access to human hearts, and not merely to human intellects. Even though it would not seem so in the beginning, you will gradually have to find the way to the hearts of people by speaking out of the power that comes to you when you raise your consciousness to the point of grasping matter as permeated by spirit. Without coming to the consciousness that all matter is imbued with spirit, you cannot achieve a really living conception of God.

But if you want to speak in the full sense of your intention, then what you say must be an outer expression of what is meant in the Prologue to the Gospel of John: "In the beginning was the Word …" The way in which the "Word," the "Logos," is presented there points out that the Logos was present before matter came into being, and matter proceeded from the Logos. You must unite this knowledge with the other: that, when you speak, you can let resound from your words what you yourself experience in your heart and soul when, through spiritual insight, you feel the divine within you and prepare yourself for the duty of preaching in god-sensing meditation. In this living dedication to speaking—not only in the abstract preparation of the content of your teaching—but in this meditative preparation for every single sermon, the power must arise in you through which you can achieve the building of community.

This is what I wanted to impress upon you today. I ask you to take it up in such a way that it is felt more than thought. I hope that it will be allowed for us to continue these studies when we come together again.

Now it is likely that yesterday some of you still had one or two things you wished to bring into the discussion.

Emil Bock: I thought yesterday evening that today we could present the text for the publicity.† I do not know, however, if it can remain in this form.

Rudolf Steiner: We will, in any case, stay in touch; and even if you leave today, you will let me know if I am to give advice, so that I can do so. Do you have an idea of the essentials that should be included in this publicity?

Emil Bock: As far as we have thought about it, we want to take the approach that we begin with the idea of the predicament of religious life in relation to intellectualism. Then we would refer to the need for a new worldview in which religion is possible: the need to achieve a religious renewal precisely through a worldview renewal. We want further to point out how we think of this as occurring through an enlivening of the pictorial, imaginative element, and so on. We could then say something about the fact that it has to do with a special renewal of Christianity. We also want to say that we intend to work in relation to ecclesiastical work. Then a transition must be found for an appeal to the joy of giving. We can do this only if the possibility of a free spiritual life exists. Spiritual life must be freed through a deed, that is, through a contribution. Thereby spiritual life shall be free in one area—to begin with in the realm of religion. As far as I could tell, this was the line of thought with which we were in agreement at the moment. We were not sure, however, whether or not we have captured the right ideas.

Rudolf Steiner: You have a number of ideas, which are, in any case, correct. I would only point out—so that you find the right tone and substance—the following: everything that comes from Anthroposophy stands on the ground of reality and always aims never to lose the ground of reality. The Movement for the Threefold Social Organism† began in the spring of 1919, at the time when, especially across Central Europe, there was an expectant mood among many sections of the population. Of course, the expectant mood was different in various places, but it was there. I simply wish to say that a majority of people believed that we had been thrown into chaos, and that we must progress by harmonizing societal forces in a reasonable way. This mood was quite widespread when I began working for the Threefold Social Organism in April 1919.

Now, at that time, growing out of the form that I gave my lectures on the threefold impulse, I quite often closed these lectures with the statement that what is meant there must be made a reality very soon, because it could very soon be too late. You can find this formulation, "It could very soon be too late," stated frequently in the transcripts of the lectures given at that time. It was the time when people still could have set up something in the form that I formulated, if the opposition had not grown so strong, and had not become such a great power. Now the situation today is that since that time a reactionary wave has arisen in Central Europe. It is stronger than one thinks, and we must take it absolutely seriously. This does not affect the *principle* of the threefold impulse. It will last. But the way in which we sought to realize it at that time will no longer work. What is thought out of the reality of the time is thought out for that time only, and we would enter into abstraction if we did not want to accept or see this. Today we are at the point where, in order to come out of the chaos, we must say that we must seek new forms. If we want to present the Threefold Social idea, we can no longer approach the world with the same formulas. Today it is absolutely, unconditionally important that we find above all something that can lead to some light. As uncomfortable as it might sound, what we need today is to shine a light into the whole world of untruthfulness that permeates our spiritual life. We must shine a light into the untruthfulness of the spiritual life. That is the one thing: the negative thing. The positive thing is that, as quickly as possible, we must bring one part of the Threefold Social Organism—the freeing of spiritual life—to fulfillment. Because we cannot initiate the Threefold Social Order in the form with which we began to do so in 1919, we must work less abstractly with the task of threefolding. The opposition to it is too great today. Only knowing what the power of the time is contains what can still protect us from the "null," as Spengler called it. Only this knowledge can protect us from the approach of the calamity, the downfall. You must see to it that you advance the establishment of an independent spiritual life.

Economists are so bogged down and corrupted in their views that there is no question of their understanding the Threefold Social Organism: they can never be moved to accept it. How little the Threefold Social Organism is understood in the area of economics confronts us to a terrible degree. Let me give you an example: in the beginning, when we held a meeting about the threefold impulse here in Stuttgart, the well-known chairman of a well-known party—we had formed a large committee, and he was on it—came to me and said, "As far as threefolding is concerned, it would certainly be quite wonderful if we do it, but for the time being no one understands it. People understand it only when you speak to them about it"—I say this not from a lack of modesty, but only to illustrate something by this example— "and nothing can be built that is based on only two eyes. We know that in fifteen to twenty years the last of what we still have will succumb to a calamity. We could still delay or check this calamity today if we went ahead with the Threefold Social Organism. But no one else knows about it. So we would rather use old ideas for the next fifteen to twenty years than use your threefold idea."

This is an example of the understanding that the politics of the issue produced. We can only hope that we can begin to collect the last remnants of spiritual impulses and, through them, try to free spiritual life in the realms—the sub-areas—of religion, art, and science. Each of the three parts of the Threefold Social Organism has three sub-areas. The three sub-areas or parts of the spiritual realm are religion, science, and art. If we can succeed in freeing spiritual life then—perhaps sooner than we think—there will be people who come on their own, based on the model of free spiritual life, to an understanding of equality in the political life, and of brotherhood in economic life. The first thing is therefore to work with all our strength for the independence of the one part of the Threefold Social Organism. For the time being, the important thing is to work to free the religious realm. This is what you must do. We must not use the word "threefolding" abstractly, but must use it concretely by placing the highest value on freeing one area that has been particularly ruined by untruthfulness. It would be an illusion if we were not to see how rapidly we are heading toward calamity or collapse. If one looks at the facts, one actually cannot imagine that we could continue doing business in the way we are doing it very much longer. The interest on the debts of the German Reich for last year (1920–21) is 85 billion Reich marks, and that is only the interest and not the debt itself. It is said that taxes for the residents of Central Europe must be raised threefold. How could anyone manage it? There are people today who pay 60 percent of their income in taxes. If they had to pay three times as much in taxes, they would have to pay 180 percent of their income. I ask you to think about how anyone should be able to pay 180 percent of their income, and how the logic of reality must look to people who speak about public affairs. We are about to slip into the most terrible chaos. Furthermore, we must say that today matters are still always presented falsely.

A while ago I held a lecture for a group of industrialists† and pointed out the true fact that city budgets are on the verge of failing. These city budgets have managed to maintain themselves, because the savings banks were able to make the necessary correction. But you can only go so far with a correction of this kind, and then the coffers are empty. You can keep an old coat if you do not have the means to buy a new one. You keep wearing the old clothes, just as one today keeps carrying on the old economic practices. But one day the old clothes will fall off your body. It is only an illusion when people feel comfortable and speak of progress. We are absolutely in decline.

If we can rescue spiritual life, then civilization will also be saved. But it is necessary to become conscious again of how times change. Do not misunderstand me. I am not saying that we must drop the Threefold Social impulse. However, the way we pursued it in 1919, the way it would have been possible then by the establishment of the three parts of the threefold order next to one another is no longer possible. Today we have to rescue what can still be rescued—and that is what is present in human souls. We must, of course, try to attain the freeing of spiritual life.

And so we come to an end.

Emil Bock: Since we are finished, let me express on behalf of the participants in this course our honest, heartfelt thanks. We cannot put it into words, but we believe we have tried to make a start to manifest it through our work. We are indeed grateful, and gratitude can be rendered only through deeds. I believe I can speak from the hearts of the participants when here, as it were, in a small rousing of our forces, I make a promise that we will do what we are able to do.

Rudolf Steiner: I do not need to say anything more, except that it has provided me with a deep, inner satisfaction that you have found your way to this work. May there grow, especially out of this work, something that is of value in the Anthroposophical life. It will be quite significant, if precisely that part of spiritual life, which is your part, is stimulated through this Anthroposophical life. I hope that we understand one another inwardly, and that we remain united in the work and meet again. Till we meet again!

APPENDIX

Blackboard Drawings

*

Notebook Entries

*

Promotional Piece
with facsimilie of the rough draft

*

Chronological Overview

*

List of Participants

Plate 1

Third and fourth lectures, June 14, 1921, Stuttgart

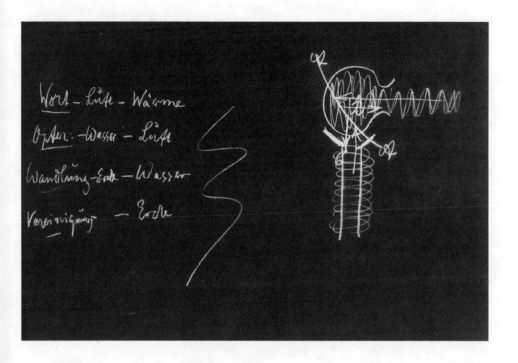

Plate 2

Fourth lecture, June 14, 1921, Stuttgart

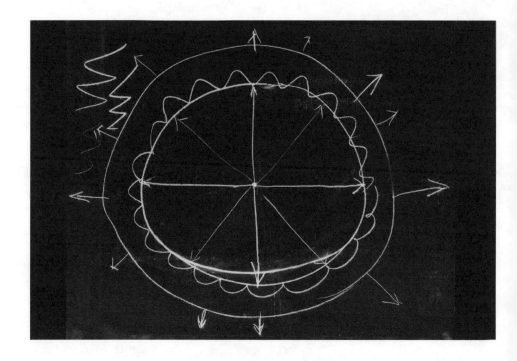

Plate 3

Sixth lecture, June 16, 1921, Stuttgart

Notebook Entries

Theology/ Goodness in the Word through the image
Hilarius: per mansuetudinem / mentis nostrae habitat / Christus in nobis. –
Overcoming the self: Goodwill improves human beings. – praedicate evangelium =
Appeal to the feeling life: Clique formation. Communities want to be held together by
what is objective. –

Develop the spiritual mood in relation to knowing. The work of the human being into a spiritual matter –

Brotherhoods / In knowing, something from the spirit. Receive – in the ritual. Give in return – life in the spirit

Act of office = 1.) divine existence – 2.) to live love – 3.) active, working love. –

Faith: one must know that which one believes.

Bock: Practical: from the church or the Anthroposophical communities.
Discussions: All ways – loose union –
        Office – letters
        Central office = Berlin. Money under the name of Der Kommonde Tag.

Rel. 13. Juni 1921:

Soziale Gemeinschaft unvollkommen —

In relation to June 13, 1921 (Discussion): Social community imperfect –

The theodicy question – Trinity, creation, the Fall, salvation = grace = (birth – death).
Chosen relationship, or elective affinity.
Perfection. Evil.
Perfection or completion presupposes a state of being imperfect or incomplete.
Evil presupposes that it is the foundation of something good –
Death – recognized as the prerequisite of consciousness –

Knowledge must not give up, but expand sense perceptions – is also not to prove, but to experience, also the suprasensible, what is seen spiritually.
God and immortality. Soul – body =
One must build the sermon on selflessness (state of not yet being born, before birth) and not on egotism – on life after death.

Theology. June 15, 1921
The public work. Course for 100 people –
Brochures 3 articles: 1. Cultural situation; 2. Ritual; 3. Communication of the doctrine/
Rituals. Anthroposophy. Religious renewal. Registry Office, Berlin.
Lectures Haass-Berkow

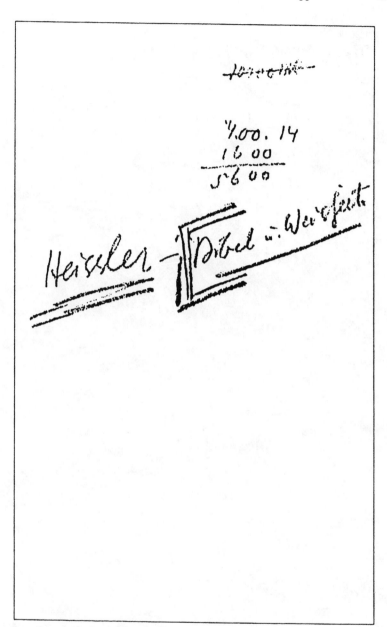

Heis[s]ler – Bible and Wisdom.

With Facsimilies of the rough draft of the promotional piece
in the handwriting of Gottfried Husemann
and corrections by Rudolf Steiner

A Way to the Necessary Renewal of Religion

The form in which religious life is lived today is not such that it could express what underlies contemporary humanity's religious will. Human beings could unite in their most sacred feelings if they could let these feelings live in community. But the antiquated form of religious life prevents this from happening. This is why we do not have religious community, but rather religious parties. Religion can thrive, however, only in community.

Today, from the most varied perspectives, attention is repeatedly drawn to the connection of these facts with the dreadful social upheavals of our time, and the healing of our circumstances is often thought to depend on a renewal of religious life. In order to bring this about, we must contemplate how we came to such a fragmentation and hollowing out of the religious realm.

We can follow, first of all, how over the past four hundred years intellectualism as the youngest of the human soul forces underwent an impressive development, on the one hand, producing, in a beneficial way, a new culture through technology and industry. We can see how it wants to make the individual independent and free. On the other hand, we can also follow how, in a dangerous way, it took the place of the old religious practices based on ritual and symbolism with the result that, since the Reformation, a sermon- and doctrine-oriented church arose. The process of fragmentation, which began with the separation of Protestantism from Catholicism, continues to intensify, but the facts of the course of evolution show that, if we want to take seriously the demand of our age for freedom of personal conviction, we cannot found community on creed and doctrinal content. Anything about which opinions are possible must lead to the individualizing and atomizing of community—but only a united community builds a basis for religion. Any attempt at renewal, insofar as it proceeds from differences in doctrine and opinion, leads to the expansion of sectarianism.

The development of the intellectual forces led to the concept of causality—which is justified in the sense world—being extended to the whole of reality. Because of this development, the existence of a suprasensible, divine-spiritual world became an impossibility, and religion appears to be an illusion. The more the knowledge of the universe was built simply on mere natural scientific ideas, the less room remained for any of the religious riches that were handed down. The reality and meaning of the symbolism that sprang from old philosophical forces was no longer recognized. Doctrine and the need for information stepped to the forefront. This whole relationship is not yet grasped by enough people today, yet understanding of precisely this is necessary for a healing of our cultural life.

The destiny of the will to rejuvenate religion—which appears everywhere today—depends on whether people, while preserving their personal freedom in relation to philosophical questions and the doctrine of the church, can find their way back to living in pictures—images—and symbols. We must find a way of knowing that can penetrate into the suprasensible realm where concepts form themselves into pictures, which can form the foundation of a unifying ritual, and where the causality of the sense world no longer is valid or effective. Today we can develop a way of knowing of this kind, and here we may point to Anthroposophical spiritual science, without immediately wanting to find or base a dogma in or on it. Out of knowledge gained in this way, a ritual can be formed once more that provides the form of religious life appropriate for our age, one that will lead human beings, in the experience of their most sacred feelings, to unity, and lets the creeds seem unimportant.

We must solve our social and cultural problems. But only those people will be able to do so who, beyond their imaginative life and their ideals, can summon the substance of their will to create and sacrifice. A number of people are now courageously prepared to tread the path of religious renewal that presents itself. Because a craving for schematizing and bureaucracy still interferes today with spiritual life and the free use of spiritual forces, and because the religious communities relate to one another like economic competitors, the work that must be done for the benefit of humanity before it is too late is made unbelievably difficult. If there is freedom in this realm, the necessary work in the economic field will also have to be done. This is how much this corresponds to the deepest, most burning need of our fellow human beings. Because we want first to create freedom, we must turn—with the request for help and collaboration with regard to financial needs—to those people who deem a renewal of religion to be necessary, and to whom our way appears to be what will lead to the overcoming of the difficulty.

Ein Weg zur notwendigen religiösen Erneuerung

ausgehen kann von Lehrunterschieden und Meinungen, führt zur Erweiterung des Sektierertums.

Auf der andern Seite hat die Entfaltung der intellektualistischen Kräfte dazu geführt, daß eine für die sinnliche Welt berechtigte Auffassung von dem Causalnexus auf die ganze Wirklichkeit ausgedehnt wurde, wodurch die Existenz einer übersinnlichen, göttlich-geistigen Welt ausgeschlossen wird und ~~als~~ die Religion als eine Illusion der Menschen erscheint. Je mehr aus bloßen Daten naturwissenschaftlichen Vorstellungen die Erkenntnis vom Weltall aufgebaut wurde, desto weniger blieb in diesem Rahmen Platz für alles, was an religiösem Gut noch überliefert war. Die aus alten Anschauungskreisen entsprungene Symbolik wurde in ihrer Wirklichkeitsbedeutung nicht erkannt, der Lehrgehalt und das Aufklärungsbedürfnis der Menschen traten in den Vordergrund. ←

das Schicksal des religiösen Meinungsstreites, der heute überall zu Tage

tritt, hängt davon ab, ob man unter Wahrung der persönlichen Freiheit in bezug auf Weltanschauungsfragen und das Lehrgut der Kirche ~~der Kirche~~ den Weg zurückfinden kann zum Leben im Bilde und in der Symbolik. Eine Erkenntnis muß gefunden werden, die in das Gebiet vordringen kann, wo die Begriffe zu solchen Bildern sich gestalten, die einem einigenden Kultus zugrunde gelegt werden ~~müssen~~ können, und wo die Causalität dieser sinnlichen Welt nicht mehr gilt.
Eine solche Erkenntnis kann heute ausgebildet werden, wobei wir auf den Versuch der anthroposophischen Geisteswissenschaft hinweisen.
~~Aus einer solchen Erkenntnis~~ läßt sich wiederum ein Kultus gestalten, der die zeitgemäße Form des religiösen Lebens abgeben ~~würde~~ ~~wird~~, der die Menschen im Erleben ihres Heiligsten

ohne sofort wieder auf freien Boden eine Dogmatik führen zu wollen.

of the origin of the course in this volume, as well as further
courses that Rudolf Steiner held for the Movement
for Religious Renewal

February 7, 1920

The twenty-one-year-old philosophy student,Werner Klein came to
Dornach with his friends, Martin and Elisabeth Borchart. The three
friends listened to Rudolf Steiner's evening lecture (*What Is Needed in
These Urgent Times*) [CW 196]. Afterward Werner Klein asked Rudolf
Steiner for a personal conversation. This took place the following day.

February 8, 1920

Conversation of Werner Klein with Rudolf Steiner: In the course of
the conversation, Klein asked the question: "Has the time come to
prepare the way for a third Christianity, the Johannine Christianity?"
Klein reports about his meeting with Rudolf Steiner in his book,
Leben...wofür [Life...why], Hamburg 1979):

"In the evening we heard his lecture in the *Schreinerei* [Carpentry
shop], as the building was a large room set aside for this event. The
talk consisted, to an amazing extent, of a tirade against his followers (at the end of the lecture of February 8, 1920 [CW 196]). The
address, as surprising as it was, did me a lot of good, as one can easily
imagine. After the lecture I gathered my courage and approached the
almost delicate-looking man with dark eyes. He had already noticed
me. I made a short military bow. At the same time I asked for a
conversation. It was granted to me the next day.

"The conversation took place in front of a huge, powerful wooden
sculpture in the workshop. It was that figure upon which Rudolf
Steiner sculpted until the last days of his life. The conversation began
with general discussions about the Middle Ages and the Crusades.
When the moment came to bring my questions, I began by saying

that they concerned a theme which, in light of his views, he would most likely have to reject. But I still wanted to pose the questions, in order [perhaps] to hear his opinion.

"I said, 'In my philosophical studies I have become acquainted with the German Idealistic thinker, Schelling. He differentiated between Petrine, Pauline, and Johannine Christianity. He saw in them stages and paths of the one Spirit moving within the Christian realms. Petrine Christianity evidently appeared in Rome, not least through the power of the keys and the judgment sword of this church. The Pauline Christianity, in its rejection of justification through deeds and its conviction that only belief in the merciful grace of God can justify us, is just as transparent as the stigma of the Protestant Church. Also, it—as the second possible Christianity—seems to me to be outdated, and set aside by history. Question: Has the time come to prepare the way for a third Christianity, the Johannine Christianity? I see this Christianity essentially as a call for the maturity of the human spirit and its essential identity with the eternal. We are called to the power of the spirit springing from within ourselves. "God is spirit, and those who worship him shall worship him in spirit and in truth" (John 4:24). He is no longer to be worshipped only in Jerusalem, or at some other preferential place, or in the buried forms of the fathers. From this comes the task, not to wipe out Christianity, but quite the opposite: to increase and intensify it, and to read its documents in a new way. With this, Christianity began, in a certain sense, for the first time.'

"Rudolf Steiner listened attentively. Then he straightened and spoke with a thoughtful, clear voice: 'If you want to do this and find the necessary forms for it—the forms let themselves be found—this then signifies something great for humanity.' That was it. It was spoken. After a pause, as if returning to daily life, in a somewhat more lively fashion he added: 'You were right when you said that I cannot do that. My task is a different one. I have to bring spiritual science and speak to human beings out of it. I must remain with that. What you see is great and necessary, but you must do it yourself.'

"The words went through me like a stroke of joy. He saw the historical-religious task and affirmed it. It was the most that I could expect, although right here a seed of misunderstanding may have lain.

'The forms let themselves be found.' On this February morning a kind of Gentleman's Agreement was made between the leader of spiritual science and me. I had his consent. Also about the name of Johannine Christianity there was no doubt. Some people will wonder why I stress this so much, but it has to do with the life task I have set for myself. It concerned John and the John element. It was a matter of a third stage of Christianity. It was left to me, because it was not Rudolf Steiner's task.

"I saw my life's path before me. There was enough to study and contemplate. Much was to be entrusted to the ideas occurring in the spirit in its further development. It seemed to me at that time that in approximately forty years' time, the ideas and recommendations would be ready for me to make them public."

February 8, 1920

A theology student in Basel, Gertrud Spörri, posed the following question to Rudolf Steiner: "Is there a possibility for Anthroposophy to work within the church?" (from a letter by Gertrud Spörri to Marie Steiner on January 3, 1930.) Concerning her conversation with Rudolf Steiner, Gertrud Spörri reported:

"In April of the same year (1920) I asked Rudolf Steiner for a conversation. I had completed my maturation exams, and was enrolled to study theology in Basel. Dr. Steiner received me in front of the Christ sculpture. I told him that my goal was to study theology, in order later to serve Anthroposophy—when possible within the church, but if not, then outside of it. Rudolf Steiner then said: 'It would be quite possible to achieve something within the church, if a large number of young theologians attain pastoral positions.' In those days the first Architects' Course (March 21–April 9, 1920) was taking place. Dr. Steiner spoke of the possibility of a similar course for young theologians: 'In such a course, one could speak with the young people in a much more intimate manner than is possible as yet with the doctors.'"

April 1920–March 1921

Both Werner Klein and Gertrud Spörri evidently considered their respective conversations with Rudolf Steiner as a private concern.

Neither of them spoke of them even once with their close friends. This changed only the following year.

April 3–10, 1921

In Dornach two college courses took place (*The Fourth Dimension* [CW 76]). Werner Klein and Gertrud Spörri met one another during this course.

Report of Werner Klein, quoted according to Hans-Werner Schroeder in *Die Christengemeinschaft—Entstehung, Entwicklung, Zielsetzung* [The Christian Community—origin, development, goal], Stuttgart 1990:

"In the college course at Easter 1921 at the Goetheanum, I met Miss Spörri. She was a theologian. I poured out on her my whole bottled-up feelings concerning this study. I wanted to know what she actually wanted and hoped for. She felt pressed to defend her position and brought a statement from Rudolf Steiner. He had said to her that, concerning religious questions about the future, a course could be held with a yet more intimate character than was the case, for instance, with the doctors."

April–May 1921

Gertrud Spörri and Werner Klein decided to look for other like-minded people to join them in asking Rudolf Steiner for a course.

Week of Whitsun 1921

In Stuttgart, interested students from Marburg, Berlin, and Tübingen met together and worked on the content of a community letter to Rudolf Steiner.

May 1921

The following letter was written and given to Rudolf Steiner (the quote from Rudolf Steiner was taken from the lecture of February 20, 1917, in *Building Stones for an Understanding of the Mystery of Golgotha* [CW 175]):

"We are convinced that humanity today wants to attain spiritual development. Because of this and because 'The living practice of religion within human community enkindles spiritual consciousness,' we, the undersigned students, see a direction for activity that perhaps will have to be taken up out of the Anthroposophical Movement.

"We are reticent about the idea of priesthood as it is connected with what has existed so far in the church. It is a question for us as to whether something similar or something different must take its place. Because we believe that all further questions, about religious practice and work can be posed correctly only after this first question has been answered, we ask you to address this question.

"From the answer, the individuals listed below will be able to decide if they can fulfill the tasks needed."

Stuttgart, May 22, 1921

Werner Klein, student of philosophy
Gertrud Spörri, student of theology
Ludwig Köhler, student of theology
Gottfried Husemann, student of chemistry, earlier theology

"Those who have declared themselves of like mind:

Robert Spörri	theological candidate	Zürich
Wilhelm Clormann	theological candidate	Mannheim
Ludwig Nonnemacher	theological student	Mannheim
Walter Gradenwitz	theological student	Wiesbaden
Martin Borchart	theol. & phil. student	Marburg
Rudolf Meyer		Hamburg
Richard Gitzke	theological student	Berlin
Otto Franke	theological student	Berlin
Horst Münzer	theol. & phil. student	Berlin
Emil Bock	theological candidate	Charlottenburg
Eberhard Kurras	theological candidate	Saaleck (Thüringen)
Ernst Umlauff	student of philosophy	Breslau
Otto Becher	House Teacher	Holzmindening

Some signatures are missing."

Da nach unserer Überzeugung die Entfaltung des Geist-
bewußtseins dasjenige ist, was die gegenwärtige Menschheit zunächst
werden will und da außerdem „Religion in ihrem lebendigen
Leben, in ihrem lebendigen Erübrigsein innerhalb der menschlichen
Gesellschaft das Geistbewußtsein erfaßt", sehen die unterzeichneten
Studenten aus diesen Tatsachen eine Richtung sich ergeben für die
Tätigkeit, die sie aus der anthroposophischen Bewegung heraus vielleicht
auszuüben haben.

Da wir an den heute mit der Ausübung der Religion
verbundenen Begriff des Priestertums nur mit einer gewissen Scheu
herangehen können, solange einerseits dasselbe nur abgeleitet wird
von dem, was bis heute als priesterliche oder kirchliche Institution
angenommen ist und da wir andererseits nicht wissen, ob überhaupt
etwas ähnliches oder wie etwas anderes an dessen Stellen treten
muß; da wir schließlich glauben, daß alle weiteren Fragen nach
dem, was mit religiöser Übung und religiöser Betätigung um-
schreiben würde und nach dem, was als religiöses Milieu das
menschliche Leben von der Geburt bis zum Tode zu umgeben hat,
erst richtig gestellt werden können, nachdem auf diese erste Frage
eingegangen worden ist, bitten wir Herrn dr. Steiner von Hagen,
uns über diese Frage Auskunft zu geben.

Aus einer Antwort kann sich für den einzelnen ergeben, ob er
in diesem Zusammenhang Aufgaben zu erfüllen im Stande ist.

Stuttgart, den 22. Mai 1921

Werner Klein, stud. philos.
Gertrud Spörri, stud. theol.
Ludwig Köhler, stud. theol.
Gottfried Husemann, stud. chem. früher theol.

Bitte wenden!

In demselben Sinne haben eine Erklärung abgegeben:

Robert Spörri, cand. theol. Zürich
Wilhelm Cloormann, cand. theol. Mannheim
Ludwig Nonnenmacher, stud. theol. Mannheim
Walter Gradenwitz, stud. theol. Wiesbaden
Martin Borchart, stud. phil. et theol. Marburg
Rudolf Meyer, Hamburg
Richard Gitzke, stud. theol. Berlin
Otto Franke, stud. theol. Berlin
Horst Münzer, stud. phil. et theol. Berlin
Emil Bock, cand. theol. Charlottenburg
Eberhard Kurras; cand. theol. Saaleck (Thüring.)
Ernst Nunläuff, stud. phils. Breslau
Otto Becher, Hauslehrer, Holzminden

Es fehlen noch einige Unterschriften.

May 24, 1921

In a conversation with Werner Klein and Gertrud Spörri, Rudolf Steiner agreed to do a course in the middle of June.

June 12–16, 1921

The course presented in this volume was held. Participants: Eighteen students and five teachers who gave free religious instruction in the Waldorf school. (See the participant list later in this volume.)

June–September 1921

More people interested in a second course on religious renewal were found, increasing the size of the group.

September 26–October 10, 1921

In Dornach a course was held for theologians, with over one hundred participants present. In twenty-nine lectures and discussion periods, Rudolf Steiner spoke about the way spirit-knowledge can be brought into religious work and gave the first texts for forming a new ritual.

August 2, 1922

In Dornach a meeting was held at which Pastor Dr. Friedrich Rittelmeyer, Pastor Dr. Christian Geyer, and Lizent Emil Bock gave an orientation to those present concerning the upcoming founding of the Movement for Religious Renewal—planned for the following month. Rudolf Steiner gave a short talk. See *Beiträge zur Rudolf Steiner Gesamtausgabe* [Contributions to Rudolf Steiner's collected works], number 110, *The Spiritual Hierarchies and Their Reflection in the Physical World. Zodiac, Planets, and Cosmos.*

September 1922

Forty-five people—among them was the Protestant pastor Dr. Friedrich Rittelmeyer—went to Dornach to found the Movement for Religious Renewal. Rittelmeyer decided to become a coworker and to take on the leadership conferred on him. In accordance with an earlier suggestion from Rudolf Steiner, the Movement for Religious Renewal was named "The Christian Community." Rudolf Steiner accompanied the founding of The Christian Community with lectures, question-and-answer sessions, and an introduction to the new ritual.

July 11–14, 1923

Rudolf Steiner held four lectures in Stuttgart for the priests of The Christian Community.

September 1924

Among the last lectures that Rudolf Steiner gave in his life were a course for priests of The Christian Community on the Apocalypse of John, *Book of Revelation*, 18 lectures in Dornach, September 5–22, 1924 [CW 346], and a course for doctors and priests on pastoral medicine, *Broken Vessels*, 11 lectures, September 8–18, 1924 [CW 318].

List of the Participants

of the course held in Stuttgart, June 12–16, 1921

*Otto Becher	(1891–1954)	Teacher
*Emil Bock	(1895–1959)	theology candidate
*Martin Borchart	(1894–1971)	student of philosophy & theology
Wilhelm Clormann	(1889–1976)	theology candidate
*Otto Franke	(1897–1956)	student of theology
*Rudolf Frieling	(1901–1986)	student of theology
Fritz Gawandtka	(1900–?)	
*Richard Gitzke	(1896–1989)	student of theology
*Walter Gradenwitz	(1898–1960)	student of theology
*Gottfried Husemann	(1900–1972)	student of chemistry
*Thomas Kändler	(1901–1957)	student of theology
*Werner Klein	(1898–1984)	student of philosophy
*Ludwig Köhler	(1900–1985)	student of theology
*Eberhard Kurras	(1897–1981)	theology candidate
*Rudolf Meyer	(1896–1985)	theology candidate
Ludwig Nonnenmacher	(1897–?)	student of theology
*Gertrud Spörri	(1894–1968)	student of theology
Ernst Umlauff	(1896–?)	student of philosophy

At Rudolf Steiner's request:

Marie Steiner
and from the Waldorf school, those teachers who gave the free
religious instruction:

Ernst Uehli	(1875–1959)	7th Class
Herber Hahn	(1890–1970)	Classes 3a, 3b, 4a, 4b, 6, 9, 10
Leonie von Mirbach	(1890–1973)	Classes 1a, 1b, 2a, 2b

*Wilhem Ruhtenberg	(1888–1954)	Classes 5a, 5b, 8
Paul Baumann	(1887–1964)	music arrangements for the services and later, free religious instruction

And toward the end of the course:

*Hermann Heisler	(1876–1962)	Protestant pastor

* These individuals became priests of The Christian Community.

EDITORIAL AND REFERENCE NOTES

Concerning the Quality of the Documents for the German Edition

The publishers of the German edition preface their work by remarking that in publishing any of Rudolf Steiner's lectures—his spoken words—the editors are wholly dependent on the individual human beings who made the stenographical record or took notes on what Steiner said. The quality of the surviving text of Steiner's lectures thus always depends on the stenographer or note-taker's proficiency in stenography and notetaking; and also, equally importantly, on their ability to hear and understand what was said. Since Rudolf Steiner rarely reviewed the final text of his lectures, the possibility always arises of errors and omissions. In this case, that danger is more than usually present, for the original stenographic notes unfortunately no longer exist. The editors therefore had to rely on the first transcription of these notes because they had nothing to refer to.

The stenographer, Karl Lehofer, was a conscientious young man, a co-worker in the Scientific Research Institute of the *Kommende Tag*, but not a very practiced stenographer. When speakers spoke slowly, he could follow; but when they spoke more quickly, as they often did, he could not keep up and his handwriting fell apart and the legibility of his record suffered grievously. There were parts that even he could not decipher.

The German edition, prepared by Ulla Trapp and Paul G. Bellmann with the help of Hella Wiesberger and Klas Diederich, was based on the uncorrected first draft of Karl Lehofer's transcript, which had been typed and sent to various participants in the course without Lehofer having a chance to review it or work through any unclarities. The German editors did their best to make as accurate a text on this basis as they could and consulted a private printing of this course prepared by The Christian Community in 1978 to make comparisons. They did not feel justified, however, in making any adjustments for the sake of fluidity or smoothness. In this English edition, we have done what we can in this direction, while still striving to remain true to the original quality of the text. So, the text is now (we believe) quite readable and understandable.

Page 5 "Ritschl school of thought"
See Gustav Ecke's *Die theologische Schule Albrecht Ritschls und die evangelische Kirche der Gegenwart* [The theological school of Albrecht Ritschl and the protestant or evangelical church of the present], 2 volumes, Berlin 1897/1903. Concerning Albrecht Ritschl (1822–1889) himself, see Otto Ritschl's *Albrecht Ritschls Leben* [Albrecht Ritschl's life], 2 volumes. Bonn 1892/96. Ritschl taught Church History in Bonn, and then from 1864 on he taught systematic theology in Göttingen. His main work was *Die christliche Lehre von der Rechtfertigung und Versöhnung* [The Christian doctrine on justification and reconciliation], 3 volumes. Bonn 1870–74, fourth edition 1895–1902.

Page 7, "Paul's Letters would have to be omitted from the Gospels"
Paul's Letters are not a part of the Gospels, but of the New Testament. It could be that Rudolf Steiner actually referred to the New Testament here, and that it was an error on the part of the stenographer to refer to the Gospels.

Page 9, "Strauß'... [Old and new belief]"
David Friedrich Strauß: *Der alte und der neue Glaube. Ein Bekenntnis* [The old and the new belief. A creed], Bonn 1872.

Page 10, "'Ignorabimus'... Ranke in relation to the question of Christ"
"As I speak this name, 'Jesus Christ', I must, even though I am believed to be a good Protestant Christian, protest against the presumption that I could here undertake to talk about the religious Mystery, which, as incomprehensible as it is, cannot be ascertained historically. Just as little as I can deal with the Father God, just as little also can I do so with the Son God. The concepts of debt, satisfaction or amends, and redemption belong to the realm of theology and to the creed connecting the soul with the Godhead. For the historian it can only be a matter of making visible the combination of the world-historical moments in which Christianity appeared and through which its effect was determined." (Leopold von Ranke, *Weltgeschichte* [World history], 3rd edition, 3rd part: "Das altrömische Kaisertum" [The ancient Roman empire], Leipzig 1883).

Page 10, "natural causality"
Rudolf Steiner spoke in two lectures about human life as the struggle against natural causality and about overcoming natural causality with moral impulses. These two lectures, held shortly after the course given in this volume, were as follows: the lecture of July 24, 1921, in GA 206; and the lecture of September 5, 1921, in *Fruits of Anthroposophy* (CW 78).

Page 11, "insight into repeated earth lives"
See, for example, the lectures in *Reincarnation and Karma* (CW 135).

Page 11, "life between death and rebirth"
See the lecture cycle by that title (CW 141) held in Berlin and the lecture cycle held in Vienna: *The Inner Nature of the Human Being and Life between Death and Rebirth* (CW 153).

Page 12, "the Clausius formula"
This refers to the second principle of thermodynamics by German physicist Robert Clausius (1822–1888).

Page 16, "Kant-LaPlace theory"
This theory came from Kant's *Universal Natural History and Theory of the Heavens* (1755), or from the "nebulous theory," which established and explained it. Also from *Exposition du système du monde* (1796) by LaPlace.

Page 17, "ritual"
This term, as used in this volume, refers to the religious service for the sacraments.

Page 21, "Goethe's *Fairytale of the Green Snake and the Beautiful Lily*"
Contained originally within Goethe's novel, *Conversations of the German Immigrants*. First published in 1795 in Schiller's magazine, *Die Hor* [Comes from *horae*, which means literally "the hours," but in Greek mythology they are the goddesses of the seasons]; and in the special edition of Rudolf Steiner's lectures on the fairytale, published with the title of *Goethes geheime Offenbarung in seinem Märchen von der Grüne Schlange und der schöne Lilie*, Dornach 1982. See also his essay in *Goethe's Spiritual Nature and Its Revelation in Faust and through the Fairytale of the Snake and the Lily* (CW 22).

Page 23, "in my *Outline of Esoteric Science*"
(CW 13).

Page 23, "Christ Group"
See the lecture held in Berlin on June 10, 1915, in *The Destinies of Individuals and of Nations* (CW 157).

Page 23, "such people as Bruhn"
Wilhelm Bruhn was a private lecturer and academic counselor in Kiel. He held lectures on "Theosophie und Anthroposophie." These were published together under the same title.

Page 29, "to create a Threefold Social Organism"
See the following: *Towards Social Renewal* (CW 23); *The Renewal of the Social Organism* (CW 24); the lectures for the members of the Anthroposophical

Society in GA 185a–193; GA 196–200; as well as the lectures on the social life and the Threefold Social Organism in GA 328–341.

Page 30, "I lectured in Colmar on the 'Bible and Wisdom'"
These lectures were held on November 19 and November 21, 1905. Transcripts of the lectures do not exist. The first lecture was titled "Die Weisheitslehre des Christentums im Lichte der Theosophie," [The wisdom-teachings of Christianity in the light of Theosophy]. See also Rudolf Steiner's lecture of March 5, 1920, in Stuttgart, contained in *Polarities in the Evolution of Mankind* (CW 197).

Page 34, "in a practical manner out of the impulse of threefolding"
See the note for page 29, especially the lectures on the social life and the Threefold Social Organism in GA 328–341.

Pages 38–39, "we must feel clearly that marriage itself … find their form within social life"
In this long section, as an example of the tasks that befall the pastor in the sense of community-building, Rudolf Steiner speaks about marriage from the viewpoints that result from the various realms of social threefolding.

Whether Rudolf Steiner expressed himself so tersely at this place in the lecture, or whether the brevity of the presentations is because of something lacking in the stenography, can no longer be ascertained, since the original notes of the stenographer no longer exist. One cannot rule out the possibility that the stenographer summarized a text that had gaps in it into a shorter text.

For information on the content, refer to:
(1) Rudolf Steiner's letter of February 1913 to Baron Ferdinand von Paungarten, in which he explains why marriage is not only the "personal affair of the individuals marrying, but rather of "the whole of the social matrix." For this, see letter number 618 in *Briefe II* [Correspondence II] GA 39.
(2) Rudolf Steiner's lecture of November 16, 1908, in Berlin, in *The Being of Man and his Future Evolution* (CW 107).
(3) The lecture of December 14, 1908, in Stuttgart, in GA 108.

Page 40, "since the formal dogmatic decree of infallibility"
See the note for page 47.

Page 41, "*The Philosophy of Freedom*"
(CW 4). See also Otto Palmer's book, *Rudolf Steiner on his Book "The Philosophy of Freedom,"* Tr. Marjorie Spock, SteinerBooks: Great Barrington, MA 2007.

Page 41, "one of the first … critics, who wrote about my *Philosophy of Freedom*"
Robert Zimmerman wrote in *The Athenaeum*, Number 4380, London, July 7, 1894: "The tendency of the day is to run into extremes. For example, Rudolf Steiner

in his book entitled *Philosophie der Freiheit* [The Philosophy of Freedom] and Bruno Wille in his *Philosophie der Befreiung* [Philosophy of the freeing-up] start from Nietzsche's standpoint, but go far beyond him, and end in a theoretical anarchy, which, even in the domain of practice, allows of no moral prescriptions."

Page 45, "Anthroposophy as such will simply soon be opposed in unbelievable ways"
See, for example, Louis M. I. Werbeck: *Eine Gegnerschaft als Kulturverfallserscheinung* [An opposition as sign of decay of culture], 2 volumes, Stuttgart 1924. Also Karl Heyer: *Wie Man Gegen Rudolf Steiner Kämpft* [How one fights against Rudolf Steiner], Stuttgart 1932.

Page 45, "when we founded the Waldorf school"
The Independent Waldorf School in Stuttgart, Germany, was founded in 1919 through the initiative of industrialist Dr. Emil Molt of the Waldorf Astoria Cigarette Factory, in connection with the Movement for the Threefold Social Organism.

Page 45, "Anthroposophical religious instruction that was 'free'"
See "Zur religiöse Erziehung, Wortlaute Rudolf Steiners as Arbeitsmaterial für Waldorfpädagogen," [On religious instruction. Rudolf Steiner's words as study and work material for Waldorf teachers], in typescript only, Stuttgart 1985.

Page 47, "the German emperor"
Wilhelm II came to Switzerland in September 1912.

Page 47, "Old Catholicism came into being"
The dogma of the infallibility of the pope resulted from the Vatican Council of 1869–1870:

> "After long, agitated debates, after the pope allowed the minority to leave, the 'Constitutio de ecclesia' was approved on July 18, 1870, with a vote of 533 for and 2 against. As of that time, it is dogma that the pope has the direct power and jurisdiction over the whole of the church, and that the doctrinal decisions given 'ex cathedra' by the pope on faith and customs are infallible. The infallibility rests on the divine support and counsel that is promised to the pope in Saint Peter.... After the council had spoken, all of the Catholic bishops subjected themselves to the new dogma. In opposition, among the educated Catholics of Germany, proceeding out of the circles of the Catholic universities, there arose *Old Catholicism*. It was a continuing education of the old church that rejected the pope-church. It won over, however, only a minority of people and was not able to stop the pope-church from the path it had taken." (Karl Heussi, Kompendium der Kirchengeschichte [Compendium of the church history], 16th edition, Tübingen 1981.

Compare August Bernhard Hasler's *Wie der Papst unfehlbar wurde. Macht und Ohnmacht eines Dogmas*, [How the pope became infallible. Power and powerlessness of a dogma], Munich/Zurich 1979. See also, by Johann Friedrich von Schulte (one of the leaders of the Old Catholics): *Der Altkatholizismus*, [The Old Catholicism], Gießen 1887.

Page 47, "in Switzerland, where the Old Catholicism has survived much more than elsewhere"
On December 1, 1872, in Switzerland, at a conference in Olten, Rome-free congregations were founded by the opponents of the Vatican resolutions. In 1875 these congregations united to become the *Christ Catholic Church*. Its peak was in 1876, with 73,830 members in 55 parishes. Compare the book by Eduard Herzog (a bishop of the Swiss Old Catholics): *Beiträge zur Vorgeschichte der Christkatholischen Kirche der Schweiz* [Contributions to the early history of the Christ Catholic Church in Switzerland], Bern 1896; and that by Gschwind: *Geschichte der Enstehung der Christkatholischen Kirche der Schweiz* [The history of the origin of the Christ Catholic Church in Switzerland], 2 volumes, 1904/10.

Page 48, "Dr. Rittelmeyer"
Friedrich Rittelmeyer (1872–1938). He was a well-known preacher in Nuremburg from 1902 to 1916; and then at the "New Church" in Berlin. From 1911 he had a personal connection with Rudolf Steiner; and in 1924 he published *Vom Lebenswerk Rudolf Steiners* [From Rudolf Steiner's life and work]. Co-founder and first *Erzoberlenker* [head of the church] of The Christian Community, which was founded on September 16, 1922. See Rittlemeyer's *Aus meinem Leben* [From my life], Stuttgart 1937, and *Rudolf Steiner Enters My Life*, Floris Books. See also Gerhard Wehr's *Friedrich Rittelmeyer. Religiöse Erneuerung als geistiger Brüchenschlag zwischen den Zeiten* [Friedrich Rittelmeyer. Religious renewal as spiritual bridge between the times], Wies/Südschwarzwald [South Black Forest], 1985.

Page 50, "Werner Klein"
Werner Klein (1898–1984). He completed his abitur ("high school" maturation certification) at the age of 16 and immediately enlisted in the military. After his experiences in the war and a debilitating illness, he studied philosophy in Marburg. He became a member of the Anthroposphical Society in the fall of 1919. His question addressed to Rudolf Steiner in February 1920 (See pp. xvii and 206) can be seen as having given the first impetus for this present course to come about. Klein played a substantial role in co-founding The Christian Community in 1922, and as *Oberlenker* [leader of a specified region of the church] in Bremen and Hamburg. During his time of service in The Christian Community, he bore the additional forename of "Johannes" [John]. In 1929, for private reasons, he separated from The Christian Community, and then lived as a scholar in Hamburg.

Page 52, *"Der Kommende Tag"*
A public, limited company (1920–1925) for the promotion and support of economic and spiritual values. An associative undertaking in the sense of the Threefold Social Order impulse. It was founded on March 13, 1920. Rudolf Steiner was president of its board until 1923. The intention for this initiative, according to a business report from 1921, was "to build a seed for a new economic life on an associative basis." The company had to be liquidated gradually, as a result of the general economic crisis (inflation) beginning in 1925.

Page 57, "One might think of Heisler"
Hermann Heisler (1876–1962). Protestant theologian. In 1912, after twelve years of service as a pastor, he gave up his pastoral profession and studied philosophy and natural science in Tübingen. During WWI, he was appointed to an abandoned parish, where he already began preaching about reincarnation and karma. In 1917 he received his doctorate with the work "Das Ewige im Zeitlichen. Grundzug einer geistgemaßen Weltauffassung. Eine Untersuchung über der Substanzproblem" [The eternal in the temporal. Outline of a spiritual conception of the world. An examination of the problem of substance]. (Letter from Heisler to Rudolf Steiner on March 25, 1917). After occupying himself for several years with Theosophical thought, he joined the Anthroposophical Society in 1917 and supported Anthroposophy with everything he said and wrote from then on. In the foreword to the second edition (1919) of his sermon collection—*Lebensfragen* [Life questions]—he wrote: "… it is the deepest conviction of [this] author that the spirit of anthroposophically oriented spiritual science, as it was given to our time by Rudolf Steiner, is the only remedy for reenlivening the dead religious feeling of our time…." After WWI, Heisler was active in the Movement for the Threefold Social Order and gave many lectures on Anthroposophy. In 1919 he published *Anthroposophie und Christentum* [Anthroposophy and Christianity]. Called by Rudolf Steiner on June 13/14, 1921, to attend the course held for young theologians, he worked untiringly to support the coming into being of the Movement for Religious Renewal, at first through fundraising in order to create a financial footing for the movement. He became a priest of The Christian Community in November 1922.

Page 59, "Adolf Harnack"
Adolf Harnack (1851–1930). German Protestant theologian. Leading representative of the liberal direction. Professor of church history in Leipzig, Gießen, Marburg, and especially in Berlin (1888–1921). His main works: *Lehrbuch der Dogmengeschichte* [Textbook of the history of dogma], 3 volumes, Freiburg 1886–1890 (reprint of the 4th edition of 1909–1910 in Darmstadt 1983); *Geschichte der altchristlichen Literatur* [History of the old Christian literature], 3 volumes, Leipzig 1893–1904, 2nd edition in 1958; and *Das Wesen des Christentums* [The nature of Christianity], Leipzig 1900 (several editions).

See also the book by his daughter, Agnes von Zahn-Harnack: *Adolf Harnack*, Berlin 1936, 2nd edition in 1951.

Page 59, "A man, who can say that Christ can be taken out of the Gospels and that only the Father has a place in them"
Literally: "It is no paradox and also not 'rationalism', but the simple expression of fact, as it stands in the Gospels: not the Son, but the Father alone belongs in the Gospel, as Jesus proclaimed." (From *Das Wesen des Christentums* [The nature of Christianity], lecture 8).

Page 60, "Gideon Spicker"
Gideon Spicker (1840–1912). Former Capuchin monk, professor of philosophy in Münster in Westfalen; he wrote, among other things: *Kant, Hume und Berkeley. Eine Kritik der Erkenntnistheorie* [Kant, Hume, and Berkeley. A critique of the theory of knowledge], Berlin 1875; *Lessings Weltanschauung* [Lessing's philosophy], Leipzig 1883; *Die Ursache des Verfalls der Philosophie in alter und neuer Zeit* [The cause of the decline of philosophy in olden and modern times], Leipzig 1892; *Der Kampf zweier Weltanschauungen. Eine Kritik der alten und neuesten Philosophie mit Einschluß der christlichen Offenbarung* [The conflict of two world philosophies. A critique of the ancient and most modern philosophies, including the Christian revelation], Stuttgart 1898; *Versuch eines neuen Gottbegriffes* [Attempt at a new concept of God], Stuttgart 1902; and *Vom Kloster ins akademische Lehramt. Schicksale eines ehemaligen Kapuziners* [From the cloister into the academic teaching profession. Destiny of a former Capuchin monk], Stuttgart 1908.

Page 60, "Community Movement"
A religious movement within the Protestant movement that broke off from the Lutheran Church. Having its roots in the Reformation and pietism, it developed in the second half of the nineteenth century. Noteworthy among its various groups and churches are the Methodist Church, the Salvation Army, and most likely the various other Protestant churches.

Page 60, "this little piece about the personality of Jesus"
Friedrich Rittelmeyer: *Jesus: Ein Bild in vier Vorträgen* [Jesus: a picture in four lectures], Ulm 1912.

Page 61, "Weinel's conception"
Heinrich Weinel (1874–1936). From his work, *Jesus im neunzehten Jahrhundert* [Jesus in the nineteenth century]: "Freely, it is not to Christ of the past, the God-human of the old dogma, but to Jesus of Nazareth that men of our time come for his answers to their questions concerning their cares. This simple and courageous man was hidden a long, long time in the brilliant glory of the King of Heaven...."

Page 62, "since Rittelmeyer published his book, which is a collection"
Vom Lebenwerk Rudolf Steiners. Eine Hoffnung neuer Kultur [From Rudolf Steiner's life and work. A hope for a new culture], with contributions from

various authors and published by Friedrich Rittelmeyer, Berlin 1921 (third edition done in the same year).

Page 62, "[Association for Anthroposophical College Work]"
This was the uniting, in July 1920 in Stuttgart, of the various student groups studying anthroposophically oriented spiritual science in Germany and Switzerland. See also the pamphlet "Bestrebungen und Ziele des Bundes für Anthroposophische Hochschularbeit" [The strivings and goals of the Association for Anthroposophical College Studies], Stuttgart (no date available).

Page 63, "the ideas that Spengler described in his *Decline of the West*"
Oswald Spengler (1880–1936). Philosopher of history and culture. Teacher of mathematics from 1908–1911, after which he was a freelance writer. He became famous immediately upon publishing the first volume of *Decline of the West* in German in 1918. The second volume followed in 1922. See Rudolf Steiner's essays on Spengler's *Decline of the West* in GA 36 and his lectures on the same topic in GA 198, GA 204, and *The Mystery of the Trinity* (CW 214).

Page 64, "absolutely not at all doomed to destruction"
An error occurred when the text was being copied by The Christian Community and there stood in the text: "…that must be further fought against."

Page 65, "Mr. Husemann"
Gottfried Husemann (1900–1972). At age 19, he was introduced to Anthroposophy by his brother, Friedrich Husemann. In May 1922 he participated in the writing of the community letter to Rudolf Steiner (See pp. xix and 208-211). He was one of the co-founders of The Christian Community in the fall of 1922. In 1930 he became the leader of the priest seminary and in 1933 an *Oberlenker*. For more on his biography, see *Die Christengemeinschaft* [The Christian Community], 44th edition, No. 7, July 1972.

Page 65, "agendas"
Austrian term meaning "tasks" or "duties."

Page 71, "the theologian Schmiedel"
Otto Schmiedel (b. 1858) In his work *Die Hauptprobleme der Leben-Jesu Forschung* [Research of the main problems concerning the life of Jesus], Tübingen 1902, he wrote: "We have as a substantial characteristic of the presentations of the life story of the founders and the salvation-personalities that, with pious zeal, they glorify the personality in question—yes, in fact, deify him. The more this tendency increases, just all the more does the report lose its historical quality and becomes legend. Let us turn it about-face! Let us find passages in the Gospels that express something about Jesus in contrast or opposition to what strives to glorify him; which, however, later Gospels have turned around or have done away with, because they take offence at the lack

of glory. Thus, one can be sure that the passages that do not glorify Jesus are ancient and real."

See also Rudolf Steiner's lecture of December 28, 1919, in Cosmic New Year (CW 195), and his lecture of October 30, 1920, in *The New Spirituality and the Christ Experience of the Twentieth Century*, (CW 200).

Page 71, "psychiatric research into the Gospels"
For instance, the following: from de Loosten, *Jesus Christus vom Standpunkt des Psychiaters* [Jesus Christ in the view of the psychiatrist], Bamberg 1905; from Binet-Sanglé, *La Folie de Jesus* [The delusions of Jesus], 4 volumes, Paris 1910; from E. Rasmussen, *Jesus. Eine vergleichende psycho-pathologische Studie* [Jesus: a comparative psycho-pathological study], Leipzig 1905; and from Schaefer, *Jesus in psychiatrischer Beleuchtung* [Jesus in the light of psychiatry], Berlin 1910.

Page 73, "attempts such as Overbeck's"
Franz Overbeck (1837–1905). Protestant theologian. In 1864 he was a private lecturer in Jena, and from 1870–1897, a professor of theology in Basel. He wrote *Über die Christlichkeit unser heutigen Theologie* [About the Christian nature of our theology today], Leipzig 1873, 2nd edition in 1903; *Vorgeshcihte und Jugend der mittelalterlichen Scholastik* [Early history and youth of scholasticism of the middle ages], 1917; and *Selbstbekenntnisse* [Confessions], published by E. Fischer, 1941.

Page 74, "we were not founding a school that taught a particular philosophy"
See the lecture of December 30, 1921, given in Dornach, *Soul Economy* (CW 303).

Page 74, "Ernst Uehli"
Ernst Uehli (1875–1959). See the note for page 105.

Page 75, "such a Sunday service…and also a ritual for children…"
The texts for these services, as they were given by Rudolf Steiner, have as yet not been printed.

Page 77, "school of William James"
The students of the American pragmatist, William James (1842–1910).

Page 82, "Klinckowström"
See Rudolf Steiner's presentations on this in the lecture of April 4, 1916, Berlin, in *The Present and Past in the Human Spirit* (CW 167) and the lecture of December 24, 1916, Dornach, in *The Karma of Untruthfulness I* (CW 173).

Page 83, "There is today even a Jesuit book"
From Christian Kunz: *Die liturgischen Verrichtungen des Zelebranten* [The liturgical work of the celebrant], second edition, Regensburg and Rome 1914. It is

the same as the fourth book of *Handbuches der priestlichen Liturgie nach dem römischen Ritus* [Handbook of the priestly liturgy according to the Roman rites] by C. King.

Page 84, "prompted me to bring some parts of the Catholic rituals used today into the original form that lay in them"

Hugo Schuster (1876–1925). As a young business man in St. Gallen, he took part in 1903/1904 in the initiative to build up the Anthroposophical work in Switzerland, for example, in the founding of the branches in St. Gallen, Bern, and Basel. He joined the Theosophical Society in 1905 and was one of Rudolf Steiner's personal students. Through Steiner's presentations on Christ he felt impelled toward the priesthood, and so studied theology as of 1913.

Schuster was friends with the Old Catholic pastor Constantin Neuhaus. Neuhaus wrote the following to Rudolf Steiner on January 30, 1914: "Today Mr. Schuster from Binningen told me that you will soon come to Basel for about four weeks. I would be deeply grateful if you would grant an audience to Mr. Schuster and me together. We both would like to attain more clarity about the Eucharist and about eschatological questions. Theology fails there, whereas we are convinced that esotericism gives satisfying solutions...."

Nothing more is known about the conversation or about further conversations which, without a doubt, took place over the following years. Both Schuster and Neuhaus were often in Dornach. Both were members of the Anthroposophical or Theosophical Societies for many years and knew Rudolf Steiner personally for a long time.

In mid-1918 Hugo Schuster was ordained as a priest of the Old Catholic Church. His first charge was in Basel. During that time he received from Rudolf Steiner the burial ritual. Rudolf Steiner had often given the memorial talk at the burial ceremony for members of the Anthroposophical Society, but had never celebrated a burial ritual himself. After a member of the society would officiate as priest, there was a collaboration. On one such occasion Schuster celebrated the burial with a ritual that Rudolf Steiner had given him for the first time. This was on January 14, 1919, at the grave of Marie Leyh. Rudolf Steiner then gave the memorial talk (See GA 261).

More services for the dead in collaboration with Steiner followed. According to a letter by Marie Steiner, Rudolf Steiner spoke at burials and cremations of members "when relatives asked him to. In the beginning, they were isolated cases. Because they gradually increased in number, and in the meantime he had given the ritual to the priests who had turned to him for the service, he wanted the matter to be handled in this manner because he wanted to practice the profession of priest just as little as he wanted to practice medicine."

In 1919 Rudolf Steiner had begun to translate anew the Mass ritual for Pastor Schuster. On April 20, 1919, immediately before his departure for Stuttgart, where the next day in a meeting of the signatories of the "Appeal to the German People and the Cultural World," the Movement for the Threefold

Social Organism had its beginning, Rudolf Steiner sent the first part of the Mass—up to the offertory. The accompanying letter read: "Dornach, April 20.1919, My Dear Pastor Schuster! Enclosed you are receiving first the part of the Mass that is already finished enough to give to you. I will, however, take it with me on my trip, and now that my book *Towards Social Renewal* (CW 23) is done, it is my opinion that all of it will reach your hands soon. Please do not be upset with me that you are receiving so little of it for the time being. It is moving forward. Best regards, Rudolf Steiner." The further parts followed between June and October of 1921. (See also Steiner's comments in the discussion hour of this course on June 14, 1921.)

Hugo Schuster and Constantin Neuhaus participated in the course for theologians in the fall of 1921, and in the preliminary discussions for the founding of The Christian Community. Neither of them could decide to become co-workers, which they communicated to Friedrich Rittelmeyer at the beginning of September 1922. Schuster soon afterward became ill and died in January 1925.

How much Rudolf Steiner valued Hugo Schuster is shown in the following letter: "Goetheanum, January 14, 1925. My Dear Mrs. Geering-Christ! Many thanks for your letter. I am deeply shaken by our dear friend [Hugo Schuster] leaving the physical plane. You may be sure that I will be with him in thought. He was a devoted Anthroposophist. And precisely the beginnings of the movement in Switzerland owes him a great deal of gratitude—a great deal. Please communicate what I am writing here, with my best greetings, also to Mr. Geering-Christ. With best regards, Rudolf Steiner."

Page 85, "protein is always on its way into chaos"
See the lecture of July 1, 1921, in GA 205, as well as the lecture of May 17, 1923, in *Man's Being, His Destiny, and World Evolution* (CW 226).

Page 88, "on the basis of my 'Cultural Appeal'"
See Rudolf Steiner's talks and discussions in giving advice about the cultural council to be founded (in Stuttgart on May 29; June 7 & 21; July 10 & 25; and September 1919. These are planned for GA 332.

Page 89, "I spoke once with a man, who was quite important for his exegeses"
Which person is referred to here could not be ascertained. It could be the exegete, Franz Xaver Pölzl (1840–1914). In 1882 he became the successor of Carl Werner in his teaching position in New Testament Bible Study at the University of Vienna. His highly respected main work: *Kurzgefaßter Kommentar zu den vier hl. Evangelien* [Abridged commentary on the four Gospels], 4 volumes, Graz 1880–1893.

Page 90, "Professor Bickell"
Gustav Bickell (1838–1906). Son of the teacher of cannon law and statesman, Johann Wilhelm Bickell (1799–1848). He studied Protestant theology and

linguistics at the University of Marburg. In 1865 he converted to Catholicism and, after studying Catholic theology, he was ordained into the priesthood in Fulda in 1867. In 1871 he was appointed by the philosophy faculty of Münster as associate professor of Oriental languages and the comparison of Indo-Germanic languages. In 1874 Bickell became a full professor of Old Christian archeology and Semitic languages on the theological faculty of Innsbruck, where he co-founded the *Zeitschrift für katolische Theologie* [Magazine for Catholic theology], and in 1876 he achieved his doctorate in theology. Carl Werner, the Viennese researcher of the history of theology and philosophy, mediated Bickell's call to Innsbruck. In 1891 he attained the teaching position for Comparative Speech Research and Oriental Philology and Ancient Knowledge on the philosophy faculty of the University of Vienna. He worked there as an Orientalist until his death in 1906.

Page 90, "I had a conversation about forty years ago with a Catholic theologian"
Wilhelm Neumann (1837–1919). Academic researcher from the Cistercian Order. In 1855 he was in the Lilienfeld Monastery, and then in 1858 he transferred to the Heiligenkreuz Monastery, where he was professor of Old Testament Bible studies from 1861–1874. In 1874 he was appointed as associate professor of the Semitic languages and the high exogese of the Old Testament of the Catholic theological faculty at the University of Vienna. He then became full professor in these fields. In 1899/1900 he became the Rector Magnificus (former title for the director of a college or university) of the University of Vienna. He wrote many publications on Middle Eastern and Eastern Studies and on Christian art. His scholarship and knowledge was astounding. His friend, the philosopher and theologian Laurenz Müllner, said of him: "Neumann knows the whole world and three villages in addition." See also Fl. Watzl's *Die Cisterzienser von Heiligenkreuz* [The Cistercians of Heiligenkreuz (Holy Cross Monastery)], Graz 1898. See also Rudolf Steiner's *Autobiography* (CW 28).

Page 90, "the immaculate conception of Mary"
The dogma of the immaculate conception of Mary was proclaimed in the papal bull of December 8, 1854: "Ineffebilis Deus" [Ineffable God]. It states near the end of the document: "We declare, pronounce, and define that the doctrine which holds that the most Blessed Virgin Mary, in the first instance of her conception, by a singular grace and privilege granted by Almighty God, in view of the merits of Jesus Christ, the Savior of the human race, was preserved free from all stain of original sin, is a doctrine revealed by God and therefore to be believed firmly and constantly by all the faithful."

Page 91, "the church historian at the University of Vienna"
Josef Kopallik (1849–1897). He was the former student and later friend of Carl Werner.

Page 91, "I have held whole lectures in the form of a legend"
For example, the lecture of January 6, 1918, "The New Isis Legend," in *Ancient Myths and the New Isis Mystery* (CW 180).

Page 91, "My booklet 'The Nature of the Arts' is presented wholly in pictures"
The lecture in Berlin on October 28, 1909, was published in 1910 as a pamphlet. It was reprinted in *Art and the Knowledge of Art* (CW 271).

Page 92, "Ludwig Laistner"
Ludwig Laistner (1845–1896). First a vicar, then a private tutor, and from 1881 on a freelance writer. In 1889 he was a literary advisor for Haus Cotta in Stuttgart. His two volumes of *Das Rätsel der Sphinx. Grundzüge einer Mythengeschichte* [The riddle of the Sphinx. Characteristics of a history of myths] appeared in Berlin in 1889.
The ending of this lecture, as it was taken down by a stenographer, had gaps in it and had to be added to by the editors of the German edition. The documents used for this are statements about Ludwig Laistner by Rudolf Steiner in his *Autobiography* (CW 28), as well as the following lectures: March 8, 1906, in *Anthroposophy and the Riddle of the World* (CW 54); March 9, 1911, on "Moses" in GA 60; and January 4, 1915, in GA 64.

Page 96, "systems of forces go through the entire universe"
See the lecture of October 26, 1909, held in Berlin and contained in *A Psychology of Body, Soul & Spirit* (CW 115); and the lecture of January 12, 1921, held in Stuttgart (GA 323).

Page 99, "three murderers"
See what Rudolf Steiner related about the three traitors in his handwritten copy of the "Temple Legend," published in *Freemasonry and Ritual Work* (CW 265).

Page 99, "a man depicted with the head of a bull and a woman with the head of a lion"
Compare the lecture held in Dornach on October 10, 1915, in *The Occult Movement in the Nineteenth Century* (CW 254).

Page 100, "with regard to form, the human being is ..."
Rudolf Steiner spoke in more detail about the various stages of the evolution of the members of the human being in the lecture held in Cologne on December 27, 1907. Contained in *Myths and Legends, Occult Signs and Symbols* (CW 101), as well as the lecture held in Munich on March 20, 1916, in GA 174a.

Page 101, "and Wagner says of the poodle: 'Er zweifelt'"
In *Faust I* ("Before the Gate") by Johann Wolfgang von Goethe.

Page 101, *"Himmlatzer"*
A common Austrian expression in dialect, meaning "lightning without thunder."

Page 102, *"dun horse"*
The source of this story could not be ascertained.

Page 102, "Ernst Müller"
Ernst Müller (1880–1954). A mathematician, writer, and scholar of Hebrew and the Kabbala. In his youth he spent several years in Palestine. He served many years as librarian of the Jewish Library in Vienna. Later he immigrated to England. See also Emil Bock's letter to Frieda Müller about the death of Dr. Ernst Müller in *Emil Bock, Briefe* [Letters].

Page 103, "ancient Greeks did not have a perception of color in the sense that we have"
See "Die geschichtliche Entwicklung der Farbwahrnehmung" in GA 291a, a supplement to *Color* (CW 291). See also W. Schultz's *Das Farbenempfindungssystem der Helenen* [The system of color sensing among the ancient Greeks], Leipzig 1904.

Page 105, "what Mr. Uehli will have told you today"
At this time, he was editor of the weekly *Dreigliederung des sozialen Organismus* [Threefolding of the social organism] and a teacher of religion at the Independent Waldorf School in Stuttgart. The report mentioned could have been an orientation concerning the Sunday service in the Waldorf school. Compare *Der Lehrkreis um Rudolf Steiner in der ersten Waldorf Schule 1919–1925. Lebensbilder und Erinnerungen* [The circle of teachers around Rudolf Steiner in the first Waldorf school 1919–1925. Life pictures and memories], Stuttgart 1977.

Page 106, "Paul Baumann"
Paul Baumann (1887–1964). He was a member of the first college of teachers of the Independent Waldorf School in Stuttgart. Mainly he gave music instruction and was responsible for the music for school events. In later years he also gave free religious instruction. Also, see the book indicated in the note above.

Page 107, "which then is backed up in the hearing"
Concerning the forming of the organ of hearing, see Rudolf Steiner's lecture of December 9, 1922 (GA 218).

Page 108, "Bach"
Johann Sebastian Bach (1685–1750).

Page 109, "Debussy"
Claude Achille Debussy (1862–1918).

Page 109, "Richard Wagner"
Richard Wagner (1813–1883).

Page 110, "Quaker movement"
The Quakers, the Society of Friends, the Religious Society of Friends, founded in 1649 by George fox in opposition to the state church. He founded Christian lay-community.

Page 111, "Emil Bock: We have heard that there are already rituals in existence"
On the occasion of the death of the Swiss pastor of the Old Catholic Church, the burial ritual was given in September 1918. See Rudolf Steiner's talk on September 22, 1918 in GA 261. Steiner also translated a part of the Catholic Mass from the Latin for Hugo Schuster. The first part was done in 1919; the last part, in the time between June and September 1921. This is included in GA 343a. Steiner gave a text for the baptism ritual to the Protestant Pastor Johannes Geyer, who was a teacher in the Waldorf School in Stuttgart. And in 1921 he gave baptism and marriage rituals to Pastor Wilhelm Ruhtenberg, teacher in the Waldorf School in Stuttgart. Further, at this time there were three texts for services for children of the Waldorf School: the Sunday service (1920); the Christmas service (1920); and confirmation (1921).

Page 111, "a member of our movement"
Hugo Schuster. See the note for page 84.

Page 112, "The rest…was interrupted by the World War"
See *Freemasonry and Ritual Work* (CW 265).

Page 115, "Socrates"
Socrates (470–399 B.C.E.).

Page 117, "I had a friend, who was an excellent Protestant pastor"
Presumably Max Christlieb. See Rudolf Steiner's statements about him in his *Autobiography* (CW 28) and in *Briefe: 1890–1925* [Correspondence] (GA 39).

Page 117, "Luther frock"
A black "frock" with a stand-up collar, which is worn by the Lutheran clergy.

Page 119, "read a good translation of the discourses of Buddha"
For instance, *Die Reden Gotamo Buddhos* [The discourses of Gautama Buddha], 3 volumes, Munich 1896–1902; and 1922, and more after that. Translated by Karl Eugen Neumann.

Page 123, "such personalities as Newman, the English cardinal"
John Henry Newman (1801–1890), English.

Page 123, "as Weinel did"
See the note for page 61.

Page 123–124, "He could not accomplish this until he realized..."
In his essay, "Essay in Aid of a Grammar of Assent," 1870, Newman wrote (in literal translation of the German translation of the original): "This thought-world (of Christian belief/faith is the extension and result of some words, such as spoken by the Fisherman of Galilee.... Reason has not subjected itself to faith; it served faith and supported it. Reason explained its (faith's) documents. It turned uneducated farmers into philosophers and theologians and has drawn out the words, conclusions, and meanings of which its immediate listeners had no inkling. It is much more disconcerting that St. John should be a Theosophist than that St. Peter should be a ruler. This is the peculiar phenomenon of the Gospel and a sign of its divinity."

Page 124, "And from this he arrives at a special view of Christianity's evolution or development"
This most likely has to do with Newman's "Essay on the Development of Christian Doctrine," 1845.

Page 124, "Scheler"
Max Scheler (1874–1928). In 1919 he was called to be professor of philosophy and sociology at the newly opened University of Cologne. Rudolf Steiner met Scheler in 1904 or 1905 in Jena and debated with him on the epistemoligical justification of spirit-knowledge. See Steiner's *Autobiography* (CW 28). That Steiner followed Scheler's further path—whom Steiner deemed to be "among the sharpest thinkers of the time"—can be seen in the many statements in the lectures of May 1, 1917, in *Building Stones for an Understanding of the Mystery of Golgotha* (CW 175); of October 13, 1918, in GA 184; and of July 13, 1919, in GA 192; of October 2, 1920, in *The Boundaries of Natural Science* (CW 322).

Page 126, "the cleverest people of the nineteenth century fought against immortality ..."
See the statements by David Friedrich Strauß about "Lokal für die abgeschiedenen Menschen," [Space for the departed human beings] in *Der alte und neue Glaube* [The old and new belief].

Page 129, "the Gospel tells of the one born blind is translated as follows"
John 9: 1–3. See Rudolf Steiner's *The Gospel of John in Relation to the Other Three Gospels* (CW 112).

Page 130, "There was a poet who wrote in the Austrian dialect"
Ignaz Franz Castelli (1781–1862), Viennese poet. See Rudolf Steiner's *Briefe* [Correspondence] (GA 38).

Page 131, "grace"
The stenographic notes about the concept of grace were apparently full of holes. For a better understanding, refer to Rudolf Steiner's lecture, "Erbsünde und Gnade," [Original sin and grace], in GA 127. Also, the end of the lecture of May 29, 1905, in *The Temple Legend* (CW 93).

Page 135, "Heaven and Earth will pass away, but my Word will not pass away"
Matthew 24:35; Mark 13:31; Luke 21:33.

Page 135, "'Not I, but Christ in me'"
Galatians 2:20.

Page 138, "events planned in Stuttgart?"
A congress for the general public was planned and held on August 28–September 7, where Rudolf Steiner gave the lecture cycle *Anthroposophie, ihre Erkenntniswürzeln und ihre Lebensfrüchte*, partially translated and published as *Fruits of Anthroposophy*, CW 78.

Page 140, "Last fall we successfully held the college course [*Hochschulkurs*]"
The first Anthroposophical college course was held in Dornach, from September 26–October 16, 1920.

Page 141, "Easter Course"
The second Anthroposophical college course, held in Dornach, from April 3–10, 1921.

Page 142, "Heinzelmann"
Professor of Theology in Basel.

Page 142, "The Swiss are intensely conservative"
See Hans Hasler's, *Rudolf Steiner über die Schweiz*, [Rudolf Steiner about Switzerland], Dornach 1988.

Page 143, "events from August 20th to 27th"
This was the Summer Course (Summer Art Course).

Page 145, "brochure"
"Ein Weg zur notwendigen religiösen Erneuerung" [A way to necessary renewal of religion].

Page 145, "Haas-Berkow-Truppe [Troupe]"
The theater troupe led by Gottfried Haas-Berkow (1888–1957) was widely known during his time. The troupe travelled throughout Germany, Switzerland, Sweden, and Holland. It also worked actively for Anthroposophy. The members

of this troupe participated in the Drama Course in Dornach in September 1924. Most joined the Goetheanum Ensemble.

Page 146, "in connection with the congress"
It is concerned with the planning for the public congress: Kultur-Ausblicke der anthrpopsophischen Bewegung" [Cultural prospects of the Anthroposophical movement], which took place August 28–September 7, 1921, in Stuttgart.

Page 147, "Pastor Geyer"
Dr. Christian Geyer (1862–1929). Main preacher in the Sebald Church in Nuremburg. Friend and comrade-in-arms of F. Rittelmeyer. Wrote *Theosophy und Religion*, Nuremburg 1918. See Emil Bock's *Zeitgenossen–Weggenossen–Wegbereiter* [Contempoary–comrade on the path–pioneer], Stuttgart 1959; and Wilhelm Kelber's, "Zu Christian Geyers 100. Geburtstag" [For Christian Geyer's 100th birthday] in *Die Christengemeinshcaft* [The Christian Community], Volume 34, Issue 10, October 1962.

Page 147, "a written piece by Dr. Heisler"
Hermann Heisler, *Anthroposophie und Christentum. Ein Versuch zur Verständigung* [Anthroposophy and Christianity: an attempt for understanding], Constance/Leipzig 1919.

Page 148, "Gogarten, for instance, says, 'Yes, Anthroposophy wants to found religions'"
See Friedrich Gogarten, *Rudolf Steiners "Geisteswissenschaft" und das Christentum* [Rudolf Steiner's "spiritual science" and Christianity], Stuttgart 1920.

Page 149, "[Life work]"
See the note for page 62.

Page 149, "No one besides Geyer"
Christian Geyer wrote the section: ""Rudolf Steiner und die Religion," [Rudolf Steiner and religion] (*Lebenswerk* [Life Work]).

Page 149, "Schairer"
Dr. Immanuel Schairer, pastor in Nagold.

Page 149, "Reverend Klein"
Paul Klein (1871–1957). Pastor in Mannheim. Longtime member and temporary branch director of the Anthroposophical Society in Mannheim. Not he, but his son, Gerhard Klein, participated in the founding of The Christian Community. See Gerhard Klein, "Pfarrer Paul Klein und Rudolf Steiner" [Pastor Paul Klein and Rudolf Steiner] in *Mitteilungen aus der anthroposophischen Arbeit in Deutschland* [News from the Anthroposophical work in Germany]. Volume 21, Issue 2, St. John's Tide 1967.

Page 149, "Sauter"
Ludwig Sauter, pastor in Lachen/Pfalz. Member of the Theosophical Society, and then the Anthroposophical Society from 1909.

Page 149, "Jundt in Mannheim"
E.B. Jundt, pastor in Mannheim/Neckrau.

Page 150, "In Berlin I gave lectures t... "the Bible and Wisdom,'"
The Berlin lectures, "Bible and Wisdom" I and II, held on November 12 and 14, 1908, were published in *How Does One Find the Spirit?* (CW 57).

Page 150, "Neither Bruhn nor Gogarten"
Wilhelm Bruhn, *Theosophie und Anthroposophie* [Theosophy and Anthroposophy], 1921; Friedrich Gogarten, see the note for page 148; *Friedreich Laun, Moderne Theosophie und katholisches Christentum* [Modern Theosophy and Catholic Christianity], Rottenburg 1920.

Page 151, "Professor Traub"
Friedrich Traub in the article: "Die Lehre Rudolf Steiners" [The teaching of Rudolf Steiner] Sunday insert in the *Schwäbischen Merkur*, April 30, 1921.

Page 151, "[Stuttgart Evangelical Sunday paper]"
Number 19 from May 8, 1921, report of the annual meeting of the Evangelic Church Association, at which Pastor Jehle held a lecture, "The Anti-church Streams of the Present."

Page 151, "called him the reincarnation of Bernard of Clairvaux"
More detailed exposition in the lecture of June 16, 1921, published in *Menschenwerden, Weltenseele und Weltengeist* [Human development, world-soul, world-spirit] (GA 205).

Page 151, "it has been made impossible for us to cultivate what has to do with ritual any further"
See *Freemasonry and Ritual Work: The Misraim Service* (CW 265).

Page 152, "In Seiling's brochure"
Max Seiling, *Die anthroposophosche Bewegung und ihr Prophet* [The Anthroposophical Movement and its prophet], Leipzig 1918.

Page 153, "Franz Brentano"
Franz Brentano (1838–1917). Ordained a Catholic priest in 1864. Appointed professor of philosophy in Würzburg in 1864. He left the priesthood in 1873 on grounds of faith (against the dogma of infallibility) and relinquished his professorship in Würzburg. In 1874 he was appointed professor of philosophy in Vienna. In 1879, he left the Catholic Church. In 1880 came his marriage

to Ida von Lieben and the loss of the professorship in Vienna. However, until 1895, he continued to teach there as private lecturer. See Rudolf Steiner's obituary for him, "Franz Brentano," in *Von Seelenrätseln* (GA 21); and the four essays on Franz Brentano in *Der Goetheanumgedanke inmitten der Kulturkrisis der Gegenwart* (GA 36), Dornach 1961.

Page 153, "sauber"
Today this word means "clean."

Page 154, "Rittelmeyer has now written about Anthroposophy and the renewal of religion"
This essay with the title "Anthroposophie und religiöse Erneuerung" [Anthroposophy and religious renewal] was published in September 1921 in the monthly *Die Tat* [The deed], Jena, Volume XIII, Issue 6.

Page 154, "a fund-raising flyer"
"A Way to the Necessary Renewal of Religion." See p. 247-255.

Page 155, "Keyserling's cause"
The Society for Free Philosophy of Darmstadt, or the School of Wisdom of Count Hermann von Keyserling (1880–1946). Founded in 1919.

Page 156, "Rudolf Meyer"
Rudolf Meyer (1896–1985) studied theology and philosophy in Kiel and Göttingen. He became acquainted with Anthroposophy in 1916 and worked from 1919 on as an anthroposophical speaker in North Germany. In his own words, he sought "within its (Anthroposophy's) scope to specially advocate a new Christianity." Meyer participated in all the preparatory steps for the founding of The Christian Community and was ordained at the end of October 1922 in Hamburg. At the advice of Rudolf Steiner he went to Breslau with Rudolf von Koschutzki and Kurt von Wistinghausen. For biographical details see the obituary of Michael Heidenreich in *Die Christengemeinschaft* [The Christian Community], Volume 57, Issue 9, September 1985.

Page 159, "Mr. Posadzy"
Ludwig Posadzy, born in Poland in Szymborze, district of Inowrazlaw (Hohensalza), then Province of Posen, in 1878. Studied philosophy in Berlin. Met Rudolf Steiner in 1905.

Page 159, "write about Herder"
Ludwig Posadzy, *Der Entwicklungsgeschictliche Gedanke bei Herder* [Herder's idea of the history of development], Posen 1906.

Page 159, "quoting from my *Christianity as Mystical Fact*"
Christianity as Mystical Fact was not quoted in the printed version of the

dissertation. However, *Friedrich Nietzsche, Fighter Against his Time* was quoted. Further, in his biography in his dissertation, Ludwig Posadzy pointed out his article, "L. Cl. Saint Martin, F. Bauder, und A, Mickiewicz im Kampfe gegen die modern Philosophie" [L. Cl. Saint Martin, F. Bauder, and A, Mickiewicz in the battle against philosophy], where he wrote: "This work appeared in Rudolf Steiner's Theosophical magazine: *Lucifer-Gnosis* (1905, No. 25–28)." It is possible that this had something to do with the fact that his dissertation was rejected.

Page 159, "Braun"

Otto Braun (1885–1922). Private lecturer in Münster, a professor of philosophy in Basel. He picked up the thread of Schelling and wrote, among other things: *Schellings geistige Wandlungen in den Jahren 1800–1810* [Schelling's spiritual transformation in the years of 1800–1810], Leipzig 1906; and *Hinauf zum Idealismus! Schellingstudien* [Upward to idealism! Schelling studies], Leipzig 1908.

Page 159, "Altemüller"

Otto Altemüller. The dates of his lifespan are not known. He studied philosophy at that time. He took part in the theology course in the fall of 1921 (the second course, given for those wanting to found a renewal of religion). He wrote a work for his exams, the topic of which Rudolf Steiner suggested: "Klarstellung und Kritik der Willenstheorie Theodor Ziehens" [Clarification and critique of Theodor Ziehen's will theory]. In 1924 he became a class teacher at the Waldorf school in Hamburg-Wandsbek and also gave the free religious instruction there.

Page 160, "Mrs. Plincke"

Violetta Plincke (1883–1968). In the summer of 1921 she became a teacher in the Waldorf school in Stuttgart, and in 1924 she went to England. See *Der Lehrerkreis um Rudolf Steiner in der ersten Waldorfschule 1919–1925* [The circle of teacher around Rudolf Steiner 1919–1925], Stuttgart 1977.

Page 160, "[Bible and Wisdom]"

See the note for page 150.

Page 160, "in the article in which Traub"

See the note for page 151.

Page 161, "One of our members..."

Possibly Roman Boos is meant here.

Page 161, "Frohnmeyer's booklet"

D. Johannes Frohnmeyer, *Die theosophische Bewegung* [The Theosophical movement], Stuttgart 1920.

Page 162, "Eighth General Ecumenical Council of 869"
At the Eighth Ecumenical Council of Constantinople in 869 C.E. it was decreed by Pope Hadrian II against Photus that the human being has a reasonable, knowing soul (*unam animam rationabilien et intellectualem*), so that a spiritual principle in the human being may no longer be spoken of. From then on the spiritual was looked upon as only a characteristic of the soul. Rudolf Steiner spoke about this doing away with the spirit in the most varied connections: May 15, 1917, in *The Karma of Untruthfulness* (CW 174); May 20, 1917, in *Death as Metamorphosis of Life* (CW 182); October 4, 1919, in GA 191; November 21, 1919, in *Mission of Michael* (CW194), etc.

Page 163, "Wilhelm Wundt"
Wilhelm Wundt (1832–1920) was a psychologist and philosopher. He studied medicine in Tübingen, Heidelberg, and Berlin from 1851–1856. In 1857 he received his certificate of qualification to be a professor in Heidelberg, and in 1864 he served there as associate professor. In 1874 Wundt was professor of inductive philosophy in Zürich. In 1875 he was full professor of philosophy in Leipzig, where he founded the first institute for experimental psychology. Among other things, he wrote *Grundzüge der physiologischen Psychologie* [Basic physiological psychology] and *Grundriß der Psychologie* [Outline of psychology].

Page 165, "what was then called science or Mathesis"
"The great teachers of Gnosis, especially Plato and Pythagoras, stress that Gnosis is nothing other than the truth of Mathesis, the mystery of the formed and geometrically understood number and size (Größe)." (Eugen Heinrich Schmitt: *Die Gnosis. Grundlagen der Weltanschauung einer edleren Kultur* [Foundations of the worldview of a noble culture], Volume I, Leipzig 1903. See also Rudolf Steiner's "Mathematik und Okkultismus" [Mathematics and esotericism], (his own report of his lecture, given at the Congress of the Federation of European Sections of the Theosophical Society in Amsterdam on June 21, 1904), published in GA 35.

Page 165, "Augustine went through decadent Manichaeism"
See Aurelius Augustine's *Confessions*, especially Book 3. See also Rudolf Steiner's lecture of November 11, 1904, in Berlin, published in *The Temple Legend* (CW 93).

Page 165–166, "Harnack and others expressed their doubts"
See Adolf Harnack's *Zur Quellenkritik der Geschichte des Gnosticismus* [On the critique of the sources of the history of Gnosis], Tübingen 1873.

Page 166, "Hilgenfeld"
Adolf Hilgenfeld (1823–1907). Protestant theologian. In 1869 he became an associate professor in Jena, and in 1890, full professor of the New Testament Exegese. He and Otto Pfleiderer were the last significant representatives of the Tübingen school.

Page 166, "the writings of General von Gleich"
The opposing writing of General Major Gerold von Gleich: *Rudolf Steiner als Prophet* [Rudolf Steiner as prophet], Ludwigsburg 1921.

Page 166, "Lord's Prayer…but deliver us from evil"
Rudolf Steiner speaks in detail about the Lord's Prayer in the following lectures: Berlin on January 28 and February 18, 1907, contained in *Original Impulses of Spiritual Science* (CW 96), as well as February 4, 1907 in Karlsruhe and March 6, 1907 in Cologne, contained in GA 97.

The Waldorf school teacher Rudolf Treichler reported in his booklet *Wege und Umwege zu Rudolf Steiner* [Paths and roundabout ways to Rudolf Steiner] the following:

> I must think especially of a visit to my class by Rudolf Steiner; it is written deeply in my heart. It was an English class, and I had—as I then later always repeated—taken the children through the Lord's Prayer and had begun to have them learn it.
>
> Dr. Steiner entered just as we had spoken the closing words, "For this is the kingdom, the power, and the glory—forever and ever." As we finished Dr. Steiner stood up, went to the blackboard, picked up the chalk, and said to the children: "You have just spoken the beautiful closing words of the Lord's Prayer in English, and you, of course, also know it in German. Now, every royal kingdom encompasses a certain area, has a certain size." Along with these words, he drew a circle on the board. "And where is the power of this kingdom?" The children answered that it is in the middle. "Yes, it is in the middle of the circle, and the glory, the radiance, which rays out from this kingdom, shines outward far and wide!" Thereby he drew something like rays of radiance and light all around the circle. And then he continued: "Yes, now what does this all look like?" After a brief hesitation the children called out: "Like the Sun!" Rudolf Steiner, visibly pleased, said: "Yes, it is the Sun." He then left. We kept his drawing on the blackboard for a long time as a kind of living greeting from him to the class.

Page 168, "before Emperor Justinian closed the last of the Greek schools of philosophy"
The Eastern Roman Emperor Justinian I closed the Athenian Academy of Philosophy in 529.

Page 168, "Gondishapur"
The Academy of Gondishapur in Mesopotamia. See Rudolf Steiner's lecture in Dornach on October 12, 1918, in GA 184.

Page 169, "John Scotus Eriugena"
John Scotus Eriugena (810–877). He did not hold a secular or a religious office.

Around 850 he was called to the court or royal school of Karl des Kahlen in Paris, where he taught liberal arts. His main writing is *De divisione naturae* [On the arrangement or division of nature], which was written in 862–866.

Page 169, "then came the time of the Scholastics, of Albertus Magnus and Thomas Aquinas"
See Rudolf Steiner: *The Redemption of Thinking* (CW 74).

Page 169, "The great quarrel between Nominalism and Realism"
See the chapter "The Philosophies in the Middle Ages" in *The Riddles of Philosophy* (CW 18); and the lecture of January 27, 1923 in GA 220.

Page 171, "such as Oetinger"
Friedrich Christoph Oetinger (1702–1782). Swabian pastor, philosopher, and Theosophist.

Page 171, "'All material manifestations are the last manifestations of the spirit.'"
This sentence is also known in the following form: "Matter is the end result of the ways of God." Although in Oetinger's Bible and enigmatic dictionary (1776), it says under the entry "Leib" [Body]: "The bodily element is the end result of the work of God," the first version above was used already during his lifetime. Compare also with both of Rudolf Steiner's lectures in Berlin on December 14, 1915, in *Destinies of Individuals and Nations* (CW 157) and the lecture of March 20, 1917, in *Building Stones for an Understanding of the Mystery of Golgotha* (CW 175).

Page 171, "when Justinian executed the final act ..."
See the note for page 168.

Page 172, "Roger Bacon"
Roger Bacon (1214–1294). Franciscan friar. Taught at Oxford University.

Page 172, "in Spinoza's philosophy, which, in turn, had such a great influence on Goethe"
See Rudolf Steiner's *Nature's Open Secret* (CW 1).

Page 173, "text for the publicity"
See pp. 195-203.

Page 174, "The Movement for the Threefold Social Organism"
See the note for page 29.

Page 177, "A while ago I held a lecture for a group of industrialists"
This lecture has as yet not been found.

RUDOLF STEINER'S COLLECTED WORKS

The German Edition of Rudolf Steiner's Collected Works (the Gesamtausgabe [GA] published by Rudolf Steiner Verlag, Dornach, Switzerland) presently runs to over 354 titles, organized either by type of work (written or spoken), chronology, audience (public or other), or subject (education, art, etc.). For ease of comparison, the Collected Works in English [CW] follows the German organization exactly. A complete listing of the CWs follows with literal translations of the German titles. Other than in the case of the books published in his lifetime, titles were rarely given by Rudolf Steiner himself, and were often provided by the editors of the German editions. The titles in English are not necessarily the same as the German; and, indeed, over the past seventy-five years have frequently been different, with the same book sometimes appearing under different titles.

For ease of identification and to avoid confusion, we suggest that readers looking for a title should do so by CW number. Because the work of creating the Collected Works of Rudolf Steiner is an ongoing process, with new titles being published every year, we have not indicated in this listing which books are presently available. To find out what titles in the Collected Works are currently in print, please check our website at www.steinerbooks.org, or write to SteinerBooks 610 Main Street, Great Barrington, MA 01230:

Written Work

CW 1	Goethe: Natural-Scientific Writings, Introduction, with Footnotes and Explanations in the text by Rudolf Steiner
CW 2	Outlines of an Epistemology of the Goethean World View, with Special Consideration of Schiller
CW 3	Truth and Science
CW 4	The Philosophy of Freedom
CW 4a	Documents to "The Philosophy of Freedom"
CW 5	Friedrich Nietzsche, A Fighter against His Own Time
CW 6	Goethe's Worldview
CW 6a	Now in CW 30
CW 7	Mysticism at the Dawn of Modern Spiritual Life and Its Relationship with Modern Worldviews
CW 8	Christianity as Mystical Fact and the Mysteries of Antiquity
CW 9	Theosophy: An Introduction into Supersensible World Knowledge and Human Purpose
CW 10	How Does One Attain Knowledge of Higher Worlds?
CW 11	From the Akasha-Chronicle
CW 12	Levels of Higher Knowledge

Public Lectures

CW 78   Anthroposophy, Its Roots of Knowledge and Fruits for Life
CW 79   The Reality of the Higher Worlds
CW 80   Public lectures in various cities, 1922
CW 81   Renewal-Impulses for Culture and Science–Berlin College Course
CW 82   So that the Human Being Can Become a Complete Human Being
CW 83   Western and Eastern World-Contrast. Paths to Understanding It
         through Anthroposophy
CW 84   What Did the Goetheanum Intend and What Should
         Anthroposophy Do?

Lectures to the Members of the Anthroposophical Society

CW 88   Concerning the Astral World and Devachan
CW 89   Consciousness–Life–Form. Fundamental Principles of a Spiritual-
         Scientific Cosmology
CW 90   Participant Notes from the Lectures during the Years 1903-1905
CW 91   Participant Notes from the Lectures during the Years 1903-1905
CW 92   The Occult Truths of Ancient Myths and Sagas
CW 93   The Temple Legend and the Golden Legend
CW 93a   Fundamentals of Esotericism
CW 94   Cosmogony. Popular Occultism. The Gospel of John.
         The Theosophy in the Gospel of John
CW 95   At the Gates of Theosophy
CW 96   Origin-Impulses of Spiritual Science. Christian Esotericism in the
         Light of New Spirit-Knowledge
CW 97   The Christian Mystery
CW 98   Nature Beings and Spirit Beings – Their Effects in Our Visible
         World
CW 99   The Theosophy of the Rosicrucians
CW 100   Human Development and Christ-Knowledge
CW 101   Myths and Legends. Occult Signs and Symbols
CW 102   The Working into Human Beings by Spiritual Beings
CW 103   The Gospel of John
CW 104   The Apocalypse of John
CW 104a From the Picture-Script of the Apocalypse of John
CW 105   Universe, Earth, the Human Being: Their Being and
         Development, as well as Their Reflection in the Connection
         between Egyptian Mythology and Modern Culture
CW 106   Egyptian Myths and Mysteries in Relation to the Active Spiritual
         Forces of the Present
CW 107   Spiritual-Scientific Knowledge of the Human Being
CW 108   Answering the Questions of Life and the World through
         Anthroposophy

CW 267   Soul-Exercises: Vol. 1: Exercises with Word and Image
Meditations for the Methodological Development of Higher
Powers of Knowledge, 1904-1924
CW 268   Soul-Exercises: Vol. 2: Mantric Verses, 1903-1925
CW 269   Ritual Texts for the Celebration of the Free Christian Religious
Instruction. The Collected Verses for Teachers and Students of
the Waldorf School
CW 270   Esoteric Instructions for the First Class of the School for Spiritual
Science at the Goetheanum 1924, 4 Volumes
CW 271   Art and Knowledge of Art. Foundations of a New Aesthetic
CW 272   Spiritual-Scientific Commentary on Goethe's "Faust" in Two
Volumes. Vol. 1: Faust, the Striving Human Being
CW 273   Spiritual-Scientific Commentary on Goethe's "Faust" in Two
Volumes. Vol. 2: The Faust-Problem
CW 274   Addresses for the Christmas Plays from the Old Folk Traditions
CW 275   Art in the Light of Mystery-Wisdom
CW 276   The Artistic in Its Mission in the World. The Genius of
Language. The World of the Self-Revealing Radiant Appearances
– Anthroposophy and Art. Anthroposophy and Poetry
CW 277   Eurythmy. The Revelation of the Speaking Soul
CW 277a The Origin and Development of Eurythmy
CW 278   Eurythmy as Visible Song
CW 279   Eurythmy as Visible Speech
CW 280   The Method and Nature of Speech Formation
CW 281   The Art of Recitation and Declamation
CW 282   Speech Formation and Dramatic Art
CW 283   The Nature of Things Musical and the Experience of Tone in the
Human Being
CW284/285 Images of Occult Seals and Pillars. The Munich Congress of
Whitsun 1907 and Its Consequences
CW 286   Paths to a New Style of Architecture. "And the Building Becomes
Human"
CW 287   The Building at Dornach as a Symbol of Historical Becoming
and an Artistic Transformation Impulse
CW 288   Style-Forms in the Living Organic
CW 289   The Building-Idea of the Goetheanum: Lectures with Slides from
the Years 1920-1921
CW 290   The Building-Idea of the Goetheanum: Lectures with Slides from
the Years 1920-1921
CW 291   The Nature of Colors
CW 291a Knowledge of Colors. Supplementary Volume to "The Nature of
Colors"
CW 292   Art History as Image of Inner Spiritual Impulses

SIGNIFICANT EVENTS
IN THE LIFE OF RUDOLF STEINER

1829:   June 23: birth of Johann Steiner (1829-1910)—Rudolf Steiner's father—in Geras, Lower Austria.

1834:   May 8: birth of Franciska Blie (1834-1918)—Rudolf Steiner's mother—in Horn, Lower Austria. "My father and mother were both children of the glorious Lower Austrian forest district north of the Danube."

1860:   May 16: marriage of Johann Steiner and Franciska Blie.

1861:   February 25: birth of *Rudolf Joseph Lorenz Steiner* in Kraljevec, Croatia, near the border with Hungary, where Johann Steiner works as a telegrapher for the South Austria Railroad. Rudolf Steiner is baptized two days later, February 27, the date usually given as his birthday.

1862:   Summer: the family moves to Mödling, Lower Austria.

1863:   The family moves to Pottschach, Lower Austria, near the Styrian border, where Johann Steiner becomes stationmaster. "The view stretched to the mountains...majestic peaks in the distance and the sweet charm of nature in the immediate surroundings."

1864:   November 15: birth of Rudolf Steiner's sister, Leopoldine (d. November 1, 1927). She will become a seamstress and live with her parents for the rest of her life.

1866:   July 28: birth of Rudolf Steiner's deaf-mute brother, Gustav (d. May 1, 1941).

1867:   Rudolf Steiner enters the village school. Following a disagreement between his father and the schoolmaster, whose wife falsely accused the boy of causing a commotion, Rudolf Steiner is taken out of school and taught at home.

1868:   A critical experience. Unknown to the family, an aunt dies in a distant town. Sitting in the station waiting room, Rudolf Steiner sees her "form," which speaks to him, asking for help. "Beginning with this experience, a new soul life began in the boy, one in which not only the outer trees and mountains spoke to him, but also the worlds that lay behind them. From this moment on, the boy began to live with the spirits of nature...."

1869:   The family moves to the peaceful, rural village of Neudorfl, near Wiener-Neustadt in present-day Hungary. Rudolf Steiner attends the village school. Because of the "unorthodoxy" of his writing and spelling, he has to do "extra lessons."

1870:   Through a book lent to him by his tutor, he discovers geometry: "To grasp something purely in the spirit brought me inner happiness. I know that I first learned happiness through geometry." The same tutor allows him to draw, while other students still struggle with their reading and writing. "An artistic element" thus enters his education.

1871:   Though his parents are not religious, Rudolf Steiner becomes a "church child," a favorite of the priest, who was "an exceptional character." "Up to the age of ten or eleven, among those I came to know, he was far and away the most significant." Among other things, he introduces Steiner to Copernican, heliocentric cosmology. As an altar boy, Rudolf Steiner serves at Masses, funerals, and Corpus Christi processions. At year's end, after an incident in which he escapes a thrashing, his father forbids him to go to church.

1872:   Rudolf Steiner transfers to grammar school in Wiener-Neustadt, a five-mile walk from home, which must be done in all weathers.

1873-75: Through his teachers and on his own, Rudolf Steiner has many wonderful experiences with science and mathematics. Outside school, he teaches himself analytic geometry, trigonometry, differential equations, and calculus.

1876:   Rudolf Steiner begins tutoring other students. He learns bookbinding from his father. He also teaches himself stenography.

1877:   Rudolf Steiner discovers Kant's *Critique of Pure Reason*, which he reads and rereads. He also discovers and reads von Rotteck's *World History*.

1878:   He studies extensively in contemporary psychology and philosophy.

1879:   Rudolf Steiner graduates from high school with honors. His father is transferred to Inzersdorf, near Vienna. He uses his first visit to Vienna "to purchase a great number of philosophy books"—Kant, Fichte, Schelling, and Hegel, as well as numerous histories of philosophy. His aim: to find a path from the "I" to nature.

October 1879-1883: Rudolf Steiner attends the Technical College in Vienna—to study mathematics, chemistry, physics, mineralogy, botany, zoology, biology, geology, and mechanics—with a scholarship. He also attends lectures in history and literature, while avidly reading philosophy on his own. His two favorite professors are Karl Julius Schröer (German language and literature) and Edmund Reitlinger (physics). He also audits lectures by Robert Zimmerman on aesthetics and Franz Brentano on philosophy. During this year he begins his friendship with Moritz Zitter (1861-1921), who will help support him financially when he is in Berlin.

1880:   Rudolf Steiner attends lectures on Schiller and Goethe by Karl Julius Schröer, who becomes his mentor. Also "through a remarkable combination of circumstances," he meets Felix Koguzki, an "herb gatherer" and healer, who could "see deeply into the secrets of nature." Rudolf Steiner will meet and study with this "emissary of the Master" throughout his time in Vienna.

1881:   January: "... I didn't sleep a wink. I was busy with philosophical problems until about 12:30 a.m. Then, finally, I threw myself down on my couch. All my striving during the previous year had been to research whether the following statement by Schelling was true or not: *Within everyone dwells a secret, marvelous capacity to draw back from the stream of time—out of the self clothed in all that comes to us from outside—into our innermost being and there, in the immutable form of the Eternal, to look into ourselves.* I believe, and I am still quite certain of it, that I discovered this capacity in myself; I had long had an inkling of it. Now the whole of idealist philosophy stood before me in modified form. What's a sleepless night compared to that!"

Rudolf Steiner begins communicating with leading thinkers of the day, who send him books in return, which he reads eagerly.

July: "I am not one of those who dives into the day like an animal in human form. I pursue a quite specific goal, an idealistic aim—knowledge of the truth! This cannot be done offhandedly. It requires the greatest striving in the world, free of all egotism, and equally of all resignation."

August: Steiner puts down on paper for the first time thoughts for a "Philosophy of Freedom." "The striving for the absolute: this human yearning is freedom." He also seeks to outline a "peasant philosophy," describing what the worldview of a "peasant"—one who lives close to the earth and the old ways—really is.

1881-1882: Felix Koguzki, the herb gatherer, reveals himself to be the envoy of another, higher initiatory personality, who instructs Rudolf Steiner to penetrate Fichte's philosophy and to master modern scientific thinking as a preparation for right entry into the spirit. This "Master" also teaches him the double (evolutionary and involutionary) nature of time.

1882:   Through the offices of Karl Julius Schröer, Rudolf Steiner is asked by Joseph Kurschner to edit Goethe's scientific works for the *Deutschen National-Literatur* edition. He writes "A Possible Critique of Atomistic Concepts" and sends it to Friedrich Theodore Vischer.

1883:   Rudolf Steiner completes his college studies and begins work on the Goethe project.

1884:   First volume of Goethe's *Scientific Writings* (CW 1) appears (March). He lectures on Goethe and Lessing, and Goethe's approach to science. In July, he enters the household of Ladislaus and Pauline Specht as tutor to the four Specht boys. He will live there until 1890. At this time, he meets Josef Breuer (1842-1925), the coauthor with Sigmund Freud of *Studies in Hysteria*, who is the Specht family doctor.

1885:   While continuing to edit Goethe's writings, Rudolf Steiner reads deeply in contemporary philosophy (Edouard von Hartmann, Johannes Volkelt, and Richard Wahle, among others).

1886:   May: Rudolf Steiner sends Kurschner the manuscript of *Outlines of Goethe's Theory of Knowledge* (CW 2), which appears in October, and which he sends out widely. He also meets the poet Marie Eugenie Delle Grazie and writes "Nature and Our Ideals" for her. He attends her salon, where he meets many priests, theologians, and philosophers, who will become his friends. Meanwhile, the director of the Goethe Archive in Weimar requests his collaboration with the *Sophien* edition of Goethe's works, particularly the writings on color.

1887:   At the beginning of the year, Rudolf Steiner is very sick. As the year progresses and his health improves, he becomes increasingly "a man of letters," lecturing, writing essays, and taking part in Austrian cultural life. In August-September, the second volume of Goethe's *Scientific Writings* appears.

1888:   January-July: Rudolf Steiner assumes editorship of the "German Weekly" (*Deutsche Wochenschrift*). He begins lecturing more intensively, giving, for example, a lecture titled "Goethe as Father of a New Aesthetics." He meets and becomes soul friends with Friedrich Eckstein (1861-1939), a vegetarian, philosopher of symbolism, alchemist, and musician, who will introduce him to various spiritual currents (including Theosophy) and with whom he will meditate and interpret esoteric and alchemical texts.

1889:   Rudolf Steiner first reads Nietzsche (*Beyond Good and Evil*). He encounters Theosophy again and learns of Madame Blavatsky in the Theosophical circle around Marie Lang (1858-1934). Here he also meets well-known figures of Austrian life, as well as esoteric figures like the occultist Franz Hartman and Karl Leinigen-Billigen (translator of C.G. Harrison's *The Transcendental Universe*.) During this period, Steiner first reads A.P. Sinnett's *Esoteric Buddhism* and Mabel Collins's *Light on the Path*. He also begins traveling, visiting Budapest, Weimar, and Berlin (where he meets philosopher Edouard von Hartman).

1890:   Rudolf Steiner finishes volume 3 of Goethe's scientific writings. He begins his doctoral dissertation, which will become *Truth and Science* (CW 3). He also meets the poet and feminist Rosa Mayreder (1858-1938), with whom he can exchange his most intimate thoughts. In September, Rudolf Steiner moves to Weimar to work in the Goethe-Schiller Archive.

1891:   Volume 3 of the Kurschner edition of Goethe appears. Meanwhile, Rudolf Steiner edits Goethe's studies in mineralogy and scientific writings for the *Sophien* edition. He meets Ludwig Laistner of the Cotta Publishing Company, who asks for a book on the basic question of metaphysics. From this will result, ultimately, *The Philosophy of Freedom* (CW 4), which will be published not by Cotta but by Emil Felber. In October, Rudolf Steiner takes the oral exam for a doctorate in philosophy, mathematics, and mechanics at Rostock University, receiving his doctorate on the twenty-sixth. In November, he gives his first lecture on Goethe's "Fairy Tale" in Vienna.

1892:   Rudolf Steiner continues work at the Goethe-Schiller Archive and on his *Philosophy of Freedom*. *Truth and Science*, his doctoral dissertation, is published. Steiner undertakes to write introductions to books on Schopenhauer and Jean Paul for Cotta. At year's end, he finds lodging with Anna Eunike, née Schulz (1853-1911), a widow with four daughters and a son. He also develops a friendship with Otto Erich Hartleben (1864-1905) with whom he shares literary interests.

1893:   Rudolf Steiner begins his habit of producing many reviews and arti-
        cles. In March, he gives a lecture titled "Hypnotism, with Reference
        to Spiritism." In September, volume 4 of the Kurschner edition is
        completed. In November, *The Philosophy of Freedom* appears. This year,
        too, he meets John Henry Mackay (1864-1933), the anarchist, and
        Max Stirner, a scholar and biographer.

1894:   Rudolf Steiner meets Elisabeth Förster Nietzsche, the philosopher's
        sister, and begins to read Nietzsche in earnest, beginning with the as yet
        unpublished *Antichrist*. He also meets Ernst Haeckel (1834-1919). In the
        fall, he begins to write *Nietzsche, A Fighter against His Time* (CW 5).

1895:   May, *Nietzsche, A Fighter against His Time* appears.

1896:   January 22: Rudolf Steiner sees Friedrich Nietzsche for the first and
        only time. Moves between the Nietzsche and the Goethe-Schiller
        Archives, where he completes his work before year's end. He falls out
        with Elisabeth Förster Nietzsche, thus ending his association with the
        Nietzsche Archive.

1897:   Rudolf Steiner finishes the manuscript of *Goethe's Worldview* (CW
        6). He moves to Berlin with Anna Eunike and begins editorship of
        the *Magazin fur Literatur*. From now on, Steiner will write countless
        reviews, literary and philosophical articles, and so on. He begins lectur-
        ing at the "Free Literary Society." In September, he attends the Zionist
        Congress in Basel. He sides with Dreyfus in the Dreyfus affair.

1898:   Rudolf Steiner is very active as an editor in the political, artistic, and
        theatrical life of Berlin. He becomes friendly with John Henry Mackay
        and poet Ludwig Jacobowski (1868-1900). He joins Jacobowski's
        circle of writers, artists, and scientists—"The Coming Ones" (*Die
        Kommenden*)—and contributes lectures to the group until 1903. He
        also lectures at the "League for College Pedagogy." He writes an article
        for Goethe's sesquicentennial, "Goethe's Secret Revelation," on the
        "Fairy Tale of the Green Snake and the Beautiful Lily."

1888-89: "This was a trying time for my soul as I looked at Christianity. . .
        . I was able to progress only by contemplating, by means of spiritual
        perception, the evolution of Christianity . . . . Conscious knowledge of
        real Christianity began to dawn in me around the turn of the century.
        This seed continued to develop. My soul trial occurred shortly before
        the beginning of the twentieth century. It was decisive for my soul's
        development that I stood spiritually before the Mystery of Golgotha in
        a deep and solemn celebration of knowledge."

1899:   Rudolf Steiner begins teaching and giving lectures and lecture cycles
        at the Workers' College, founded by Wilhelm Liebknecht (1826-
        1900). He will continue to do so until 1904. Writes: *Literature and
        Spiritual Life in the Nineteenth Century; Individualism in Philosophy;
        Haeckel and His Opponents; Poetry in the Present;* and begins what will
        become (fifteen years later). *The Riddles of Philosophy* (CW 18). He
        also meets many artists and writers, including Käthe Kollwitz, Stefan

Zweig, and Rainer Maria Rilke. On October 31, he marries Anna Eunike.

1900: "I thought that the turn of the century must bring humanity a new light. It seemed to me that the separation of human thinking and willing from the spirit had peaked. A turn or reversal of direction in human evolution seemed to me a necessity." Rudolf Steiner finishes *World and Life Views in the Nineteenth Century* (the second part of what will become *The Riddles of Philosophy*) and dedicates it to Ernst Haeckel. It is published in March. He continues lecturing at *Die Kommenden*, whose leadership he assumes after the death of Jacobowski. Also, he gives the Gutenberg Jubilee lecture before 7,000 typesetters and printers. In September, Rudolf Steiner is invited by Count and Countess Brockdorff to lecture in the Theosophical Library. His first lecture is on Nietzsche. His second lecture is titled "Goethe's Secret Revelation." October 6, he begins a lecture cycle on the mystics that will become *Mystics after Modernism* (CW 7). November-December: "Marie von Sivers appears in the audience...." Also in November, Steiner gives his first lecture at the Giordano Bruno Bund (where he will continue to lecture until May, 1905). He speaks on Bruno and modern Rome, focusing on the importance of the philosophy of Thomas Aquinas as monism.

1901: In continual financial straits, Rudolf Steiner's early friends Moritz Zitter and Rosa Mayreder help support him. In October, he begins the lecture cycle *Christianity as Mystical Fact* (CW 8) at the Theosophical Library. In November, he gives his first "Theosophical lecture" on Goethe's "Fairy Tale" in Hamburg at the invitation of Wilhelm Hubbe-Schleiden. He also attends a tea to celebrate the founding of the Theosophical Society at Count and Countess Brockdorff's. He gives a lecture cycle, "From Buddha to Christ," for the circle of the *Kommenden*. November 17, Marie von Sivers asks Rudolf Steiner if Theosophy does not need a Western-Christian spiritual movement (to complement Theosophy's Eastern emphasis). "The question was posed. Now, following spiritual laws, I could begin to give an answer...." In December, Rudolf Steiner writes his first article for a Theosophical publication. At year's end, the Brockdorffs and possibly Wilhelm Hubbe-Schleiden ask Rudolf Steiner to join the Theosophical Society and undertake the leadership of the German section. Rudolf Steiner agrees, on the condition that Marie von Sivers (then in Italy) work with him.

1902: Beginning in January, Rudolf Steiner attends the opening of the Workers' School in Spandau with Rosa Luxemburg (1870-1919). January 17, Rudolf Steiner joins the Theosophical Society. In April, he is asked to become general secretary of the German Section of the Theosophical Society, and works on preparations for its founding. In July, he visits London for a Theosophical congress. He meets Bertram

Keightly, G.R.S. Mead, A.P. Sinnett, and Annie Besant, among others. In September, *Christianity as Mystical Fact* appears. In October, Rudolf Steiner gives his first public lecture on Theosophy ("Monism and Theosophy") to about three hundred people at the Giordano Bruno Bund. On October 19-21, the German Section of the Theosophical Society has its first meeting; Rudolf Steiner is the general secretary, and Annie Besant attends. Steiner lectures on practical karma studies. On October 23, Annie Besant inducts Rudolf Steiner into the Esoteric School of the Theosophical Society. On October 25, Steiner begins a weekly series of lectures: "The Field of Theosophy." During this year, Rudolf Steiner also first meets Ita Wegman (1876-1943), who will become his close collaborator in his final years.

1903: Rudolf Steiner holds about 300 lectures and seminars. In May, the first issue of the periodical *Luzifer* appears. In June, Rudolf Steiner visits London for the first meeting of the Federation of the European Sections of the Theosophical Society, where he meets Colonel Olcott. He begins to write *Theosophy* (CW 9).

1904: Rudolf Steiner continues lecturing at the Workers' College and elsewhere (about 90 lectures), while lecturing intensively all over Germany among Theosophists (about a 140 lectures). In February, he meets Carl Unger (1878-1929), who will become a member of the board of the Anthroposophical Society (1913). In March, he meets Michael Bauer (1871-1929), a Christian mystic, who will also be on the board. In May, *Theosophy* appears, with the dedication: "To the spirit of Giordano Bruno." Rudolf Steiner and Marie von Sivers visit London for meetings with Annie Besant. June: Rudolf Steiner and Marie von Sivers attend the meeting of the Federation of European Sections of the Theosophical Society in Amsterdam. In July, Steiner begins the articles in *Luzifer-Gnosis* that will become *How to Know Higher Worlds* (CW 10) and *Cosmic Memory* (CW 11). In September, Annie Besant visits Germany. In December, Steiner lectures on Freemasonry. He mentions the High Grade Masonry derived from John Yarker and represented by Theodore Reuss and Karl Kellner as a blank slate "into which a good image could be placed."

1905: This year, Steiner ends his non-Theosophical lecturing activity. Supported by Marie von Sivers, his Theosophical lecturing—both in public and in the Theosophical Society—increases significantly: "The German Theosophical Movement is of exceptional importance." Steiner recommends reading, among others, Fichte, Jacob Boehme, and Angelus Silesius. He begins to introduce Christian themes into Theosophy. He also begins to work with doctors (Felix Peipers and Ludwig Noll). In July, he is in London for the Federation of European Sections, where he attends a lecture by Annie Besant: "I have seldom seen Mrs. Besant speak in so inward and heartfelt a manner...." "Through Mrs. Besant I have found the way to H.P. Blavatsky."

September to October, he gives a course of thirty-one lectures for a small group of esoteric students. In October, the annual meeting of the German Section of the Theosophical Society, which still remains very small, takes place. Rudolf Steiner reports membership has risen from 121 to 377 members. In November, seeking to establish esoteric "continuity," Rudolf Steiner and Marie von Sivers participate in a "Memphis-Misraim" Masonic ceremony. They pay forty-five marks for membership. "Yesterday, you saw how little remains of former esoteric institutions." "We are dealing only with a 'framework'... for the present, nothing lies behind it. The occult powers have completely withdrawn."

1906: Expansion of Theosophical work. Rudolf Steiner gives about 245 lectures, only 44 of which take place in Berlin. Cycles are given in Paris, Leipzig, Stuttgart, and Munich. Esoteric work also intensifies. Rudolf Steiner begins writing *An Outline of Esoteric Science* (CW 13). In January, Rudolf Steiner receives permission (a patent) from the Great Orient of the Scottish A & A Thirty-Three Degree Rite of the Order of the Ancient Freemasons of the Memphis-Misraim Rite to direct a chapter under the name "Mystica Aeterna." This will become the "Cognitive Cultic Section" (also called "Misraim Service") of the Esoteric School. (See: *From the History and Contents of the Cognitive Cultic Section* (CW 264). During this time, Steiner also meets Albert Schweitzer. In May, he is in Paris, where he visits Edouard Schuré. Many Russians attend his lectures (including Konstantin Balmont, Dimitri Mereszkovski, Zinaida Hippius, and Maximilian Woloshin). He attends the General Meeting of the European Federation of the Theosophical Society, at which Col. Olcott is present for the last time. He spends the year's end in Venice and Rome, where he writes and works on his translation of H.P. Blavatsky's *Key to Theosophy*.

1907: Further expansion of the German Theosophical Movement according to the Rosicrucian directive to "introduce spirit into the world"—in education, in social questions, in art, and in science. In February, Col. Olcott dies in Adyar. Before he dies, Olcott indicates that "the Masters" wish Annie Besant to succeed him: much politicking ensues. Rudolf Steiner supports Besant's candidacy. April-May: preparations for the Congress of the Federation of European Sections of the Theosophical Society—the great, watershed Whitsun "Munich Congress," attended by Annie Besant and others. Steiner decides to separate Eastern and Western (Christian-Rosicrucian) esoteric schools. He takes his esoteric school out of the Theosophical Society (Besant and Rudolf Steiner are "in harmony" on this). Steiner makes his first lecture tours to Austria and Hungary. That summer, he is in Italy. In September, he visits Edouard Schuré, who will write the introduction to the French edition of *Christianity as Mystical Fact* in Barr, Alsace. Rudolf Steiner writes the autobiographical statement known as the "Barr Document." In *Luzifer–Gnosis*, "The Education of the Child" appears.

1908: The movement grows (membership: 1150). Lecturing expands. Steiner makes his first extended lecture tour to Holland and Scandinavia, as well as visits to Naples and Sicily. Themes: St. John's Gospel, the Apocalypse, Egypt, science, philosophy, and logic. *Luzifer-Gnosis* ceases publication. In Berlin, Marie von Sivers (with Johanna Mücke (1864-1949) forms the *Philosophisch-Theosophisch* (after 1915 *Philosophisch-Anthroposophisch*) *Verlag* to publish Steiner's work. Steiner gives lecture cycles titled *The Gospel of St. John* (CW 103) and *The Apocalypse* (104).

1909: *An Outline of Esoteric Science* appears. Lecturing and travel continues. Rudolf Steiner's spiritual research expands to include the polarity of Lucifer and Ahriman; the work of great individualities in history; the Maitreya Buddha and the Bodhisattvas; spiritual economy (CW 109); the work of the spiritual hierarchies in heaven and on Earth (CW 110). He also deepens and intensifies his research into the Gospels, giving lectures on the Gospel of St. Luke (CW 114) with the first mention of two Jesus children. Meets and becomes friends with Christian Morgenstern (1871-1914). In April, he lays the foundation stone for the Malsch model—the building that will lead to the first Goetheanum. In May, the International Congress of the Federation of European Sections of the Theosophical Society takes place in Budapest. Rudolf Steiner receives the Subba Row medal for *How to Know Higher Worlds*. During this time, Charles W. Leadbeater discovers Jiddu Krishnamurti (1895-1986) and proclaims him the future "world teacher," the bearer of the Maitreya Buddha and the "reappearing Christ." In October, Steiner delivers seminal lectures on "anthroposophy," which he will try, unsuccessfully, to rework over the next years into the unfinished work, *Anthroposophy (A Fragment)* (CW 45).

1910: New themes: *The Reappearance of Christ in the Etheric* (CW 118); *The Fifth Gospel; The Mission of Folk Souls* (CW 121); *Occult History* (CW 126); the evolving development of etheric cognitive capacities. Rudolf Steiner continues his Gospel research with *The Gospel of St. Matthew* (CW 123). In January, his father dies. In April, he takes a month-long trip to Italy, including Rome, Monte Cassino, and Sicily. He also visits Scandinavia again. July-August, he writes the first mystery drama, *The Portal of Initiation* (CW 14). In November, he gives "psychosophy" lectures. In December, he submits "On the Psychological Foundations and Epistemological Framework of Theosophy" to the International Philosophical Congress in Bologna.

1911: The crisis in the Theosophical Society deepens. In January, "The Order of the Rising Sun," which will soon become "The Order of the Star in the East," is founded for the coming world teacher, Krishnamurti. At the same time, Marie von Sivers, Rudolf Steiner's coworker, falls ill. Fewer lectures are given, but important new ground is broken. In Prague, in March, Steiner meets Franz Kafka (1883-1924) and Hugo Bergmann (1883-1975). In April, he delivers his paper to the

Philosophical Congress. He writes the second mystery drama, *The Soul's Probation* (CW 14). Also, while Marie von Sivers is convalescing, Rudolf Steiner begins work on *Calendar 1912/1913*, which will contain the "Calendar of the Soul" meditations. On March 19, Anna (Eunike) Steiner dies. In September, Rudolf Steiner visits Einsiedeln, birthplace of Paracelsus. In December, Friedrich Rittelmeyer, future founder of the Christian Community, meets Rudolf Steiner. The *Johannes-Bauverein*, the "building committee," which would lead to the first Goetheanum (first planned for Munich), is also founded, and a preliminary committee for the founding of an independent association is created that, in the following year, will become the Anthroposophical Society. Important lecture cycles include *Occult Physiology* (CW 128); *Wonders of the World* (CW 129); *From Jesus to Christ* (CW 131). Other themes: esoteric Christianity; Christian Rosenkreutz; the spiritual guidance of humanity; the sense world and the world of the spirit.

1912: Despite the ongoing, now increasing crisis in the Theosophical Society, much is accomplished: *Calendar 1912/1913* is published; eurythmy is created; both the third mystery drama, *The Guardian of the Threshold* (CW 14) and *A Way of Self-Knowledge* (CW 16) are written. New (or renewed) themes included life between death and rebirth and karma and reincarnation. Other lecture cycles: *Spiritual Beings in the Heavenly Bodies and the Kingdoms of Nature* (CW 136); *The Human Being in the Light of Occultism, Theosophy, and Philosophy* (CW 137); *The Gospel of St. Mark* (CW 139); and *The Bhagavad Gita and the Epistles of Paul* (CW 142). On May 8, Rudolf Steiner celebrates White Lotus Day, H.P. Blavatsky's death day, which he had faithfully observed for the past decade, for the last time. In August, Rudolf Steiner suggests the "independent association" be called the "Anthroposophical Society." In September, the first eurythmy course takes place. In October, Rudolf Steiner declines recognition of a Theosophical Society lodge dedicated to the Star of the East and decides to expel all Theosophical Society members belonging to the order. Also, with Marie von Sivers, he first visits Dornach, near Basel, Switzerland, and they stand on the hill where the Goetheanum will be. In November, a Theosophical Society lodge is opened by direct mandate from Adyar (Annie Besant). In December, a meeting of the German section occurs at which it is decided that belonging to the Order of the Star of the East is incompatible with membership in the Theosophical Society. December 28: informal founding of the Anthroposophical Society in Berlin.

1913: Expulsion of the German section from the Theosophical Society. February 2-3: Foundation meeting of the Anthroposophical Society. Board members include: Marie von Sivers, Michael Bauer, and Carl Unger. September 20: Laying of the foundation stone for the *Johannes Bau* (Goetheanum) in Dornach. Building begins immediately. The third mystery drama, *The Soul's Awakening* (CW 14), is completed.

Also: *The Threshold of the Spiritual World* (CW 147). Lecture cycles include: *The Bhagavad Gita and the Epistles of Paul* and *The Esoteric Meaning of the Bhagavad Gita* (CW 146), which the Russian philosopher Nikolai Berdyaev attends; *The Mysteries of the East and of Christianity* (CW 144); *The Effects of Esoteric Development* (CW 145); and *The Fifth Gospel* (CW 148). In May, Rudolf Steiner is in London and Paris, where anthroposophical work continues.

1914: Building continues on the *Johannes Bau* (Goetheanum) in Dornach, with artists and coworkers from seventeen nations. The general assembly of the Anthroposophical Society takes place. In May, Rudolf Steiner visits Paris, as well as Chartres Cathedral. June 28: assassination in Sarajevo ("Now the catastrophe has happened!"). August 1: War is declared. Rudolf Steiner returns to Germany from Dornach—he will travel back and forth. He writes the last chapter of *The Riddles of Philosophy*. Lecture cycles include: *Human and Cosmic Thought* (CW 151); *Inner Being of Humanity between Death and a New Birth* (CW 153); *Occult Reading and Occult Hearing* (CW 156). December 24: marriage of Rudolf Steiner and Marie von Sivers.

1915: Building continues. Life after death becomes a major theme, also art. Writes: *Thoughts during a Time of War* (CW 24). Lectures include: *The Secret of Death* (CW 159); *The Uniting of Humanity through the Christ Impulse* (CW 165).

1916: Rudolf Steiner begins work with Edith Maryon (1872-1924) on the sculpture "The Representative of Humanity" ("The Group"—Christ, Lucifer, and Ahriman). He also works with the alchemist Alexander von Bernus on the quarterly *Das Reich*. He writes *The Riddle of Humanity* (CW 20). Lectures include: *Necessity and Freedom in World History and Human Action* (CW 166); *Past and Present in the Human Spirit* (CW 167); *The Karma of Vocation* (CW 172); *The Karma of Untruthfulness* (CW 173).

1917: Russian Revolution. The U.S. enters the war. Building continues. Rudolf Steiner delineates the idea of the "threefold nature of the human being" (in a public lecture March 15) and the "threefold nature of the social organism" (hammered out in May-June with the help of Otto von Lerchenfeld and Ludwig Polzer-Hoditz in the form of two documents titled *Memoranda*, which were distributed in high places). August-September: Rudolf Steiner writes *The Riddles of the Soul* (CW 20). Also: commentary on "The Chemical Wedding of Christian Rosenkreutz" for Alexander Bernus (*Das Reich*). Lectures include: *The Karma of Materialism* (CW 176); *The Spiritual Background of the Outer World: The Fall of the Spirits of Darkness* (CW 177).

1918: March 18: peace treaty of Brest-Litovsk—"Now everything will truly enter chaos! What is needed is cultural renewal." June: Rudolf Steiner visits Karlstein (Grail) Castle outside Prague. Lecture cycle: *From Symptom to Reality in Modern History* (CW 185). In mid-November,

Emil Molt, of the Waldorf-Astoria Cigarette Company, has the idea of founding a school for his workers' children.

1919: Focus on the threefold social organism: tireless travel, countless lectures, meetings, and publications. At the same time, a new public stage of Anthroposophy emerges as cultural renewal begins. The coming years will see initiatives in pedagogy, medicine, pharmacology, and agriculture. January 27: threefold meeting: " We must first of all, with the money we have, found free schools that can bring people what they need." February: first public eurythmy performance in Zurich. Also: "Appeal to the German People" (CW 24), circulated March 6 as a newspaper insert. In April, *Toward Social Renewal* (CW 23)—"perhaps the most widely read of all books on politics appearing since the war"—appears. Rudolf Steiner is asked to undertake the "direction and leadership" of the school founded by the Waldorf-Astoria Company. Rudolf Steiner begins to talk about the "renewal" of education. May 30: a building is selected and purchased for the future Waldorf School. August-September, Rudolf Steiner gives a lecture course for Waldorf teachers, *The Foundations of Human Experience (Study of Man)* (CW 293). September 7: Opening of the first Waldorf School. December (into January): first science course, the *Light Course* (CW 320).

1920: The Waldorf School flourishes. New threefold initiatives. Founding of limited companies *Der Kommende Tag* and *Futurum A.G.* to infuse spiritual values into the economic realm. Rudolf Steiner also focuses on the sciences. Lectures: *Introducing Anthroposophical Medicine* (CW 312); *The Warmth Course* (CW 321); *The Boundaries of Natural Science* (CW 322); *The Redemption of Thinking* (CW 74). February: Johannes Werner Klein—later a cofounder of the Christian Community—asks Rudolf Steiner about the possibility of a "religious renewal," a "Johannine church." In March, Rudolf Steiner gives the first course for doctors and medical students. In April, a divinity student asks Rudolf Steiner a second time about the possibility of religious renewal. September 27-October 16: anthroposophical "university course." December: lectures titled *The Search for the New Isis* (CW 202).

1921: Rudolf Steiner continues his intensive work on cultural renewal, including the uphill battle for the threefold social order. "University" arts, scientific, theological, and medical courses include: *The Astronomy Course* (CW 323); *Observation, Mathematics, and Scientific Experiment* (CW 324); the *Second Medical Course* (CW 313); *Color*. In June and September-October, Rudolf Steiner also gives the first two "priests' courses" (CW 342 and 343). The "youth movement" gains momentum. Magazines are founded: *Die Drei* (January), and—under the editorship of Albert Steffen (1884-1963)—the weekly, *Das Goetheanum* (August). In February-March, Rudolf Steiner takes his first trip outside Germany since the war (Holland). On April 7, Steiner receives a letter regarding "religious renewal," and May 22-23, he agrees to address the question in a practical way. In June, the Klinical-Therapeutic Institute opens in Arlesheim under the direction of Dr. Ita Wegman. In August, the Chemical-Pharmaceutical Laboratory opens in Arlesheim (Oskar Schmiedel and Ita Wegman, directors). The Clinical Therapeutic Institute is inaugurated in Stuttgart (Dr. Ludwig Noll, director); also the Research Laboratory in Dornach (Ehrenfried Pfeiffer and Gunther Wachsmuth, directors). In November-December, Rudolf Steiner visits Norway.

1922:   The first half of the year involves very active public lecturing (thousands attend); in the second half, Rudolf Steiner begins to withdraw and turn toward the Society—"The Society is asleep." It is "too weak" to do what is asked of it. The businesses—*Der Kommende Tag* and *Futurum A.G.*—fail. In January, with the help of an agent, Steiner undertakes a twelve-city German tour, accompanied by eurythmy performances. In two weeks he speaks to more than 2,000 people. In April, he gives a "university course" in The Hague. He also visits England. In June, he is in Vienna for the East-West Congress. In August-September, he is back in England for the Oxford Conference on Education. Returning to Dornach, he gives the lectures *Philosophy, Cosmology, and Religion* (CW 215), and gives the third priest's course (CW 344). On September 16, The Christian Community is founded. In October-November, Steiner is in Holland and England. He also speaks to the youth: *The Youth Course* (CW 217). In December, Steiner gives lectures titled *The Origins of Natural Science* (CW 326), and *Humanity and the World of Stars: The Spiritual Communion of Humanity* (CW 219). December 31: Fire at the Goetheanum, which is destroyed.

1923:   Despite the fire, Rudolf Steiner continues his work unabated. A very hard year. Internal dispersion, dissension, and apathy abound. There is conflict—between old and new visions—within the society. A wake-up call is needed, and Rudolf Steiner responds with renewed lecturing vitality. His focus: the spiritual context of human life; initiation science; the course of the year; and community building. As a foundation for an artistic school, he creates a series of pastel sketches. Lecture cycles: *The Anthroposophical Movement; Initiation Science* (CW 227) (in England at the Penmaenmawr Summer School); *The Four Seasons and the Archangels* (CW 229); *Harmony of the Creative Word* (CW 230); *The Supersensible Human* (CW 231), given in Holland for the founding of the Dutch society. On November 10, in response to the failed Hitler-Ludendorf putsch in Munich, Steiner closes his Berlin residence and moves the *Philosophisch-Anthroposophisch Verlag* (Press) to Dornach. On December 9, Steiner begins the serialization of his *Autobiography: The Course of My Life* (CW 28) in *Das Goetheanum*. It will continue to appear weekly, without a break, until his death. Late December-early January: Rudolf Steiner refounds the Anthroposophical Society (about 12,000 members internationally) and takes over its leadership. The new board members are: Marie Steiner, Ita Wegman, Albert Steffen, Elizabeth Vreede, and Guenther Wachsmuth. (See *The Christmas Meeting for the Founding of the General Anthroposophical Society* (CW 260). Accompanying lectures: *Mystery Knowledge and Mystery Centers* (CW 232); *World History in the Light of Anthroposophy* (CW 233). December 25: the Foundation Stone is laid (in the hearts of members) in the form of the "Foundation Stone Meditation."

1924:   January 1: having founded the Anthroposophical Society and taken over its leadership, Rudolf Steiner has the task of "reforming" it. The process begins with a weekly newssheet ("What's Happening in the Anthroposophical Society") in which Rudolf Steiner's "Letters to Members" and "Anthroposophical Leading Thoughts" appear (CW 26). The next step is the creation of a new esoteric class, the "first class" of the "University of Spiritual Science" (which was to have been followed, had Rudolf Steiner lived longer, by two more advanced classes). Then comes a new language for Anthroposophy—practical, phenomenological, and direct; and Rudolf Steiner creates the model for the second Goetheanum. He begins the series of extensive "karma" lectures (CW 235-40); and finally, responding to needs, he creates two new initiatives: biodynamic agriculture and curative education. After the middle of the year, rumors begin to circulate regarding Steiner's health. Lectures: January-February, *Anthroposophy* (CW 234); February: *Tone Eurythmy* (CW 278); June: *The Agriculture Course* (CW 327); June-July: Speech [?] Eurythmy (CW 279); *Curative Education* (CW 317); August: (England, "Second International Summer School"), *Initiation Consciousness: True and False Paths in Spiritual Investigation* (CW 243); September: *Pastoral Medicine* (CW 318). On September 26, for the first time, Rudolf Steiner cancels a lecture. On September 28, he gives his last lecture. On September 29, he withdraws to his studio in the carpenter's shop; now he is definitively ill. Cared for by Ita Wegman, he continues working, however, and writing the weekly installments of his *Autobiography* and *Letters to the Members/Leading Thoughts* (CW 26).

1925:   Rudolf Steiner, while continuing to work, continues to weaken. He finishes *Extending Practical Medicine* (CW 27) with Ita Wegman. On March 30, around ten in the morning, Rudolf Steiner dies.

INDEX